Masters of

Russian Marxism

POLITICAL SCIENCE SERIES

Taylor Cole
Joseph La Palombara
Editors

Thornton Anderson
UNIVERSITY OF MARYLAND

Masters of
Russian Marxism

New York

APPLETON-CENTURY-CROFTS
EDUCATIONAL DIVISION
MEREDITH CORPORATION

PRINTED IN THE UNITED STATES OF AMERICA

390-03305-7

Preface

THIS BOOK is a study in the history of political ideas. It makes use of other data only in that connection. It assumes that the practical effects of these ideas, and the desirable or undesirable qualities of these effects, belong to other fields and are adequately treated elsewhere. It further assumes that the ideas of Marx and Engels themselves are also adequately treated elsewhere.

It should be recognized that the development of Marxism in Russia has been shaped by many who, at various times, have been excluded from the ranks of the orthodox. These heretics—heresy being measured by differences from the official interpretation of Lenin—are variously treated by Soviet historiography. Some, like Plekhanov, are admired for their activities and opinions prior to their differences with Lenin. Others, like Martov and Trotsky, are fantastically depreciated. In this volume the approved and the disapproved stand on equal footing, the criteria for inclusion being the originality and importance of their theoretical contributions.

The exposition of Marxist political thought, especially of Russian Marxism, has been attended by so much prejudice, pro and con, that it is desirable to permit the Russians themselves to state their positions. Each chapter, therefore, includes an exposition making use of some quotation and is followed by extensive selections from the Russians' works. Selections for which titles have been supplied are indicated by brackets. Translations made especially for this volume are indicated by the translator's name following the date and place of publication of the Russian original.

A note on the bibliographies. It goes without saying that the most extensive and important works in this field are in the Russian language. Slavic language materials have, however, been deliberately excluded from the bibliographies, on two grounds: 1) readers of Russian will have much better bibliographical aids available to them, and 2) it is desirable to suggest to others how substantial the materials are in Western languages. The lists, therefore, are selective and exclude a mass of less substantial items, especially on Lenin, Stalin, and Trotsky. On the other hand, Martov, Kollontai, and Bukharin have been grossly neglected by Western writers, and there are as yet no satisfactory studies of Khrushchev. A minus sign preceding an item indicates that it has not been available for examination.

Finally, I would like to acknowledge with appreciation the help and encouragement that have been extended to me, especially by Elizabeth Anderson and by a number of other persons and libraries, and the support provided by the General Research Board of the University of Maryland.

Thornton Anderson

Contents

Preface   v

1. INTRODUCTION   1

2. PLEKHANOV: MARXISM MEANS TWO REVOLU-
   TIONS   21

   [The Political Significance of the Peasant "Indifference
       to Politics"]   30
   True Tasks of the Socialists in Russia   32
   More on Freedom and Necessity   37
   The Rôle of the Individual   41

3. LENIN: THE PRIMACY OF THE POLITICAL   44

   [On Organization]   62
   [On the Party (Against the Mensheviks)]   65
   [On Revolutionary Tactics, 1905]   67
   [The Law of Uneven Development]   71
   Imperialism as a Special Stage of Capitalism   72
   [On Revolutionary Tactics, April, 1917]   76
   [On the State]   79
   [The "Withering" of the State]   80
   The Higher Phase of Communist Society   83
   The Immediate Tasks of the Soviet Government   85

4. MARTOV: MARXISM MEANS MASS SUPPORT   90

   [On Party Organization]   101

Materialism: Metaphysical and Dialectic   104
Marx and the State   108
The Commune of 1871   114
Marx and the Dictatorship of the Proletariat   116

5. TROTSKY: A MINORITY CAN TAKE POWER   120

[The Permanent Revolution]   135
[The Permanent Revolution in Retrospect]   139
The Organization of Labor   140
The Militarization of Labor   143
The Single Economic Plan   147
[Relations With the Peasants]   149
[The Bureaucracy]   151
[Against Socialism in One Country]   152
[The Dictatorship in Russia]   158

6. KOLLONTAI: WOMEN AND THE WORKERS   163

The New Woman   173
Communism and the Family   175
The Workers' Opposition   179

7. BUKHARIN: MARXISM AS EQUILIBRIUM ECO-
   NOMICS   190

[The Withering Away of the Class Struggle]   201
[The Alliance of Workers and Peasants]   209

8. STALIN: REVOLUTION FROM ABOVE   215

[Socialism in One Country]   226
[The Class Struggle]   230
[The Withering of the State]   233
[Basis and Superstructure]   236
Character of Economic Laws Under Socialism   238
Commodity Production Under Socialism   241
[Collective-Farm Property and Public Property]   244
[Town and Country, Mental and Physical Labor]   246
[The Transition to Communism]   249

9. KHRUSHCHEV: MARXISM MEANS MATERIAL
    ABUNDANCE   253

    Some Fundamental Questions of Present-Day Interna-
        national Development   266
    [From Socialism to Communism]   273
    From Dictatorship of the Proletariat to a State of the
        Whole People   279
    [Relations Among Socialist States]   282

Index   291

Masters of
Russian Marxism

1

Introduction

THE ATTEMPT of Nicholas I after 1825 to preserve autocracy, orthodoxy, and nationalism, by preventing the influx of ideas from western Europe, required the exclusion of Western philosophy from the university curricula. As a result the students joined in private circles for the study and discussion of the latest French and German theories. During the 1830's the groups centered around the stimulating young men Herzen and Stankevich were the most outstanding in Moscow. In the 1840's, in St. Petersburg, the Petrashevski circle, of which Dostoevski was a member, attracted attention—and arrests. In some circles the movement of thought was from Schelling through Fichte and Hegel to Kant or to Feuerbach; in others interest centered around Saint-Simon, Leroux, and Fourier. Later, after the Crimean war, native Russian thinkers absorbed an increasing proportion of the attention of such groups, Belinski, Herzen, Chernyshevski, and Bakunin being widely discussed. These study groups frequently led their members to one or another brand of socialism, but even more uniformly they produced a desire to avoid capitalism. A few individuals later became active revolutionaries, but, although many persons paid in Siberia for their participation, the circles themselves were not hotbeds of conspiracy but rather seedbeds for ideas.

Yet conspiracy was already a respectable tradition in Russia, stemming from the abortive uprising of the Decembrists, the army officers who, under the influence of the Bourbon restoration in France, tried in 1825 to make Russia a constitutional monarchy. In more recent times conspiracy was frequently con-

1

nected with the name of August Blanqui, who had given it a theoretical foundation. Control by the ruling class over all means of mass communication and education made it impossible, in Blanqui's opinion, for revolutionaries to secure majority support prior to a successful seizure of power. The revolution must, therefore, be the work of a well organized and highly disciplined conspiracy of intellectuals who only thereafter would be able to teach the proletariat (in which he included most of the peasantry) to understand its own interests and thereby to win its support. The difficulties of mass propaganda in Russia were so exactly those for which Blanqui planned that, directly and indirectly, he exerted an influence there that should not be underestimated.

The liberation of the serfs in 1861 was attended by repressive measures against the students, which inspired Herzen's call, "To the people!" These measures were also the signal for a new kind of secret society, Land and Liberty (*Zemlia i Volia*), which undertook not only to study but also to carry ideas of political rights and of socialism to the workers and peasants. After the Polish revolt of 1863, the revocation of the Polish constitution and a series of other repressive governmental measures convinced more and more people that the tsar's reforming zeal was spent, and that Alexander II had become, as had Alexander I before him, the prime obstacle to all progress. An effort to rouse the peasants of the lower Volga proved a complete fiasco, however, and by 1864 Land and Liberty had been suppressed. Few were yet willing to meet the government's violence with violence. Karakozov, who shot at the tsar in 1866, had no organized support behind him.

As Western and native ideas increasingly agitated the growing intelligentsia, however, the autocracy continued to oppose these ideas, to claim a monopoly of political wisdom, and to consider itself above public opinion. It thereby gave a strong stimulus to anarchism, the philosophic rejection of government. The concept of society without government had deep historical roots in Russia, and it still has a place in Soviet political thought.

One such root may be discerned in the old freedom of the boyars (until the fifteenth century) to desert their prince and take their allegiance elsewhere without forfeiting their estates. Another can be found among the religious sectarians, such as the Trans-Volga Elders of the sixteenth century, the Old Believers (or Raskolniks), numerous since the seventeenth, and the later Dukhobors. A third lay in the repudiation of the restraints of both landlord and tsar that recruited and maintained the Cossacks. Still a fourth was the tradition of peasant revolts, always attended by fire and murder, the most widespread of which was that of Pugachev against the Empress Catherine in 1773. And finally, and most important as a contributing stimulus, was the radical and deliberate separation of the government from the people.

These were, however, largely expressions of an intuitive conviction of traditional freedoms, in the manner of British conviction regarding "the ancient rights of Englishmen." Russian anarchism had not yet developed a philosophical foundation; it tended to be particular and negative rather than general and systematic. Mikhail Bakunin, Russia's first major exponent of anarchism as a philosophy, shared these tendencies and labored with difficulty to overcome them.

A large and powerful bulk of a man, Bakunin possessed almost boundless energy and expended it wantonly in active revolutionary endeavors in many countries; yet, in spite of his own undisciplined personality, he gave to anarchism an almost systematic program. Drawing on the spirit of Pugachev and the logic of Hegel, he argued that democracy must create a new world through revolutionary demolition of the old. He gave voice to his doctrine of pan-destruction in the famous formula, "The urge for destruction is at the same time a creative passion." [1] He called for ruthless and violent smashing of old institutions, to be followed, not by individual autarchy, but by spontaneous community cooperation and the federation of communities, in which no man obeyed aught save his own convictions. This utopian federalism without the state he had borrowed from Proudhon, and not from the Russian village community,

---

[1] Bakunin (*pseud.* Jules Elysard), "Die Reaction in Deutschland," *Deutsche Jahrbücher für Wissenschaft und Kunst,* No. 251 (October 21, 1842), p. 1002.

which he did not idealize. Another characteristic of his anarchism was the importance he attached to destruction of the
church and of the belief in God. No other idea or institution,
he thought, had such power to enslave men's minds, and therefore men.

This program was consonant, he believed, with the main features of the Russian people's ideal, which he described thus:

> The first and main feature is the conviction of the whole people
> that the land, all the land, belongs to the people who water it with
> their sweat and fertilize it with their labour. The second, just as great,
> feature is that the right to make use of it belongs not to the individual,
> but to the whole village community, *mir*, which divides it temporarily
> among individuals; the third feature is of equal importance to the first
> two; it is the quasi-absolute autonomy, the self-government of the
> village community, and the community's consequent resolute hostility
> to the state. . . . However, the ideal of the Russian people is dark-
> ened by three other features which distort its character and extremely
> hinder and retard its realization. . . . These three darkening features
> are: 1) patriarchalism, 2) the absorption of the individual by the *mir*,
> 3) faith in the tsar.[2]

The *mir*, because of its common ownership of land, occupied
the key position in the thinking of the nineteenth-century socialists. Bakunin's followers, however, accepted the positive and
neglected the negative parts of his analysis; the Marxists, in
response, did the opposite.

More of a doer than a thinker, ready always to abandon his
pen for the barricades, Bakunin was still the chief theoretical
opponent of Karl Marx in the First International. Yet he had
great respect for Marx. He translated the *Communist Manifesto*
into Russian, referred to *Capital* as a magnificent work, and
began translating it also. He saw, however, that within the International Marx wished to build a tightly disciplined proletarian
party that could be used to capture political power and to turn
the state against the old ruling classes in the "dictatorship of the
proletariat." Neither this means nor this end appealed to Bakunin. Discipline meant authority and the denial of freedom,

[2] Bakunin, *Gosudarstvo i Anarkhiia* (1873), quoted in George Plekhanov,
Selected Philosophical Works, Vol. 1 (Moscow, 1961), p. 169.

while the "dictatorship of the proletariat" was only another name for the state. The state should be destroyed, not captured; and this should be accomplished by voluntary, spontaneous cooperation of communes of workers and peasants. Among the *narodniks* (populists), and later among the Marxists, therefore, the idea of "spontaneity" was closely connected with Bakunin's anarchism.

In 1869 a completely jesuitical conspirator appeared who combined ideas of Blanqui and Bakunin with some of his own, and who felt no inhibitions in his warfare against the government. This was Nechaev, who claimed to work with Bakunin's support and was certainly financed through his efforts. In Moscow Nechaev organized a tight terroristic nucleus on the principles of rigid discipline and individual obedience to group decisions. He displayed, however, a lack of integrity toward his own followers. He persuaded the members to murder as a spy one of their own number, thinking thereby to bind them inescapably to his organization and also to gain wide publicity for the revolutionary movement. He was renounced, however, by Bakunin, who had trusted him, and by the whole spectrum of radical opinion. He was used by Dostoevski in his *Possessed,* a novel in which he attacked not only the anarchists but the whole revolutionary movement.

A more thorough theoretical formulation of the less devious elements of Nechaev's plan (centralization, discipline, terrorism, etc.) was made by Peter Tkachev, a member of his organization who edited at Geneva from 1875 to 1881 a periodical called *The Tocsin* (*Nabat*). Blighted by the connection with Nechaev, his influence was more mediate than direct, exerted through his realistic grasp of Russian conditions, but it was considerably greater than is usually supposed. The People's Will (see p. 9ff), although not connected with him, accepted much of his reasoning.

The Russian people, Tkachev believed, "is much nearer to Socialism than the peoples of Western Europe, although the latter are more educated." Three circumstances led to that position. First, "Our people . . . is permeated with the principles of common ownership [through the village commune]; it is, if one may use the term, instinctively, traditionally communist."

Second, "We have no urban proletariat, that is undoubtedly true; but, then, we also have no bourgeoisie; . . . our workers will have to fight only against the *political power*—the *power of capital* is with us still only in embryo." And finally, the state itself "appears only at a distance as a power; . . . it has no roots in the economic life of the people; it does not embody the interests of any particular estate." It was, he went on, "a state hanging in the air, so to speak, one that has nothing in common with the existing social order, and that has its roots in the past, but not in the present." [3] In his plan of action Tkachev made an amalgam of ideas drawn from Blanqui, Bakunin, and Marx. As a literary critic, writing in many journals, he was one of the most consistent exponents of economic materialism, but he rejected emphatically all theories, whether Marxian or *narodnik*, that made social change dependent upon propaganda and the stimulation of a mass movement. All such theories had, in his opinion, a common defect: the process was too slow to prevent the development of capitalism in Russia. If capital ever gained power, revolution would be indefinitely delayed or rendered permanently impossible. The abysmal ignorance of the masses dictated a different tactic, a sudden seizure of political power by a tightly disciplined, nationwide conspiracy, after disorganizing the forces of government through the general use of terror. Political revolution was a precondition for social revolution, which would be imposed from above. Once in power the socialists would expropriate the means of production, strengthen the communes against the kulaks or any intrusion of capitalism, and educate the people. As this education progressed, egotism and inequality would gradually disappear, and with them the need for a centralized state. Like Bakunin, he looked forward to a fraternal federation of self-governing communes.

Tkachev did not claim to be a Marxist nor has he been claimed by them, but in his scheme several elements later important in Russian Marxism are discernible. His plan of a political revolution from below, followed by a social revolution from above,

---

[3] "Open Letter of Petr Tkachev to Friedrich Engels" (1874), quoted in Engels, "On Social Relations in Russia," in Karl Marx and Friedrich Engels, *Selected Works*, Vol. 2 (Moscow, 1951), pp. 52, 46-47.

was similar to the two stages, "bourgeois" and then "proletarian," generally expected by the Marxists, and even more similar to the actual course of events after October, 1917; and again, the "revolution from above" was proudly claimed by Stalin in connection with the collectivization of the 1930's. Tkachev's conviction that Russia could lead the way to socialism through the resolute action of a small minority came to be Trotsky's conviction in 1905, and ultimately Lenin's also. The Marxists' explanation, that the chain of capitalism broke first at its weakest link, only states post facto what Tkachev had seen beforehand. Finally, in his urgent desire to organize and impose socialism, to forestall and prevent the entrenchment of capitalism, by democratic or undemocratic means, he again anticipated the Bolsheviks.[4]

One of Alexander II's reactionary measures, intended to prevent the spread of Western ideas, was to call home the students who had gone abroad to study. These young men and women, recalling Herzen's injunction, "To the people!" became new and much larger waves of narodniks, beginning in 1873. Most of them aimed to educate, help, and minister to the peasants or factory workers, and only a few hoped to stir up an insurrection, but by 1877 several hundred of them had been imprisoned or exiled. Thus again, as with the Decembrists, the government depleted the supply of educated and civic-minded citizens, discouraging the peaceful propagandists among them and encouraging the terrorists. The recall of students, therefore, as not infrequently happened, produced an effect opposite to that intended by the government.

Perhaps more important than any westernizing influence they may have exerted, the experience of these young men and women with the peasants was among the strongest influences favoring the growth of Marxism among the radicals. Fresh from their universities, aiming unselfishly to give their knowledge to those who needed it most and to overcome the barriers that birth or education had erected between them and the peasants, many of the narodniks, if not immediately betrayed, were met

---

[4] For an interesting comparison of Tkachev with Lenin see Nicolas Berdyaev, *The Origin of Russian Communism* (London, 1937), pp. 80-85.

with tenacious ignorance, hopeless apathy, and obstinate rejection, for which Marx's "idiocy of rural life" seemed the perfect description. In order to preserve their shaken faith in humanity some of them turned elsewhere, to the people who had left the farms and formed a new and possibly more malleable mass, the proletariat. Once there they were already halfway to Marx; by 1883 Marxists were numerous enough to organize a society of their own.

A larger number of the surviving *narodniks* attributed their failure to inadequate organization and preparation. They revived Land and Liberty in 1876 and tried to orient it toward what they believed the peasants already understood and wanted. Soon, however, under the spur of their own frustrations and of Tkachev's sense of urgency, they evolved its program rapidly in the direction of immediate political revolution. The peasants' aims might be limited to a redistribution of land and self-government in the *mir,* but the threatening development of capitalism and "the various plagues of bourgeois civilization" would make such aims visionary unless forestalled by a change in the government. To some of its members, however, this evolution toward political objectives was a heresy amounting to the abandonment of socialism, and on this argument the society divided.

The moderate wing, led by Plekhanov and Axelrod (not yet Marxists), was called Black Redistribution (*Chernyi Peredel*) from the peasants' desire for land. It favored a direct struggle for socialism through the *artel* and the *mir.* Political freedom could stand only upon a firm economic foundation, and therefore the revolutionaries should improve their propaganda and prepare the people for an economic and social revolution. To turn immediately to political subversion would not help but would greatly hinder such a revolution. Terrorism was both immoral and impractical; it would antagonize potential supporters and stimulate the government to such severe repression and vigilance that no propaganda would be possible. Moreover, even if, as the terrorists held, by such tactics a constitution and some civil liberties could be achieved, they would only be used by the bourgeoisie, as they had been in western Europe, for the exploitation of the workers and peasants. For (and here lay the real basis of the split) Plekhanov and Axelrod were convinced that capitalism was making more rapid strides than was revolution, that it was already too late to forestall it. It would, however, concentrate landownership and thus contribute to the demand for redistribution. With time on their side this group soon retreated abroad, revised their doctrine, rechristened themselves in 1883 the Emancipation of Labor, and became the first group of Russian Marxists.

The other, frankly terrorist wing, The People's Will (*Narodnaia Volia*), led by Zheliabov, had drawn an opposite conclusion from going "to the people," the conclusion that propaganda could not be carried on without some improvement in political freedom. As Zheliabov summed it up,

> The party does not strive to attain political reforms. This task should belong entirely to the men who call themselves liberals. But these men are entirely powerless in Russia, and, whatever the reasons are, they have proved incapable of giving Russia free institutions and guaranties of personal rights. However, such institutions are so necessary that no activity appears to be possible without them. Therefore, the Russian socialist party is obliged to assume the duty of crushing despotism and of giving Russia those political reforms under which a struggle of opinions will be possible.[5]

That the next, the liberal or bourgeois revolution would have to be led, not by the liberals, but by the socialists—this became an article of faith among the revolutionaries. Moreover, they were convinced that peaceful propaganda, even if it won popular acceptance, would do no good since the government was adamant in its nonrecognition policy toward public opinion. Only violence, therefore, had any prospect of bringing results. That its prospects were improving, and that the public had become more sympathetic,[6] seemed demonstrated by the example of

[5] Quoted in Paul Miliukov, *Russia and Its Crisis* (Chicago, 1905), pp. 417-418.

[6] The opportunities given the *narodniks* who were placed on trial (and not simply exiled by administrative order) to explain their motives and ideals in open court had been an educational experience for the public, which followed the trials closely.

Vera Zasulich: she had shot the St. Petersburg chief of police, admitted it, and was not only acquitted by a popular jury but even protected by the crowd afterward against attempted re-apprehension. So, confident that they were carrying out their solemn duties as citizens, giving even their lives to improve their country, members of The People's Will knit themselves into an organization as tightly disciplined as Nechaev could have wished and appointed an Executive Committee to direct the use of terror and to explain and justify it before the public. The Committee wrote that

Terroristic activity consists in the destruction of the most harmful persons in the Government, the protection of the party from spies, and the punishment of official lawlessness and violence in all the more prominent and important cases in which such lawlessness and violence are manifested. The aim of such activity is to break down the prestige of Governmental power, to furnish continuous proof of the possibility of carrying on a contest with the Government, to raise in that way the revolutionary spirit of the people and inspire belief in the practicability of revolution, and, finally, to form a body suited and accustomed to warfare.[7]

The Committee in effect assumed sovereignty, an *imperium in imperio,* and in its judicial capacity passed sentence of death upon Alexander II. For eighteen months it pursued him with resourcefulness and personal sacrifice, finally killing him with a bomb in 1881. It was not simply that the tsar was reactionary and responsible for his agents; it was rather that the first prerequisite of freedom was that the people be freed from the hypnosis of autocracy.

Yet, fantastically as they may have fought the existing government, and strong as was Bakunin's influence among them, the members of The People's Will were far from being anarchists. Their aim, "to break down the prestige of Governmental power," was not an attack upon government as such. In the manifesto published upon the "execution" of Alexander they displayed more conviction in regard to economic than to political forms,

---

[7] "A Revolutionary Manifesto. Program of The People's Will," in George Kennan, *Siberia and the Exile System,* Vol. 2 (New York, 1891), p. 498.

but they called for a national constituent assembly, which, they
hoped, would establish the following program: [8]

1. Perpetual popular representation, constituted as above described
   [by "a general vote"] and having full power to act in all national
   questions
2. General local self-government, secured by the election of all officers, and the economic independence of the people
3. The self-controlled village commune as the economic and administrative unit
4. Ownership of the land by the people
5. A system of measures having for their object the turning over to
   the laborers of all mining works and factories
6. Complete freedom of conscience, speech, association, public meeting, and electioneering activity
7. Universal right of franchise, without any class or property limitation
8. The substitution of a territorial militia for the army.

It may seem incredible to those accustomed to popular sovereignty that means could diverge as far from ends as the methods
of terrorism diverged from the seemingly conservative goals of
The People's Will. This incredulity is itself a measure of the
difference between politics in tsarist Russia and in the West.

The death of the tsar, however, produced no general uprising
and his successor, schooled by Pobedonostsev, proved even
more reactionary than Alexander II. The terrorists were forced
to reconsider the utility of terrorism, and although not officially
disavowed, it was discontinued for a decade and never regained
the primary position it had held in the underground movement.

During this decade, when the best efforts of the extreme
wing of the *narodniks* appeared to have failed so abysmally,
their moderate opponents gained in strength. It seemed that
Axelrod and Plekhanov had been right in their opposition to
terror, as they had been right in their scepticism of the peasants
as revolutionaries. By 1882, however, these leaders had evolved
into Marxists. Moreover, during this time statistics were accumulating which convinced many of the *narodniks* that capitalism had come to Russia and that they could no longer hope to

[8] *Ibid.*, p. 497.

avoid it by basing socialism on the *mir*. When this conviction dawned on them, Marxism seemed inescapable.

Marx and Engels had learned Russian in order to study the revolution developing there. In the 1870's they saw in the village commune "the finest chance ever offered by history to a people" to avoid the horrors of capitalism; but they were aware that the commune was already being eroded by capitalistic influences. It could serve as "the mainspring of Russia's social regeneration," Marx wrote to Zasulich in 1881, but only if it were protected and allowed to develop spontaneously—both impossible conditions. The following year, therefore, in their preface to Plekhanov's translation of the *Communist Manifesto*, Marx and Engels laid down a different condition: "If the Russian revolution becomes the signal for a proletarian revolution in the West, so that both complement each other, the present Russian common ownership of land may serve as the starting point for a communist development." They were then optimistic that a non-proletarian uprising in Russia would provide the spark needed to set off a proletarian revolution in Europe. Engels wrote to Zasulich (1885):

What I know or believe I know about the situation in Russia makes me think that the Russians are approaching their 1789. . . . The country is like a charged mine. . . . This is one of the exceptional cases where it is possible for a handful of people to *make* a revolution. . . . If ever Blanquism—the fantastic idea of overturning an entire society by the action of a small conspiracy—had a certain raison d'être, that is certainly so now in Petersburg.[9]

By 1893, however, Engels believed it was too late. The "impulse from without," the revolution in Europe that would have provided a socialist model for the Russians to copy, had not come about in time, and it was not possible "to develop a higher social form out of primitive agrarian communism unless—that higher form was *already in existence* in another country, so as to serve as a model."[10]

Capitalism was unavoidable, therefore, yet the proper condi-

[9] Karl Marx and Friedrich Engels, *Selected Correspondence* (Moscow, n.d.), pp. 378, 412, 459-460.
[10] *Ibid.*, pp. 546-547.

tions for a proletarian revolution lay far in the future. Marx and Engels welcomed the adherence of some of the émigrés to the International and to Marxism, but their doctrines made little headway in Russia during Marx's lifetime. There were, however, various currents of thought in Russia with strong affinity for these theories. Many of the Westerners, notably Herzen, Chernyshevski, and Bakunin, grounded their positions, as did Marx, upon the French socialists and upon Hegel and the Left Hegelians. Although they differed from Marx on other points, like him they were convinced socialists and materialists. After the defeat of Bakunin in the First International and the emergence of Marxism as the dominant brand of socialism in western Europe it was to be expected that the Westerners would attempt more seriously than before to apply Marx's ideas to Russia. On the other hand, those who, under Slavophil influence, believed most strongly in the uniqueness and mission of Russia could find in Marx a penetrating critique of Western institutions. He assured them that Western capitalism and parliamentary government were temporary phenomena destined for destruction, and thus encouraged the hope that, having so largely escaped these blights, Russia might, through a scientific understanding of the processes of history, find a unique and less arduous path to a socialist utopia. And to both Westerners and Slavophils the internationalism of Marx was congenial—to the former it confirmed their opinion that Russia was inextricably linked to the future of Europe, while to the latter it offered a new and broader prospect for their messianism.

In addition to these theoretical affinities certain features of Russian political life also gave Marxism advantages over its competitors. The privileges and restrictions of classes were more sharply defined than in the West, and Marx's program was based on class consciousness. The intelligentsia, mostly urban, generally felt isolated and rejected by both the government and the peasantry; Marxism enabled them to escape this feeling by consciously identifying themselves with the urban proletariat. The government's disregard for public opinion had convinced many that peaceful change was impossible, and Marxism, unlike some other types of socialism and unlike liberalism, called not for persuasion or reform but for class warfare and revolution. The tight grip of the autocracy upon both the social structure and the church led the revolutionaries to strike at all three; to them, as to Marx, revolution must be political, social, and religious. Finally, the long tradition of bureaucratic centralization militated against a peasant movement, necessarily decentralized, and against anarchism, in favor of a movement focused upon the more concentrated proletariat and willing to seize power at the center.

Yet far outweighing these advantages and similarities of thought were various fundamental differences between the Russian environment and that for which Marx and Engels originally wrote. To these differences, reflected in various minds, the diversity and changeability of Marxist theory in Russia are largely due.

Of first rank among these was the retarded condition of capitalistic enterprise. From this flowed several special problems for the Marxists. On the one hand the capitalists themselves lacked the independent qualities of their Western counterparts, being much more dependent upon governmental favors and contracts and correspondingly unenthusiastic about the "bourgeois" revolution called for by the Marxist pattern of history. On the other hand, the proletarians who, by this same pattern, should carry on from there, were still too few. The preponderance of peasants (almost 90 per cent) in the population being far greater than in the West, the proportion of illiteracy and the difficulties both of propaganda and of organization were also greater. Moreover, any theory that discounted this vast reservoir of both misery and strength so thoroughly as did Marxism was bound to be unsatisfactory to many revolutionaries. And finally, the delay in capitalistic development meant delay in the deterministic economic solutions promised, by the schema of Marx, as a result of capitalism, and therefore stimulated his followers to search for political short cuts. The stage was thus set for conflicts between the adherents of the deterministic and the voluntaristic strains of Marxism, between those willing to await the inexorable grinding of the economic machinery and those who wanted to put their shoulders to the wheels.

Also conducive to such conflicts was a second fundamental

peculiarity in the situation of Russia, namely the arrival of Marxism in Russia a good generation later than in the West. An
obvious result was the head start enjoyed by the ideas of Bakunin,
which in addition had the advantage of greater inherent affinity
with Russian habits and circumstances Another result, of equal
importance, was the fact that Marxism had already undergone
extensive theoretical development before it began to be accepted
in Russia—development that reflected the course of Western
events more than those of Russia and that also presented to the
Russians some inconsistencies among statements by the prophets
themselves. Marx had led the way toward revisionism by his
statement in 1872 that the revolution might come in England
and the United States by majority vote; and the economic emphasis of his later writings was different from the stress on political action in his earlier ones, such as the *Communist Manifesto*.
Yet the desire to discover short cuts through the lengthy period
of capitalism that might lie ahead gave these earlier writings
(which were, incidentally, considerably closer to Bakunin) great
appeal. Thus both the influence of Bakunin among the revolutionaries and the early works of Marx imparted to Russian Marxism a strongly voluntaristic bent, while at the same time *Capital*
and later works already available encouraged the less impatient
to embrace economic determinism.

The ultimate predominance of the voluntarists was prepared
for by a third characteristic, the widespread determination to
avoid capitalism—a determination shared by Westerners and
Slavophils, by pacifists and bureaucrats, and by the non-Marxist
revolutionaries. The laissez-faire system had so thoroughly displayed its weaknesses before the industrial revolution reached
Russia that it had few defenders there. This distaste for even
a temporary bout of capitalism was long a severe handicap to
the popularity of Marxism because a proletarian revolution pre-
supposed a great growth of capitalism to produce the proletarians. The Marxists were at times so insistent upon the necessity of this that they appeared more concerned about the
bourgeoisie than about the workers or the peasants. The migra-
tion of Struve and others from the Marxist to the liberal camp
gave some substance to that appearance. The widespread jaun-

diced attitude was well summed up by Tikhomirov, a leader
of The People's Will:

> It is quite true that in the history of certain European peoples,
> capitalism, although it gave rise to a mass of evils and misfortunes,
> nevertheless had something good as one of its consequences, namely
> the creation of large-scale production, by means of which it prepared
> the ground, to a certain extent, for socialism. But it does not follow
> from this that other countries, for instance Russia, could not have
> other ways of developing large-scale production. . . . All this com-
> pels us to think that the mode of socialization of labour which capi-
> talism was capable of is one of the worst, because, although in many
> respects it actually prepares the possibility of the socialist system, at
> the same time, by other aspects it postpones in many respects the
> moment of its advent. Thus, capitalism, together with the mechanical
> union of the workers, develops competition among them, which un-
> dermines their moral unity; in exactly the same way it tends to keep
> the workers at a much lower level of development than is possible
> according to the general condition of culture; in the same way too,
> it directly disaccustoms the workers from any control over the general
> course of production, etc.[11]

To escape from the necessity for capitalism some of the Marxists eventually accepted revolution by a minority, to them the
lesser evil. This compromise, a triumph of voluntarism, was the
basis of the theory of the "permanent revolution," by which the
capitalistic period could be telescoped into a transient phase,
hardly even a lull, between the "bourgeois" and the "proletarian"
revolutions. Yet the predominance of the voluntarists did not
mean the rout of the determinists and their disappearance from
the movement. It meant, rather, personal and variable adjustments within the movement to these two strains of Marxist
thought, a process that still continues and gives to the Soviet
Union an unpredictable quality, potentially very dynamic or very
conservative, as the voluntaristic or the deterministic strain may
prevail at a given time.

[11] Lev Tikhomirov, "What Can We Expect from the Revolution?" (1884),
quoted in George Plekhanov, *Our Differences*, in his *Selected Philosophical
Works*, Vol. 1, pp. 207-208.

BIBLIOGRAPHY

Primary Works

Bakunin, Mikhail, *God and the State* (1871; New York, 1916 [?]).
———, *L'empire knoutogermanique et la révolution sociale* (1871; Geneva, 1871). Also known as *La révolution sociale ou la dictature militaire*.
———, *Fédéralisme, socialisme et antithéologisme* (1867; Paris, 1897).
———, *The Political Philosophy of Bakunin*, G. P. Maximoff, ed. (Glencoe, Ill., 1953). Material rearranged unmercifully.
Chernov, Victor, *The Great Russian Revolution*, trans. and abridged by Philip E. Mosely (New Haven, 1936).
Chernyshevski, N. G., *L'économie politique jugée par la science* (1860), trans. by A. Tveritinov and C. de Paepe (Brussels, 1874).
———, *La possession communale du sol* (1858-1864), trans. by E. Laran-Tamarkine (Paris, 1903).
———, *Selected Philosophical Essays* (Moscow, 1953).
Herzen, Alexander, *Du développement des idées révolutionnaires en Russie* (Paris, 1851).
———, *From the Other Shore* (1847-1850), trans. by Moura Budberg (London, 1956). Contains also *The Russian People and Socialism* (1851).
———, *Selected Philosophical Works*, trans. by L. Navrozov (Moscow, 1956).
Kravchinski, S. M. (Stepniak), *Career of a Nihilist* (New York, 1889). A novel.
Lavrov, Peter, *Lettres historiques*, trans. by Marie Goldsmith (Paris, 1903).
Mikhailovski, Nikolai, *Qu'est ce que le progrès?* (1869), trans. by Paul Louis (Paris, 1897).
Tikhomirov, Lev, *La Russie politique et sociale* (Paris, 1886).
Tolstoi, Lev, *Church and State and Other Essays*, trans. by Victor Yarros and George Schumm (Boston, 1891).
———, *On Socialism* (1910), trans. by Ludvig Perno (London, 1936).
———, *The Slavery of Our Times* (1899), trans. by Aylmer Maude (Maldon, Essex, 1900).

Secondary Studies

Barghoorn, Frederick C., "The Philosophic Outlook of Chernyshevski: Materialism and Utilitarianism," *American Slavic and East European Review,* Vol. 6 (December, 1947), pp. 42-56.

Belchikov, Nikolai F., *Tschernyschewskij, eine kritisch-biographische Skizze* (Berlin, 1948). Soviet interpretation.

Bernstein, Eduard, "Karl Marx und Michael Bakunin," *Archiv für Sozialwissenschaft und sozial Politik,* Vol. 30 (January, 1910), pp. 1-29.

Billington, James H., *Mikhailovsky and Russian Populism* (Oxford, 1958).

Iakovenko, Boris, *Ein Beitrag zur Geschichte des Hegelianismus in Russland* (Prague, 1934).

Koyré, Alexandre, *Études sur l'histoire de la pensée philosophique en Russie* (Paris, 1950).

Kulczycki, Ludwig, *Geschichte der russischen Revolution,* 3 vols. (Gotha, 1910-1914).

Labry, Raoul, *Alexandre Ivanovič Herzen, 1812-1870* (Paris, 1928).

Lampert, E., *Studies in Rebellion* (London, 1957).

Laurila, Kaarle S., "Leo Tolstois politische Ansichten," *Suomalaisen Tiedeakatemian Toimituksia* (Annales Academiae Scientiarum Fennicae), Series B, Vol. 17 (Helsinki, 1923), pp. 1-158.

Lavigne, Ernest, *Introduction à l'histoire du nihilisme Russe* (Paris, 1880). Contains documents.

McLean, Hugh, and others, eds., *Russian Thought and Politics* ('s-Gravenhage, 1957).

Masaryk, Thomas G., *The Spirit of Russia,* 2 vols. (London, 1919).

Nettlau, Max, "Bakunin und die russische revolutionäre Bewegung in den Jahren 1868-1873," *Archiv für die Geschichte des Sozialismus und der Arbeiterbewegung,* Vol. 5 (1914), pp. 357-422.

Owen, Lancelot A., *The Russian Peasant Movement, 1906-1917* (London, 1937).

Paléologue, Georges M., *Les précurseurs de Lénine* (Paris, 1938).

Pyziur, Eugene, *The Doctrine of Anarchism of Michael A. Bakunin* (Milwaukee, 1955).

Rezneck, Samuel, "The Political and Social Theory of Michael Bakunin," *American Political Science Review,* Vol. 21 (May, 1927), pp. 270-296.

Rosen, Hans von, *Die social politischen Ideen Alexander Herzens* (Halle, 1893).

Scheibert, P., *Von Bakunin zu Lenin. Geschichte der russischen revolutionären Ideologien 1840-1895* (Leiden, 1956-   ).

Simmons, Ernest J., ed., *Continuity and Change in Russian and Soviet Thought* (Cambridge, Mass., 1955).

Steklow, Georg, "Alexander Herzen und Nikolai Tschernischewsky," *Archiv für die Geschichte der Sozialismus und der Arbeiterbewegung*, Vol. 8 (1918), pp. 1-39.

Valentinov, N., "Tschernychevski et Lénine," *Le contrat social*, Vol. 1 (May and June, 1957), pp. 101-110, 162-172.

Venturi, Franco, *Roots of Revolution. A History of the Populist and Socialist Movements in Nineteenth Century Russia*, trans. by Francis Haskell (London, 1960). Monumental study, to 1881.

Walter, Michael, *Tolstoi nach seinen sozialökonomischen, staatstheoretischen und politischen Anschauungen* (Zurich, 1906).

General Studies of Russian Marxism

Berdiaev, Nikolai, *The Origin of Russian Communism* (London, 1937).

Bochenski, I. M., *Der Sowjetrussische dialektische Materialismus* (Bern, 1950). Also in Italian.

————, "On Soviet Philosophy," *Review of Politics*, Vol. 13 (July, 1951), pp. 344-353.

Daniels, Robert V., *The Conscience of the Revolution. Communist Opposition in Soviet Russia* (Cambridge, Mass., 1960).

Haimson, Leopold H., *The Russian Marxists and the Origins of Bolshevism* (Cambridge, Mass., 1955).

Kelsen, Hans, *The Political Theory of Bolshevism. A Critical Analysis* (Berkeley, 1949).

Kulczycki, Ludwig, *Geschichte der russischen Revolution*, Vol. 3 (Gotha, 1914). On the early Marxists.

Lange, Max G., *Marxismus, Leninismus, Stalinismus; zur Kritik des dialektischen Materialismus* (Stuttgart, 1955).

Marcuse, Herbert, *Soviet Marxism, a Critical Analysis* (New York, 1958).

Plamenatz, John, *German Marxism and Russian Communism* (London, 1954).

Schapiro, Leonard, *The Origin of the Communist Autocracy* (Cambridge, Mass., 1955).

Schlesinger, Rudolf, *The Spirit of Post-War Russia: Soviet Ideology, 1917-1946* (London, 1947).

Somerville, John, *Soviet Philosophy. A Study of Theory and Practice* (New York, 1946).

Vostokov, P., "La philosophie russe durant la période post-révolution-naire," *Le Monde Slave*, N. S. Vol. 9, tome 4 (November-December, 1932), pp. 286-305 (on the Marxists) and pp. 432-457 (on the émigrés).

Wetter, Gustav A., *Dialectical Materialism, a Historical and Systematic Survey of Philosophy in the Soviet Union*, trans. by Peter Heath (London, 1958).

II in 1881 sent another wave of radicals into exile, and it was among such exiles in Geneva in 1883 that Plekhanov, Axelrod, Leo Deutsch, and Zasulich started the first Russian Marxist organization, the Emancipation of Labor. This continued for some twenty years, its members writing and translating materials for the circles of Marxists appearing in Russia during that time.

An effective although tediously argumentative writer, Plekhanov was too temperamental and conceited to be an effective political leader, but the revolutionary movement stood in need of ideas rather than of leaders. He was attracted to Marxism by its claim to objective, scientific validity. Moreover, he saw in it a solution for the dilemma confronting the revolutionaries as a result of the unresponsiveness of the peasants to the efforts of the *narodniks,* particularly to their supreme effort, the killing of Alexander II. Marx would have expected nothing better from them. He had pointed instead to another source of support: the industrial proletariat. His theory, therefore, both explained past failures and presented the revolutionaries with a new plan and new hope. Russia was still in its industrial infancy, but Plekhanov saw numerous signs of growing proletarian strength. He became convinced that Russia was well advanced in the Marxian pattern of evolution from feudalism through capitalism to socialism.

The platform of The People's Will was an extreme assertion of the necessity for the revolutionaries to engage in a direct political struggle with the autocracy, instead of the economic and social aims of the *narodniks.* In rejecting their approach Plekhanov did not object to political revolution, although he believed that for the people (as distinguished from the intelligentsia) economic problems were more basic. He objected not to terrorism but to exclusive dependence upon it. The People's Will not only abandoned propaganda among the people; they considered it unnecessary and, by arousing the police, they made it more difficult. Plekhanov, on the contrary, believed it to be essential, since without an understanding of socialism among the people even a successful political coup would miscarry. He condemned the terrorist program as impossible Blanquism, and in his polemics he foresaw the dilemma that confronted the Bolsheviks in 1917. If the revolutionaries retained power in their own hands, this would mean rule by a "socialist caste"; if they surrendered power to the people, this would mean only bourgeois rule.

If government by the people were really established in our country, when asked whether they needed land and whether it should be confiscated from the landlords, the self-governing people would answer that they did need it and that it must be confiscated. But if asked whether they needed the "foundation of the socialist organization," they would first answer that they did not understand the meaning of that question, and then, having understood it with great difficulty, they would answer: No, we don't need that. And as the expropriation of the big landowners is by no means equivalent to the "foundation of the socialist organization," there would not be any socialism as a result of the seizure of power by the revolutionaries.[1]

The efforts of the socialists, therefore, should be expended on propaganda and on the organization of a political party.

The strength of the working class—as of any other class—depends, among other things, on the clarity of its political consciousness, its cohesion and its degree of organization. It is these elements of its strength that must be influenced by our socialist intelligentsia. The latter must become the leader of the working class in the impending emancipation movement, explain to it its political and economic interests and also the interdependence of those interests and must prepare them to play an independent role in the social life of Russia.[2]

The socialist must "bring *consciousness* into the working class," and not simply await its development through the influence of the factory environment, as more deterministic Marxists might think. Plekhanov did not deny the influence of factory life, however, and this duty of the intellectuals to instill class consciousness did not have for him the significance it came to have for Lenin (see p. 47).

This instilling of class consciousness was closely related, nevertheless, to the emphasis Plekhanov placed on politics. The extreme power of the autocracy had led most of the revolutionaries to emphasize economic problems and to regard political reform as the province of the liberals. The People's Will reversed this

---

[1] Plekhanov, *Our Differences* (1884), in his *Selected Philosophical Works*, trans. by R. Dixon, Vol. 1 (Moscow, 1961), p. 349.
[2] Plekhanov, *Socialism and the Political Struggle* (1883), in *ibid.*, p. 117.

tendency, and on this matter Plekhanov agreed with them: "It now turned out that the exceptionalism of Russian social development consisted precisely in economic questions being and having to be solved in our country by means of state interference." [3] In Marxist theory politics was a "superstructure" resting on an economic base, and this, combined with the *narodniks'* emphasis on economic conditions, was soon to lead to "Economism"—nonpolitical Marxism in Russia. From the beginning, however, Plekhanov interpreted the scriptures differently. In the social sphere, he argued, cause and effect are reciprocally interacting concepts. Every gain in economic strength is used to gain new political strength, and this, in turn, makes possible new economic gains. So it is under capitalism, he held, and so the socialists should regard their struggle. [4]

When he embraced Marxism Plekhanov was confronted at once with the primary and hitherto overriding objection that Marxism, for Russia, meant a period of capitalism—a fate that must be avoided, all the revolutionaries had held, by taking advantage of the village commune. To this he had three main answers: 1) Russia had already taken the capitalist road and there was no escape, 2) the village commune was a false hope since its inherent tendency was to evolve toward capitalist and not toward socialist forms of landownership, and 3) the length of the capitalistic period was variable, and in Russia its rise and fall would be accelerated because technology and Marxism could be borrowed full blown from the West. [5] To many, these answers, reiterated and statistically supported, were never convincing. Marxism continued to labor under the stigma of wanting capitalism before socialism.

Plekhanov's third answer involved the question, Are there alternative paths to socialism?, which has continued to generate heat in the Marxist movement to the present day. Believing that "the development of scientific socialism is not complete" and cannot "stop at the works of Marx and Engels," he proceeded to develop it in the voluntaristic vein. The first program of the

---

[3] *Ibid.*, p. 74.
[4] *Ibid.*, pp. 80-85.
[5] Plekhanov, *Our Differences*, in *ibid.*, pp. 235-310, 378-380.

Emancipation of Labor group (1884) contained a strong claim
for a separate path for Russia. Quoting Marx's "The proletariat
of each country must, of course, first of all settle matters with
its own bourgeoisie," he went on:

> This introduces an element of variety into the programmes of the
> socialist parties in the different states, compelling each of them to con-
> form to the social conditions in its country. It goes without saying
> that the practical tasks, and consequently the programmes of the so-
> cialists, are bound to be more original and complicated in countries
> where capitalist production has not yet become dominant and where
> the working masses are oppressed under a double yoke—that of rising
> capitalism and that of obsolescent patriarchal economy.[6]

This dealt with variety in the conditions and the tasks of the
socialists, however, and not with exceptions to the Marxist pattern of history. Yet he went further, saying that "dialectical
materialism doesn't sentence any countries to anything at all."
The door was open to even more original thought by others.

Plekhanov's emphasis on the political struggle met its strongest
challenge from the "Economists" who, from 1896, began to revise
Marxism to fit better, as they thought, the realities of Russia.
Having deep historical roots in the apolitical attitudes of the
narodniks and anarchists, and stressing the economic bases of
Marx, the Economists developed directly from participation in
the economic struggles of the proletariat as advocated by the
pamphlet *On Agitation* (see p. 92). For some six years they
showed great strength, capturing the St. Petersburg Union of
Struggle after Lenin's arrest and the émigré Union of Russian
Social Democrats Abroad in spite of Plekhanov and his friends.
They enjoyed two fortuitous advantages. In the first place, nearly
all their opponents in Russia were jailed or exiled, including the
St. Petersburg leaders and the officers chosen by the First Party
Congress in Minsk in 1898. In the second, the revisionist writings
of Eduard Bernstein began, after the death of Engels, to chal-
lenge one after another of the dogmas of Marxism. The Economists were hardly as sophisticated as Bernstein, but his em-

---

6 Plekhanov, *Selected Philosophical Works*, Vol. 1, p. 402. Similar passages were included in the second draft program (1887) and in the program adopted by the Congress of 1903, but not in that of 1919.

pirical approach confirmed them in their belief that both tactics
and program could be evolved gradually in the spontaneous
economic struggle.

In 1899 the Economists published a *Credo* drawn up by Katarina Kuskova. Since many of the Economists later became
Mensheviks, these views were important in the development of
Menshevik thought, but whereas the Mensheviks expected Russian developments to parallel those of the West, Kuskova began
by contrasting Russia with the West. She found that the "fundamental law" of the labor movement was that it followed the
"line of least resistance," which in the West, with its free institutions, was political activity, while in Russia, with the oppression
of the autocracy, "the line of least resistance will never tend
in the direction of political activity."

> The economic struggle too is hard, infinitely hard, but it is possible
> to wage it; it is in fact being waged by the masses themselves. By
> learning to organise in the midst of this struggle, and coming into
> constant conflict with the political regime in the course of it, the Rus-
> sian worker will at last create what may be called the form of the
> labour movement, the organisation or organisations that will best con-
> form to Russian conditions.[7]

In the meantime the antagonism displayed by "intolerant,
negative, primitive Marxism" toward the liberals should be replaced by collaboration in "liberal opposition activity" against
the autocracy.

From various points of exile Plekhanov, Axelrod, Lenin, and
Martov thundered against these views. As firm believers in "spontaneity," in the development of the workers into socialists through
their own experiences, the Economists denied the value of ideological propaganda and of a political party dedicated to the in-
fusion of class consciousness into the workers. They thus challenged the whole pattern of Russian Marxism as Plekhanov had
conceived it. Worse still, they were prepared, unlike the other
revolutionaries, to see the bourgeoisie lead its own revolution.
They thus seemed to reduce the proletariat, in politics, to an
appendage of the bourgeoisie. No Russian Marxist had yet con-

[7] The text of the *Credo* is in V. I. Lenin, *Selected Works*, 12 vol. ed.,
Vol. 1 (London, n.d.), pp. 516-519. Quotation from p. 518.

templated a proletarian government to be installed by a bourgeois revolution, but Plekhanov's orthodox followers refused to
surrender the idea, borrowed from Zheliabov, that the revolution
must be led by the working class. The threat that the proletariat
might be taken in tow by the hated bourgeoisie, with the help
of persons claiming to be Marxists, made the organization of an
effective and disciplined political party more than ever urgent.

At this point Lenin, determined to counteract the spread of
Economism and to organize Russian Marxism, conceived the
idea that a newspaper, published abroad and smuggled all over
Russia, could serve both purposes. As a forum for opinion it
would expose error and concentrate the efforts of its adherents
on the lines of activity advocated by the best collective thought.
Being nationwide, it would lead to the union of the scattered
circles and groups into a real party. In this project he enlisted
Martov and Potresov and went to Geneva to negotiate for the
cooperation of Plekhanov and his friends.

Plekhanov, Axelrod, and Zasulich joined in the publication of
the paper, the famous *Iskra* ("The Spark"), but these negotiations had a profound disillusioning effect upon Lenin. From a
distance Plekhanov, the "founder of Russian Marxism," had been
idealized; Lenin was, he said, even "enamoured" with him and
approached him with deference. Now, face to face, the great
man seemed to his younger disciple to be suspicious and autocratic, scheming and slippery, dealing with a comrade as with
an enemy. The shock of this revelation was almost fatal to the
plan, but the initial revulsion soon turned to a response of emula-
tion. Lenin resolved thenceforth "to regard all persons 'without
sentiment'; to keep a stone in one's sling." This attitude was to
permeate Lenin's party and to weigh heavily therein against
idealism.[8]

When Lenin and Potresov approached him with their project
for the unification of the Russian Marxists, Plekhanov had just
withdrawn with his group from the Union of Russian Social
Democrats Abroad, which had been captured by the Economists.

---

[8] These negotiations are described, from Lenin's point of view, in his
"How the *Spark* Was Nearly Extinguished," *Collected Works*, Vol. 4 (New
York, 1929), Part 1, pp. 23-37.

He found Lenin too mild toward these and other revisionists, for he was utterly irreconcilable to reunion with them and similarly adamant on the Jewish Bund, which he denied was even Marxist. The concept of *Iskra* as a forum, open even to non-Marxist writers, he rejected; the editors should, he believed, shape opinion in the movement, not by superiority of argument and the convincing of opponents, but by polemics and by excluding those who disagreed. Lenin's desire for unity on a broader scale soon gave way as he learned (perhaps over-learned) from Plekhanov the limits of persuasion and the advantages of splits and the elimination of adversaries.

In this spirit the *Iskra* editors engineered the Second Party Congress in 1903. They used their prestige and their paper to prevent the calling of a congress by other groups until their following was sufficient to enable them to assemble a respectable gathering with a dependable majority. Even the driving out of groups that had to be invited, such as the Bund, was planned in advance. Yet, as happens with overwhelming majorities, the *Iskra* group itself split: this was the congress that produced the Bolsheviks and the Mensheviks, two parties instead of one.[9]

At the Congress itself Plekhanov sided with Lenin and was thus among the original Bolsheviks. He soon had second thoughts, however, as Lenin's polemics against Martov, Axelrod, and Trotsky pointed up the distinctions and conflicts between conspiracy and centralization on the one hand and propaganda and a mass party on the other. He left Lenin, taking *Iskra* with him into the ranks of the Mensheviks.

Long hoping for a restoration of unity, Plekhanov, in the years that followed, at times agreed with Lenin on specific issues, as, for example, on the continuation of illegal as well as legal party work. When the First World War forced upon Marxists everywhere a choice between patriotism and their principles, however, he immediately became a "social chauvinist," supporting the tsar's government. He justified this position by the argument that, if Russia were defeated, Germany would convert it into an agrarian province, would stifle the growth of industry and

[9] The split is discussed in more detail on pp. 50-51, 93-95.

the proletariat, and thus the prospects of Social Democracy would be set back for many years, if not indefinitely. At the opposite pole from the Bolsheviks and their policy of working to overthrow the tsar, he also broke with Martov and eventually withdrew from the Mensheviks. Thus standing aside from all important groups, he returned to Russia after the revolution of February, 1917. He rejected on principle an invitation to join the government of Kerensky, but he greeted with derision Lenin's "April Theses" (see p. 76) and did not participate in the October revolution. Gravely ill, he left Petrograd and died in Finland in June, 1918.

By his interpretations of the scriptures and of events Plekhanov had given a strongly voluntaristic bent to Russian Marxism and directed it toward political goals. Yet he tried to maintain a balance with the deterministic strain and to keep his feet firmly planted on the economic realities. Both slow development and sudden change were parts of the pattern, in his opinion; but the sudden change could come only when the time was ripe, when the evolution of the means of production had given strength to the proletariat. On these grounds he established Marxism in opposition to the *narodniks* who, in one way or another, wished to use the peasant commune as a basis for socialism, and so to skip the period of capitalism. On the same grounds, while remaining a Marxist, he opposed the later variations in Marxism itself as, in the hands of Trotsky in 1905 and of Lenin in 1917, it came to stand for sudden change without regard for the stage of development of the means of production—much in the manner of The People's Will. He was not radical enough to forget Marx's economics and to give to politics so great a degree of autonomy. Thus he was, in the end, too deterministic, too patient, to be able to maintain leadership in the movement under the conditions then prevailing in Russia.

[THE POLITICAL SIGNIFICANCE OF THE

PEASANT "INDIFFERENCE TO POLITICS"]

Plekhanov, *Istoriia Russkoi Obshchestvennoi Mysli* (1913-1915),
in his *Sochineniia*, D. Riazanov, ed., Vol. 20 (Moscow-Leningrad,
1925), trans. by Eugene Hardy. Brackets in the text refer to pages
of this edition; cf. pp. 132-152 of the French edition, *Introduction
à l'Histoire Sociale de la Russie*, trans. by Mme. Batault-Plékhanov
(Paris, 1926).

One of the remarkable peculiarities of the Russian historical process is the fact that our struggle of the classes most
often remained beneath the surface, [and] in the course of a
very long time not only did not disturb our existent political
order but, on the contrary, extraordinarily strengthened it.

Further. Estate (*pomest'e*) ownership for a long period was
economically a necessary condition for obtaining proper service
from the gentry. This was clearly understood both by the "most
humble slaves" of the Russian rulers and by their actual slaves—
the peasants. But with the development of a money economy
the situation essentially changed. The army was reorganized and
the distribution of land gave way to money wages. This also
did not escape the people's attention. Gentry landownership lost
justification in their eyes. If the enserfed peasants were convinced that their actual liberation should follow the abolition
of compulsory service of the estate owners, then they viewed
it in no way other than as liberation *with land*. . . .

When the peasant demanded seizure of the land from the
landlords, and even when he himself set out to seize it, he conducted himself not as a revolutionary but, on the contrary, as
the most confirmed conservative: he protected that agrarian base
on which the whole social-political structure of Russia had maintained itself for so long. Opposing the "black redistribution,"
the landlords rose against that base, and for that reason appeared

in the eyes of the peasant as the most dangerous of rebels. The natural result was that, proposing such a radical economic demand as the demand for land redistribution, our farmers at the same time remained absolutely alien to any sort of political radicalism. [111-113]

Peter not only consolidated the enserfment of the peasantry. Even his numerous and varied technical adoptions from the West carried our social relations not so much toward Europeanization as toward a more consequent transformation of them in the old Moscovite spirit. Wishing to stimulate the development of the productive forces of his country, he turned to that means which had such wide application in Moscovite Russia: to forced labor and compulsory service of the various classes of the population suitable for the given aims. . . . In the advanced countries of the West the spreading of factory and workshop production meant the spreading of the system of hired labor. In Russia Peter, founding factories and workshops, attached to them the neighboring peasants, which created a new kind of serfdom. [121-122]

Falling into the position of a proletarian, even though on paper he continued to be considered a peasant in the majority of cases, the Russian producer began little by little to enter that same path on which the West-European workers had long preceded him: on the path of struggle against capital. This struggle quickly developed in him a new frame of mind and aspiration, previously unheard of in Russia. And when the police state zealously defended the interests of capital, the Russian proletarian quickly lost one after the other the eternal political prejudices of the peasant that he had carried out of the village. . . .

One of the first reforms perpetrated by that counterrevolution [1906] of the gentry, which triumphed thanks to the still insufficient Europeanization of the peasantry by the previous course of economic development, was the legislative abolition of the agrarian commune. The gentry reasoned that by abolishing the agrarian commune it would kill that old agrarian tradition in the name of which the peasantry considered itself right to expropriate the landlords. And it stands to reason that sooner or later they will kill it. But together with it they will kill all the old peasant outlook, finally destroying that economic base on which for so many centuries our old political order has been based. This will hardly be in accord with the interests of the gentry but will certainly be in complete accord with the interests of the proletariat, the progressive movement of which has been and is being held back by the political inertia of the old peasantry. [125-126]

TRUE TASKS OF THE

SOCIALISTS IN RUSSIA

Plekhanov, *Our Differences*, in his *Selected Philosophical Works*, trans. by R. Dixon, Vol. 1 (Moscow, 1961), pp. 373-374, 378-380, 389-390.

"Russian socialism, as expressed in the Narodnaya Volya party," will be alien to the great tasks of European socialism until it abandons for ever its intermediary position between Bakunin's anarchism and Tkachov's Blanquism, i.e., until it acknowledges the barrenness of Mr. Tikhomirov's theoretical constructions.

But as these constructions are the last desperate attempt to revive our revolutionary theories of the good old times, our socialism, by raising itself to the height of such an acknowledgement, will cease to be *"Russian"* and will merge with world socialism "as expressed" in the works of Marx and Engels and partly in those of Lassalle.

Its supporters will then understand that:

1. The *communist* revolution of the working class cannot in any way grow out of the petty-bourgeois peasant socialism professed at present by nearly all our revolutionaries.

2. By the inherent character of its organization the rural community tends first and foremost to give place to bourgeois, not communist, forms of social life.

3. In the transition to the latter its role will be not *active,* but *passive;* it is not in a position to *advance* Russia on the road to communism; it can only *offer less resistance* to that advance than small individual landownership.

4. The initiative in the communist movement can be assumed only by the working class in our industrial centres, the class,

5. Whose emancipation can be achieved only by its own conscious efforts.

Once they have understood these simple truths, the Russian socialists "from the privileged sections" will put aside all thoughts of seizing power, leaving that to our workers' socialist party of the future. Then their efforts will be directed only *towards the creation of such a party and the removal of all conditions which are unfavourable to its growth and development. . . .*

The most usual argument against that trend—an argument which comes *from the heart* if not "from reason"—is the reference to the impossibility of the revolutionary movement developing rapidly in Russia if its chances depend only on the strength and growth of the Russian working class. This consideration gives rise, on the one hand, to the inclination towards exceptionalist programmes, and, on the other, to the fear that we have already mentioned of the revolutionaries themselves having, perhaps, to enter the service of Russian capital. This argument, of course, will not be long in being brought to bear against our reasoning.

That is why we do not think it superfluous to draw our reader's attention to the strange inconsistency of those from whom we hear objections similar to the one just quoted. That inconsistency is a palpable indication that many of Chernyshevsky's pupils have mastered only the results of his study and have not formed the slightest idea of his method.

When it is a question of the probable destiny of Russian capitalism or of its influence on our political relations, the Narodniks generally begin by pointing out the supposed indisputable fact that our capitalism is in the same stage of development as was that "in Western Europe" more than a century ago. From this it is concluded that a whole century must elapse before capitalism renders our history the same "service" as it rendered the history of the "West." That is a long time, and as our intelli-

gentsia have long been in the habit of substituting their revolutionary will for revolutionary development, they look to the
village community and refer to the possibility proved by Chernyshevsky of its immediate transition to a socialist form of communal life. Thus they invoke the probability of the *complete
omission* of one phase in social development largely because they
do not understand the possibility of that phase *being shortened.*
It does not even occur to them that the complete omission of a
particular historical period is but a particular case of its short-
ening, and that by proving the possibility of the former we at
the same time, and to a larger extent, affirm the probability of
the latter.

We have already seen above from the example of P. N. Tkachov that this gross error in logic underlay our Blanquists' programme. Unfortunately not only the Blanquists repeat it.

Many people think that the social revolution can take place
in Russia "now, or in a very remote future, perhaps never"—in
other words on the basis either of our present economic relations or of a system whose institution and consolidation are a
matter of the most hazy future. But we already know—and this
we learn from the history of that same Western Europe—that
only the first step was difficult for capitalism and that its uninterrupted advance from "West" to East is taking place with
constantly increasing acceleration. Not only the development of
capitalism in Russia cannot be as slow as it was in England, for
example, its very existence cannot be so lasting as it has been
fated to be in the "West European countries." Our capitalism
will fade before it has time to blossom *completely*—a guarantee
for which we find in the powerful influence of international relations. But neither is it possible to doubt that the course of affairs
is advancing to its more or less complete victory. Neither un-
substantiated denials of an already existing fact nor grieved
exclamations about the disintegration of the old "traditional"
forms of the people's communal life—nothing will stop the advance of a country "which has entered the road of the natural
law of its development." But this development will be more or
less slow, the birth-pangs will be more or less painful, depending
on the combination of all the social and international relations

of the country in question. The more or less favourable character of that combination for the working class depends, in turn,
on the conduct of those who have understood the meaning of
the evolution which awaits their country. . . .

In promoting the formation of the workers' party, our revolutionaries will be doing the most fruitful, the most important thing
that can be pointed to a "progressive man" in present-day Russia.
The workers' party alone is capable of solving all the contradictions which now condemn our intelligentsia to theoretical and
practical impotence. We have already seen that the most obvious
of those contradictions is at present the necessity to overthrow
absolutism and the impossibility of doing so without the support
of the people. Secret workers' organizations will solve this contradiction by drawing into the political struggle the most progressive sections of the people. But that is not enough. Growing and
strengthening under the shelter of free institutions, the Russian
workers' socialist party will solve another, not less important
contradiction, this time of the economic character. We all know
that the village community of today must give place to communism or ultimately disintegrate. At the same time, the economic
organization of the community has no springs to start it off on
the road to communist development. While *easing* our peasants'
transition to communism, the community cannot impart to it the
initiative necessary for that transition. On the contrary, the development of commodity production is more and more undermining the traditional foundations of the community principle.
And our Narodist intelligentsia cannot remove this basic contradiction in one fell swoop. Some of the village communities are
declining, disintegrating before their eyes and becoming a
"scourge and a brake" for the poorest of the community members. Unfortunate as this phenomenon may seem to the intelligentsia, they can do absolutely nothing to help the community
at present. There is absolutely no link whatever between the
"lovers of the people" and the "people." The disintegrating community is still alone on its side, and the grieving intelligentsia
are alone on theirs, neither being able to put an end to this
state of affairs. How can a way out of this contradiction be
found? Will our intelligentsia indeed have to say Bah! to all

practical work and console themselves with "utopias" of the kind
Mr. G. Uspensky likes? Nothing of the sort! Our Narodniks can
at least save a certain number of village communities if only
they will consent to appeal to the dialectics of our social development. But such an appeal is also possible only through the
intermediary of a workers' socialist party.

The disintegration of our village community is an indisputable
fact. But the speed and intensity of the process differs according
to localities in Russia. To halt it completely in places where the
community is still fresher and more stable, our Narodniks must
use the forces now being freed by breaking up of communities
in gubernias where industry is more developed. These forces are
nothing else than the forces of the rising proletariat. They, and
they alone, can be the link between the peasantry and the socialist intelligentsia; they, and they alone, can bridge the historical
abyss between the "people" and the "educated" section of the
population. Through them and with their help socialist propaganda will at last penetrate into every corner of the Russian
countryside. Moreover, if they are united and organized at the
right time into a single workers' party, they can be the main
bulwark of socialist agitation in favour of economic reforms
which will protect the village community against general disintegration. And when the hour of the decisive victory of the workers' party over the upper sections of society strikes, once more
that party, and only that party, will take the initiative in the
socialist organization of national production. Under the influence
of—and, if the case presents itself, under pressure from that
party—the village communities still existing will in fact begin the
transition to a higher, communist form. . . .

MORE ON FREEDOM AND NECESSITY

Plekhanov, *In Defense of Materialism. The Development of the Monist View of History*, trans. by Andrew Rothstein (1895; London, 1947). Brackets in the text refer to pages of this edition.

The French materialists, consistently developing their sensationalist views, came to the conclusion that man, with all his thoughts, feelings and aspirations, is the product of his social environment. In order to go further in applying the materialist view to the study of man, it was necessary to solve the problem of what conditions the structure of the social environment, and what are the laws of its development. The French materialists were unable to reply to this question, and thereby were forced to be false to themselves, and to return to the old *idealist* point of view which they had so strongly condemned: they said that environment is created by the "opinion" of men. Dissatisfied with this superficial reply, the French historians of the Restoration set themselves the task of analysing social environment. The result of their analysis was the conclusion, extremely important for science, that *political constitutions are rooted in social relations,* while social relations are determined by the *state of property*. With this conclusion there arose before science a new problem, without solving which it could not proceed: *on what then depends the state of property?* The solution of this problem proved to be beyond the powers of the French historians of the Restoration, and they were obliged to dismiss it with remarks on the qualities of human nature which explained absolutely nothing at all. The great idealists of Germany—Schelling and Hegel—who were their contemporaries in life and work, already well understood how unsatisfactory was the point of view of human nature: Hegel made caustic fun of it. They understood that the key to the explanation of the historical advance of humanity must be sought *outside* human nature. This was a great service which they rendered: but in order that that service should prove completely fruitful for science, it was necessary to show *where precisely that key should be sought.* They looked for it in the *qualities of the spirit,* in the logical *laws of development of the absolute idea.* This was a radical error of the great idealists, which returned them by roundabout ways to the point of view of human nature, since the absolute idea, as we have already seen, is nothing else than the personification of our logical process of thought. The discovery of the genius of Marx corrects this radical error of idealism, thereby inflicting on it a deadly blow: the state of property, and with it all the qualities of the social environment (we saw in the chapter of idealist philosophy that Hegel, too, was forced to recognise the decisive importance of the "state of property"), are determined, not by the qualities of the absolute spirit and not by the character of human nature, but by those mutual relations into which men of necessity enter one with another "in the social process of production of their life," i.e. in their struggle for existence. [176-177]

The *psychology* of society adapts itself to its *economy.* On the given *economic* foundation there rises up fatally the *ideological superstructure* appropriate to it. But on the other hand each new step in the development of the productive forces places men, in their daily worldly practice, in new mutual relations which do not correspond to the relations of production now growing out of date. These new and unprecedented situations reflect themselves in the psychology of men, and very strongly change it. In what direction? Some members of society defend the old order: these are the people of stagnation. Others—to whom the old order is not advantageous—stand for progress; their psychology changes in the direction of those relations of production which in time will replace the old economic relations, now growing out of date. The adaptation of psychology to economy, as you see, continues, but slow psychological evolution *precedes* economic revolution.

Once this revolution has taken place, a complete harmony is established between the psychology of society and its economy. Then on the basis of the new economy there takes place the full flowering of the new psychology. For a certain time this harmony remains unbroken, and even becomes stronger and stronger. But little by little the first shoots of a new discord make their appearance; the psychology of the foremost class, for the reason mentioned above, again outlives old relations of production: without for a moment ceasing to adapt itself to economy, it again adapts itself to the *new* relations of production, constituting the germ of the future economy. Well, are not these two sides of one and the same process? [192-193]

Man's Conquest of Necessity

Our anthropoid ancestors, like all other animals, were in complete subjection to *nature*. All their development was that completely unconscious development which was conditioned by adaptation to their environment, by means of natural selection in the struggle for existence. This was the dark kingdom of *physical necessity*. At that time even the *dawn of consciousness*, and therefore of *freedom*, was not breaking. But physical necessity brought man to a stage of development at which he began, little by little, to separate himself from the remaining animal world. He became a *tool-making animal*. The tool is an organ with the help of which man acts on nature to achieve his ends. It is an organ which subjects *necessity* to the human *consciousness*, although at first only to a very weak degree, by fits and starts, if one can put it that way. *The degree of development of the productive forces determines the measure of the authority of man over nature*. . . .

But man is not alone in his struggle with nature: the struggle with her is carried on, in the expression of Marx, by social man (der Gesellschaftsmensch), i.e. a more or less considerable social union. The characteristics of *social* man are determined at every given time by the degree of development of the productive forces, because on the degree of the development of those forces depends the entire structure of the social union. . . .

The development of the social environment is subjected to its own laws. This means that its characteristics depend just as little on the will and consciousness of men as the characteristics of the geographical environment. The productive action of man on nature gives rise to a new form of dependence of man, a new variety of his slavery: *economic necessity*. And the greater grows man's authority over nature, the more his productive forces develop, the more stable becomes this new slavery: *with the development of the productive forces there become more complex the mutual relations of men in the social process of production;* the course of that process completely slips from under their control, *the producer proves to be the slave of his own creation* (as an example, the capitalist anarchy of production).

But just as the nature surrounding man itself gave him the first opportunity to develop his productive forces and, consequently, gradually to emancipate himself from nature's yoke—so the relations of production, social relations, by the very logic of their development bring man to realisation of the causes of his enslavement by *economic necessity*. This provides the opportunity for a new and final triumph of *consciousness* over *necessity*, of *reason over blind law*.

Having realised that the cause of his enslavement by his own creation lies in the anarchy of production, the producer ("social man") organises that production and thereby subjects it to his will. Then terminates the kingdom of *necessity*, and there begins the reign of freedom, which itself proves *necessary*. The prologue of human history has been played out, history begins.

Thus dialectical materialism not only does not strive, as its opponents attribute to it, to convince man that it is absurd to revolt against economic necessity, but it is the first to point out how to *overcome* the latter. Thus is eliminated the *inevitably fatalist* character inherent in *metaphysical materialism*. And in exactly the same way is eliminated every foundation for that pessimism to which, as we saw, consistent idealist thinking leads of necessity. The individual personality is only foam on the crest of the wave, men are subjected to an iron law which can only be discovered, but which cannot be subjected to the human will, said Georg Büchner. No, replies Marx: once we have discovered that iron law, it depends on us to overthrow its yoke, it depends on us to make *necessity* the obedient slave of *reason*. [242-245]

THE ROLE OF THE INDIVIDUAL

Plekhanov, *The Role of the Individual in History* (1898), trans.
by J. Fineberg (Moscow, 1946), p. 52.

Social relationships have their inherent logic; as long as
people live in given mutual relationships they will feel, think
and act in a given way, and no other. Attempts on the part of
public men to combat this logic would also be fruitless; the
natural course of things (*i.e.*, this logic of social relationships)
would reduce all his efforts to nought. But if I know in what
direction social relations are changing owing to given changes
in the social-economic process of production, I also know in what
direction social mentality is changing; consequently, I am able
to influence it. Influencing social mentality means influencing
historical events. Hence, in a certain sense, I *can make history*,
and there is no need for me to wait while "it is being made."

BIBLIOGRAPHY

Works by Plekhanov

Anarchism and Socialism (1894), trans. by Eleanor Marx Aveling
(London, 1895).
Concerning the Evolution of the Monist View of History (1895), trans.
by Andrew Rothstein as *In Defence of Materialism* (London, 1947).
Crítica del Sindicalismo (1910), trans. by Andrés Nin (Madrid, 1934).
Essays in Historical Materialism (New York, 1940). Contains the two
essays, *The Materialist Conception of History* (1897), and *The Role
of the Individual in History* (1898), also available separately.
Essays on the History of Materialism (1896), trans. by Ralph Fox
(London, 1934).
Fundamental Problems of Marxism (1908), trans. by Eden and Cedar
Paul (London, 1929).

Le materialisme militante (1908-1910), trans. by S. Engelson (Paris, 1930). Also available in Spanish.

N. G. Tschernischewsky (Stuttgart, 1894).

Selected Philosophical Works (Moscow and London, 1961-   ). To be issued in five volumes.

La Social-Democratie et la Guerre (Paris, 1916).

Biography

–Kamenskaia, M., *Georges V. Plékhanoff* ("Publications des 'Amis de Plékhanoff," No. 2.; Paris, 1924).

Exposition

–Adler, Charles C., "The Politics of Socialism: The Thought of George V. Plekhanov," unpublished Ph.D. dissertation, Harvard University, 1958. 241 pp.

Baron, Samuel H., "George Plekhanov and the 'Emancipation of Labor' Group, 1883-1894," unpublished Ph.D. dissertation, Columbia University, 1952. 256 pp.

————, "Plekhanov on Russian Capitalism and the Peasant Commune, 1883-1885," *American Slavic and East European Review*, Vol. 12 (December, 1953), pp. 463-474.

————, "Plekhanov's Russia: The Impact of the West upon an 'Oriental' Society," *Journal of the History of Ideas*, Vol. 19 (June, 1958), pp. 388-404.

Berlin, Isaiah, "Review of George Plekhanov's *In Defence of Materialism*," *Slavonic and East European Review*, Vol. 28 (November, 1949), pp. 257-262.

Fomina, V. A., *Die philosophischen Anschauungen G. W. Plechanows*, trans. by Nikolai Shcherbina (Berlin, 1957).

Freville, Jean, Introduction to George Plekhanov, *L'art et la vie sociale* (Paris, 1950). Not in English edition.

Giusti, Wolfango, *Due secoli di pensiero politico russo* (Florence, 1943), pp. 197-206.

Haimson, Leopold H., *The Russian Marxists and the Origins of Bolshevism* (Cambridge, Mass., 1955).

Hecker, Julius F., *Russian Sociology* (New York, 1934), pp. 253-264.

Masaryk, Thomas G., *The Spirit of Russia*, 2 vols. (London, 1955). Especially Chapter 18, Vol. 2, pp. 287-377.

Treadgold, Donald W., *Lenin and his Rivals* (London, 1955).

Trotsky, Leon, "Georges Valentinovitch Plekhanov," *Quatrième Internationale,* Vol. 14 (Nos. 10-12; December, 1956), pp. 53-58.

Untermann, Ernst, *Die logischen Mängel des engeren Marxismus: Georg Plechanow et alii gegen Josef Dietzgen* (Munich, 1910).

3

Lenin:

The Primacy of the Political

LENIN'S POLITICAL THOUGHT has become the orthodox interpretation of Marxism, although his practical successes have been most outstanding when his enemies have believed him to deviate furthest from Marx, as, for example, in forcing the pace of revolution through the leadership of professionals and without regard for the "ripeness" of economic development. Inferior to Marx as an economist, but far surpassing him as a strategist, Lenin was, perhaps for that reason, inclined to stress the political forces within Russia more than the economic forces. His originality is more evident in his adaptations of Marxism to primitive circumstances than in his ideas of the philosophical bases or the ultimate aims of socialism. Living in times of rapid change, he used the writings of Marx and Engels as "guides to action." He always read them, not as prophecies the fulfillment of which must be awaited, but as descriptions of reality, which could be supplemented as new realities came on the historical scene. His own thinking evolved continuously throughout his life, perhaps most rapidly under the impact of the events of 1917 and 1918.

As if to illustrate Turgenev's divergence of *Fathers and Sons*, Lenin's father, a middle class teacher of mathematics and physics, served the autocracy faithfully enough to become director of the elementary schools of his province, a rank that raised him to the nobility, but he reared two sons who were revolutionaries. The execution of the elder of them in 1887, for participating in an ill-prepared attempt to kill Alexander III, undoubtedly con-

44

tributed to the implacable will with which the younger lived and breathed revolution until the Romanov dynasty itself was extinguished.

Lenin (Vladimir I. Ul'ianov, 1870-1924) was an outstanding student in the gymnasium of Simbirsk (now Ul'ianovsk), the provincial capital on the middle Volga, leaving in 1887 with a gold medal to begin the study of law at the University of Kazan. In less than a year, however, he was expelled and exiled from Kazan for "political activity." After a period as manager of his mother's farm, which gave him first-hand experience with the peasants, he was permitted by the government to go to St. Petersburg (but not to its university) to resume the study of law. By systematic reading for about a year he was able to pass the examinations in 1891, even ranking first among those who took them.

He then tried legal practice in Samara, Pugachev's old town, and finding much time on his hands, he applied his systematic method of study to all the subversive literature he could find. The expositions of Marxism that Plekhanov was then sending into the country so impressed him that he learned German, devoured two volumes of *Das Kapital*, and by 1893 was himself writing from that viewpoint. His first subject, significantly, was agrarian: "New Economic Trends In Peasant Life" (unpublished until 1923).

Convinced that the proletariat was the promising class, he abandoned Samara for industrial St. Petersburg, and replaced the peasant ideal of Pugachev with the "scientific" expectations of Marx and Engels. Yet from his pre-Marxian period Lenin carried over more of Pugachev than had his master, Plekhanov. Moving farther along the line of voluntarism than had Plekhanov, he accepted the conclusion of The People's Will (see p. 9) that the socialists could assume the lead in a bourgeois revolution, and actually must do so if such a revolution was to achieve such rights of democracy as universal suffrage, freedom of the press, etc.

In St. Petersburg he used the "literacy committees," or Marxist study circles for workers, to study the proletarians themselves, and issued (by hectograph) for his important pamphlet, *What* the *"Friends of the People" Are and How They Fight the Social Democrats*, a thorough criticism of the *narodniks*. After a visit to Plekhanov in Geneva he tried with Martov to consolidate the St. Petersburg Marxists into a Union of Struggle for the Liberation of Labor. These activities led to his arrest late in 1895 and to his exile in southern Siberia for three years.

During his exile he hit upon the idea of cementing the scattered Marxist circles into a nation-wide Social Democratic Party through the wide circulation of an illegal newspaper and a journal of Marxist theory published abroad and smuggled throughout Russia. Such publications, properly edited, would also serve to combat the Economists and other perversions of Marxism.

His work in St. Petersburg had convinced him that factory employment did not automatically make the workmen socialists. Already in the West the followers of Marx had found his doctrine of the increasing misery of the working class to be a qualification on his doctrine that the liberation of the workers must be accomplished by the workers themselves. In the Hainfeld Program of 1888 the Austrian Social Democrats had said, "The deterioration of the conditions of life, which degrades the worker into a dull slave, makes it impossible for him to devote strength and time to the pursuit of human goals, even of his own liberation." [1] To his aid the intellectuals must come, through party organization. "To organize the proletariat politically, to imbue it with consciousness of its situation and its tasks, to make it and keep it prepared for combat—this is the true program of the Social Democratic Workers' Party in Austria." [2] This view had been expressed by Plekhanov five years before (see p. 23), and was included by the German Social Democrats in the Erfurt Program of 1891: "To mold the struggle of the working class into a conscious and unified one, and to point out its scientifically determined goal—that is the task of the Social Democratic Party." [3] Kautsky, in his *Das Erfurter Programm* (1892),

[1] *Verhandlungen des Parteitages der Österreichischen Sozialdemokratie in Hainfeld* (Vienna, 1889), p. 50.
[2] *Ibid.*, p. 3.
[3] Wilhelm Schröder, *Handbuch der sozialdemokratischen Parteitage von 1863-1909* (Munich, 1910), p. 471.

had gone on to emphasize the dependence of the proletariat upon the intellectuals.[4] Plekhanov and the Western Marxists, however, did not see this view as being in conflict with the doctrine that men's minds are shaped by their material environment.

Lenin went further to emphasize the inadequacy of proletarian experience in shaping the minds of the workers. Arguing against the Economists in a basic pamphlet, *What Is To Be Done?* (1902), he declared, "The history of all countries shows that the working class, exclusively by its own effort, is able to develop only trade union consciousness," not class consciousness, and, far from arousing hatred for the class enemy, "trade unionism means the ideological enslavement of the workers to the bourgeoisie."[5] Marx, therefore, should not be read as a determinist. Without the guidance of the Marxists, without the leadership of professional revolutionaries, the proletarians would be as bourgeois as the peasants.[6]

Lenin went further than the Western Marxists also in the role he conceived for the party. To them the party was needed to educate the workers to class consciousness and to organize the resulting mass struggle. Lenin added the duty of serving as a fighting vanguard of the proletarian army.

This conviction, that alone the workers were nonpolitical, was fundamental to all his later adaptations of Marxism. It underlay his long controversy with the Mensheviks over the nature of the party. It made possible the separation of the vanguard from the main body of "troops" and thus the seizure and retention of power by a minority. It conditioned his attitude toward the

[4] Cf. 11th ed. (Stuttgart, 1912), pp. 235-236.

[5] V. I. Lenin, *Selected Works*, J. Fineberg, ed., Vol. 2 (London, 1936), pp. 53, 62.

[6] This was especially true in Russia, for the Russian factory worker traditionally maintained his ties with the farm. An open letter from a Moscow organizer in 1905 informed Lenin, "Even now, in spite of the fact that certain factories have been in existence for 40 to 50 years, the overwhelming majority of our 'proletariat' has not become divorced from the land. The 'village' has such a strong hold over it that none of the psychological and other prerequisites, which a 'pure' proletarian acquires in the course of collective work, develop among our proletarians." Full letter quoted in Lenin's "The Attitude of Social-Democracy Toward the Peasant Movement," *ibid.*, Vol. 3, p. 141.

"Workers' Opposition" in 1920 (see p. 131), which finally replaced revolutionary enthusiasm with party discipline. It thus led ultimately to a régime of tutelage and centralized bureaucracy instead of the freedom and equality that had been the goal. An important corollary of Lenin's denial that factory experience makes the workers socialist was his denial of the primacy of economics over politics, which Marxism had always asserted. Lenin long acted on the premise that politics was primary—at least in the short run—before he formulated this view as a theory. At the Ninth Party Congress (1920), however, with Bukharin's help he resolved the conflict with Marxism by saying that "politics is the most concentrated expression of economics." [7] He then went on to assert: "Politics can not but have precedence over economics. To argue differently means forgetting the A B C of Marxism." [8] This view enabled him, in contrast to the Mensheviks, to anticipate a proletarian revolution in Russia before the economic conditions were ripe. It brought him closer to Trotsky; it served to buttress the hegemony of the party; and ultimately it led to the concept of "revolution from above" (see p. 224f).

According to Lenin's opponents these opinions contradicted the economic causality that was essential to Marxism. For this reason, and because of his frequent emphasis upon a tightly disciplined élite and his seizure of power in 1917, they have accused Lenin of being a Blanquist rather than a Marxist. In fact, in retrospect the events of the Russian revolution may more closely correspond to the theories of Blanqui than to those of Marx. Yet Marx and Engels had opposed Blanqui's tactics, and Plekhanov, in his polemics with The People's Will, had disparaged him; the Russian Marxists, therefore, could not admit being influenced by him nor could they openly attempt to integrate his ideas into their own. They might conspire, they might revolt and seize power, they might then indoctrinate or educate the people as Blanqui had wanted to do, but it had to be done in the name of Marx. The discipline of conspiracy fitted well with Lenin's own experience and with his temperament, yet he de-

[7] *Deviatyi S"ezd RKP(B), Protokoly* (Moscow, 1960), p. 418.
[8] Lenin, "The Trade Unions, the Present Situation and the Mistakes of Comrade Trotsky," *Selected Works,* Vol. 9 (London, 1937), p. 54.

rived it not directly from Blanqui but from the conspiratorial tactics the Russian radicals had developed in response to the tsar's suppression of public opinion. Behind him was the tradition of the Decembrists, of Nechaev and Tkachev, and of The People's Will. This tradition, reinforced by Tkachev's sense of urgency in forestalling the bourgeoisie, struggled within him against the delays involved in attaining the "overwhelming majority" on which Marx, even in the *Manifesto,* had hoped to base the revolution. Yet Lenin's polemics against Trotsky after 1905 (see p. 122f) show clearly that, for all his élitist methods, he was convinced that mass support was indispensable, and thus arose the ambivalence of his desire for both discipline and majority approval. Not until 1917 did the conspirator in him, with the aid of Trotsky and the excuse of a unique opportunity, win out. Even then he clearly believed that the masses would accept his program and that collaboration with both Mensheviks and Socialist-Revolutionaries was possible. "To be successful," he wrote in September, "insurrection must rely not upon conspiracy and not upon a party, but upon the advanced class." Only as events forced the choice upon him did he definitely choose the dictatorial rather than the democratic element of his formula, "the revolutionary-democratic dictatorship of the proletariat and the peasantry."

From this lack of faith in a spontaneous working-class movement he deduced that the main element of the Russian Marxist party must be a tightly disciplined body of professionals who could lead and guide the proletariat, and not simply a broad and loose aggregation of proletarians and intellectuals. "An attack must be made by regular troops and not by a spontaneous outburst of the crowd." He expressed this deviously at the Party Congress of 1903 as a requirement that party members must be members of party organizations (Point 1 of the Rules). But when he explained the meaning of his formulation it was seen to imply more discipline than the Congress wanted, and his draft was rejected in favor of Martov's, which required only that members work "under the direction" of party organizations. Lenin did not, however, wish to confine party membership to conspirators. "It should not be thought," he told the Congress, "that Party organizations must consist solely of professional revolutionaries. We need the most diversified organizations of every type, rank and shade, starting from extremely narrow and secret ones and ending with very broad, free, *lose Organisationen.*"[9]

This was the first break in the unity of the *Iskra* bloc at the Congress, but the real split of the party into Bolsheviks and Mensheviks came on Lenin's seemingly needless insistence upon excluding Axelrod, Potresov, and Zasulich from the editorial board of the party journals. He had already learned to work with these people, so why drive them out? His motive probably lay in his changed conception of the role of *Iskra.* Before the Congress the paper had worked for a unified party, which they all wanted; this being achieved, the task was now the centralized control of a disciplined party—a task for which only Plekhanov had sympathy.

Formerly our Party was not a formally organized whole, but only the sum of separate groups, and therefore, no other relations except those of ideological influence were possible between these groups. *Now* we have become an organized Party, and this implies the establishment of authority, the subordination of lower Party bodies to higher Party bodies. . . . Refusal to accept the direction of the central bodies is tantamount to a refusal to remain in the Party, it is tantamount to disrupting the Party; it is a method of *destroying*, not of convincing.[10]

Yet Lenin badly misjudged the mood of the Congress and destroyed party unity in an attempt to strengthen it.[11]

Divergent explanations have been given to this split between

[9] *Vtoroi Ocherednoi S"ezd R S D R P, Polnyi Tekst Protokolov* (Geneva, 1903), p. 240.

[10] V. I. Lenin, *One Step Forward, Two Steps Back* (London, 1941), pp. 218, 214.

[11] Describing Lenin at this Congress, Bertram Wolfe says, "This flexible inflexibility, which made his own views the test of when it was a crime to break discipline and when it was a crime not to, did not spring from hypocrisy or arrogance or lust for power. It sprang from his unshakable conviction of his own rightness. It was selfless in the sense that for Lenin the distinction between self and the movement had become completely obliterated." Bertram D. Wolfe, *Three Who Made a Revolution* (Boston, 1955), p. 245.

Lenin and Martov. The most penetrating analysis, that of Leopold H. Haimson, finds the roots of the conflict in the problems of "consciousness" versus "spontaneity" (see p. 91ff): Lenin, because he believed that class consciousness could be developed among the workers only through party tutelage, insisted on tight organization and centralized discipline, while Martov, who believed that consciousness would develop independently through trade union experience, saw greater advantages in a mass movement.[12] The conflicts over Point 1 of the Rules and the election of the *Iskra* editors were only symptomatic of this difference. In this analysis, however, one must remember that, in 1895, Lenin and Martov had agreed on the *On Agitation* approach to the problem of consciousness (see p. 93), and subsequently had fought the Economist interpretation of that approach. Both men, in other words, had denied the sufficiency of spontaneity in the extreme form of Economism; Martov now denied the necessity of tutelage in the extreme form of Lenin's disciplined party. Both men lacked Marx's confidence that the material conditions of the workers would of themselves make them socialists, but Martov thought that this process needed less help than Lenin thought it needed from the conscious revolutionaries.

In part this difference reflected their divergent assessments of the urgency of revolution, also noticed by Haimson. Lenin, less urban in background, retained more of the *narodnik* desire to skip the stage of capitalism. As a Marxist he denied the possibility of this, but as a dedicated Russian socialist he felt the Marxist movement to be in a race against the growing bourgeoisie for the tottering sceptre of the tsar. Martov, the more consistent (or less original) Marxist, thought that historical materialism required an extended period of capitalist rule during which spontaneity could be guided to consciousness.

In any event, Lenin won his point at the Congress by virtue of the withdrawal of some delegates who had supported Martov, but Martov refused to serve on the *Iskra* board and Plekhanov soon went over to the Mensheviks. Lenin thus lost control of *Iskra* and shortly of the other Party organs as well; he was almost

[12] Leopold H. Haimson, *The Russian Marxists and the Origins of Bolshevism* (Cambridge, 1955), pp. 187-197, 209-219.

isolated in the Party, with all the influential leaders against him. Nevertheless he continued the fight for a disciplined party, with a handful of followers to whom the old conspiratorial tradition was more congenial than the Mensheviks' building of mass support. The Party thus lost its chance for unity just at a time when popular discontent was building up through famines, strikes, and the Russo-Japanese War to a really revolutionary situation. The two factions proceeded each to destroy the appeals and proposals of the other, diverting mental and physical energy that might have toppled the tsar in 1905 if it had been better utilized.

One result of this hypercritical, destructive atmosphere was that Lenin failed to grasp the significance of the most important new idea of the period, the Parvus-Trotsky theory of "permanent revolution." Lenin's views of this theory will be discussed more fully later (pp. 122f), but it may be noted here that they were less clearly negative than Stalin later made them appear. While attacking Trotsky, Lenin was influenced by events of the 1905 revolution to question, like Trotsky, many of the settled points of Russian Marxism, and on some he came very close to the Trotsky-Parvus position. The old distinction between the bourgeois revolution and the socialist revolution, for example, was blurred when he said that "in history certain particular elements of both revolutions become interwoven." The expectation of a period of capitalist rule became uncertain when he suggested that workers and peasants "will not surrender" the democratic revolution to the bourgeoisie. It seems as though he had almost seen the same vision that Trotsky had seen, but that he drew back from such a sharp break with orthodox Marxism.

Lenin was attracted, like all the émigrés, by the revolution of 1905, but he did not risk a return to Russia until the October wave of strikes promised relative safety. Arriving in November, when division was already appearing in the revolutionary ranks and the bureaucracy was regaining the initiative, he did not, as Trotsky was doing, add much to his stature.

Before his arrival, however, he gave a foretaste of the speed, so shocking to his friends in April, 1917, with which he could revise his doctrines to accommodate new facts. Awaiting passage in Stockholm, he read of the creation of the St. Petersburg soviet

—the committee that groups of workers had set up, on the tsar's invitation, to express their wishes—and immediately saw in it "the embryo of the provisional revolutionary government." In spite of his polemics against broad, nonpartisan organizations, he proposed that the soviet "choose a strong center of a revolutionary provisional government and enlarge it with the representatives of all the revolutionary parties and all the revolutionary democrats. . . . We do not fear broadness and differences of composition; rather we desire it, for without the unification of the proletariat and the peasants, without the militant union of social democrats and revolutionary democrats, complete victory is impossible." [13] He did not publish or press this new view, however,[14] and his followers, conditioned by his polemics against the Mensheviks, made a poor showing in the soviet. The soviet itself, in the absence of any other representative body and in consequence of the age-old separation of the government from the people, gained great prestige and wide support as the only elected voice of the people, yet Lenin so distrusted its Menshevik majority that he soon lost his enthusiasm for it and underestimated its importance. Even so, by 1906 he again said that "The Soviets of Workers' Deputies, etc., were *in fact* the embryo of a provisional government; power would *inevitably* have passed to them had the uprising been victorious," and he advocated study of them for future use. The next year, in combatting the revived Menshevik plan for a nonpartisan labor organization, which included the use of soviets, Lenin argued that "such institutions may actually become superfluous." [15] Later he realized his mistake and reevaluated the soviet, making it central to his plans; but his shifts of position left ambiguous guidance for his followers when the soviet reappeared in 1917.

The failure of the 1905 revolution, which was largely urban, led the Social Democrats to search more diligently for broader

[13] Lenin, *Sochineniia*, 5th ed., Vol. 12 (Moscow, 1960), pp. 63-66.
[14] He did advocate the enrollment of workers into open party organizations "by the hundreds and thousands."
[15] Lenin, *Selected Works*, Vol. 3, pp. 383, 485. On his changing attitude see Wolfe, *op. cit.*, pp. 312-318, 368-370. Trotsky, who had been its president, adhered to the opinion that "the Soviet was in reality an embryo of a revolutionary government."

support in the countryside. More than the other leaders Lenin recognized the importance of the peasants, who were an overwhelming majority of the Russian people. He labored manfully to adjust Marxism to that circumstance, seeing that the peasants, in their ardor to seize the landlords' land, "are immeasurably more imbued with direct revolutionariness" than the proletarians. He revised the formula for the "dictatorship of the proletariat" to include them, on the grounds that the coming revolution was bourgeois, not socialist, and that the proletariat alone could not govern. He studied carefully the programs of peasant groups and parties and tried to fit their desires into the Marxist program. He was unable, however, to reconcile Marxism with a genuine peasant movement, as Mao Tse-tung was later to do. While he fought with the Economists and then the Mensheviks the peasants were organized by others into the non-Marxist Socialist Revolutionary Party, and it was only by adopting the S-R land program in 1917 that he achieved the temporary support of the rural masses.[16]

In the years of disappointment that followed the failure of the 1905 revolution, which Lenin spent in the West, his conviction that Marxism had only one proper interpretation—his own—resulted in endless doctrinal disputes with Plekhanov, Martov, Trotsky, and others, and prevented the restoration of real unity in the party. Moreover, his involvement with those inside Russia (including Stalin) who supplied his faction with funds through armed robbery ("expropriation"), while attracting to him the more militant, tended to alienate from him all who thought such methods immoral or harmful to the party. These factors contributed, in 1912, to a final and irreparable breach between Bolsheviks and Mensheviks.

During this period Lenin also concerned himself with the international socialist movement. He was sufficiently impressed

---

[16] Lenin later stressed the importance of this maneuver: "We achieved victory because we adopted, not our own agrarian programme, but that of the Socialist-Revolutionaries, and actually put it into practice. Our victory lay in the fact that we carried out the programme of the Socialist-Revolutionaries; that is why it was achieved so easily." *Selected Works,* Vol. 10 (London, 1938), p. 286.

by the peculiar difficulties of Marxism in Russia to be aware that adaptation to local conditions, rather than imitation of the great German party, must be the general rule for each national party.

The international revolutionary movement of the proletariat does not proceed and cannot proceed evenly and in the same form in different countries. The thorough and all-sided utilisation of all possibilities in all spheres of activity comes only as a result of the class struggle of the workers of various countries. Every country contributes its own valuable original traits to the general stream, but in every individual country the movement suffers from some kind of one-sidedness, from some theoretical or practical shortcoming in the individual Socialist Parties.[17]

Lenin thus emphasized the limitations of separate national parties, but such passages were later to be used with good effect by the Yugoslavs in their struggle against Stalinist conformity.

During the First World War Lenin strengthened these ideas by formulating the "law of the uneven development of capitalism," by which the possibility of a socialist revolution in one country was stressed, as against simultaneous international revolution, and each national party encouraged to speed ahead on its own path. After his own party led the way, however, he tended to think of the Russian path as normal. Marxists in other countries were eager to imitate their successful comrades; soviets became popular everywhere,[18] and Lenin smiled upon them.

The idea of the Soviet power has come to life *all over the world* and is spreading among the proletariat of all countries with unprecedented rapidity. . . . Experience has proved that on some very important questions concerning the proletarian revolution, *all* countries will inevitably have to go through what Russia has gone through.[19]

He thus again left his followers an ambiguous legacy: was there only one, or more than one, path to socialism?

Lenin's influence in the Russian party revived during the War.

---

[17] *Ibid.*, Vol. 4 (London, n.d.), pp. 302-303.

[18] This to the great disgust of the Mensheviks, who considered the Bolshevik soviets to be perversions of the original soviet idea.

[19] *Ibid.*, Vol. 10, p. 68.

He resisted the upsurge of patriotism that divided the socialist movement in all countries and broke the power of the Second International. He avoided the ambivalent position of those, like Plekhanov and the liberal Miliukov, who tried both to oppose the government and to support the war. As the futility of the war grew more apparent his followers grew in strength. From his refuge in Switzerland he continued to work against the Russian rulers and the war and for a new International.

An important aspect of this work was the formulation of his doctrine of imperialism. The readiness of the workers to support bourgeois governments in the war had contradicted Marxian dogmas of international proletarian solidarity and class warfare, and had stimulated socialists in all countries to reexamine these doctrines. Some arrived at very pessimistic opinions regarding the future of revolution, seeing in the growth of international cartels an abatement of the competitive contradictions of capitalism, and pointing to the exploitation of colonial empires as the basis for a new symbiotic relationship between the proletariat and the capitalists in the advanced countries that had destroyed its will for revolution. Lenin, however, arrived at quite different conclusions. Drawing on analyses formulated by Bukharin, Kautsky, and Luxemburg, and on the data of many non-Marxist writers, he argued that the contradictions of capitalism, far from abating, were becoming more acute under imperialism, a final and economically necessary stage in the development of capitalism. This development being uneven within and between countries, no monopoly or cartel could be stable and no international agreement for the division of the world, made by the imperialist governments as agents of the capitalists, could be more than a temporary truce between wars. The "bribing" of the workers of the leading nations with profits extracted from colonial peoples did not destroy the potentialities for revolution, as he saw it; on the contrary, it served to segregate the opportunists from the real revolutionaries and to reinforce the latter by the addition of new victims of exploitation in the colonies. He thus came to the opinion that revolution might come first, not in the West where such bribery was rampant, but in backward, semi-colonial, or even colonial countries. This brought him closer to Trotsky, who had believed since 1905 that Russia could lead the way (see p. 135).[20]

This idea also brought him to question, in light of the international ramifications of capitalism in its final stage, the necessity for the capitalistic development of separate countries. This necessity had been the foundation for the expectation of two revolutions in Russia, bourgeois and proletarian. In discarding it Lenin again, belatedly and by a different route, came to an opinion that Trotsky had long held, that the two revolutions could somehow be telescoped into one.

In April, 1917, following the liberal revolution of February, Lenin returned to Petrograd with some "Theses," a bold new plan quite surprising to the "old Bolsheviks" who still thought of revolution in two stages. He proposed to carry the bourgeois revolution on into a proletarian and peasant revolution as soon as he could secure a Bolshevik majority in the Petrograd soviet. This soviet, and others throughout the country, had grassroots support and could, he now believed, take power into their own hands at will. Following Trotsky, perhaps still unconsciously, he had come to see in the soviet the counterpart of Marx's favorite revolutionary instrument, the Paris Commune of 1871 (see p. 79f). It was representative yet not parliamentary, spontaneous and broadly based yet disciplined, ready-made for the avoidance of the hesitancies of parliamentary procedure that Marx had condemned.

All through the summer, with the aid of Trotsky, he hammered away for control of the soviets. By September this propaganda, plus the mistakes of the Provisional Government and of the parties that supported it, had given the Bolsheviks a majority in the soviets of Moscow and Petrograd, and Lenin believed the country was ready to support an armed uprising. He therefore destroyed the hopes of many of his fellow Bolsheviks as well as of the Mensheviks and competing parties for a new socialist coalition ministry and for a parliamentary republic. He advanced instead another conception of government which rejected the

[20] For a complete summary of Lenin's theory of imperialism, more systematic than any he ever wrote, see Alfred G. Meyer, *Leninism* (Cambridge, Mass., 1957), pp. 235-256.

theory of the separation of executive and legislative powers and
envisioned responsibility without electoral alternatives. The new
government was to be characterized by unselfish dedication of
the leadership to the building of a socialist and then communist
society, by close contact with and responsiveness to the people
(reinforced by the recall), and by Marxian correctness of theory,
strategy, and tactics. The weakness of this conception lay in the
contradiction between dedication to Marxian aims and responsiveness to the non-Marxian masses. Yet Lenin, like Blanqui,
expected that education and experience would eliminate this
difficulty, that the achievements of the new society would erase
the prejudices inherited from the old. In proposing the land
decree of 1917, the Socialist Revolutionary program, he gave one
of his clearest expressions to both the idealism and the prag-
matism of his hour of victory:

> As a democratic government, we cannot ignore the decision of the
> rank and file of the people, even though we may disagree with it; in
> the fire of experience, applying the decree in practice, and carrying
> it out locally, the peasants will themselves understand where the truth
> lies. And even if the peasants continue to follow the Socialist-Revolu-
> tionaries, even if they give this party a majority in the Constituent
> Assembly, we shall still say, be it so. Experience is the best teacher
> and it will show who is right. Let the peasant solve this problem from
> one end and us from the other. Experience will bring us closer in the
> general stream of revolutionary creation, in the elaboration of the new
> state forms. We must follow experience; we must allow complete free-
> dom for the creative faculties of the masses.[21]

The success of the October revolution gave Lenin centralized
power in Russia and unparalleled prestige among revolutionaries
throughout the world, prestige that remains untarnished. His
opinions, nevertheless, were not always accepted by the strong
minds in his own party. Yet, in sharp contrast to his vigorous
attacks upon their doctrinal deviations, he showed great flexibility and generosity in continuing in power even those, like
Zinov'ev, Kamenev, and Bukharin, who had opposed him at most

21 *Ibid.*, Vol. 6 (London, 1936), p. 409.

critical junctures. He had little time, however, to build the new society. Counterrevolutionary uprisings and foreign invasions consumed his energies until 1921, and illness largely incapacitated him from early in 1922 until his death two years later.

Space does not permit examination of Lenin's ideas regarding all the issues and problems that faced the new government. Some of them will be touched on in the chapters that follow, but here attention will be given to his views on only one of the most important, the creation of a viable socialist economy.

The classics of Marxism gave surprisingly little guidance in this area, and the Bolsheviks, focused on achieving power, had given little attention to the problems of the exercise of power once achieved. Ill prepared and hardly aware of the magnitude of their task, they took control of an economy that was already debilitated by the war. To get it rolling again Lenin tried many different approaches, including "workers' control," "War Communism," and the New Economic Policy (N.E.P.).

The great importance of economic planning in Stalin's building of the economy poses the question of why this was not used more vigorously from the beginning. The surprising conclusion must be reached that it was blighted by Lenin's scepticism. Outside the field of electrification where he did push planning, his writings show little understanding of the importance or the problems of this approach. Reflecting the views of his *State and Revolution*, he seems to have underestimated the complexity of the economic difficulties and regarded them as soluble by piecemeal methods, such as "Workers' Control in Industry." Under this slogan, spontaneous factory committees, strongly influenced by anarcho-syndicalism, had seized factories during disputes with management all through 1917. Lenin had supported and defended the committees, but the meaning of workers' control was far from clear.

In Lenin's mind, control meant the responsibility of the managers to the workers through accounting, inspection, and auditing, not management by the workers; yet he defended the committees against the charge of syndicalism, and in June he said that "Workers' control . . . should be immediately developed . . . into complete regulation of the production and distribution of goods by the workers." [22]

The factory committees were better at disrupting the capitalist order in the interest of the revolution than they were at managing the factories. In theory they stood for centralization and the planning of industry, but in practice, like the peasants dividing the landed estates, they tended after October to think of the factories as their own, in short-range, local terms. By the spring of 1918 workers' control was almost completely discredited.

In the interest of production the government undertook to centralize workers' control by subordinating the factory committees to the trade unions and by integrating the unions into the state machinery. The unions were entrusted with the discipline and distribution of labor, the administration of the social insurance system, and other duties, and the First Congress of Trade Unions (January, 1918) resolved that the unions ought to be "organs of state power." They "ought to take on themselves the main burden of organizing production and of rehabilitating the country's shattered productive forces." [23]

The question of the independence of the unions was raised at the congress, however. It was pointed out that for them to become organs of state power would mean that their decisions would be carried out by compulsion, and that spontaneous class solidarity would thus be replaced by coercion.[24] Martov and Maiski argued that, since the revolution could only be bourgeois, not socialist, the role of the unions must remain unchanged. Martov went on:

At the present historic moment, in the present historic situation, this cannot be a government of the working class alone, but must be merely a *de facto* government connected with the heterogeneous mass of toiling people, with proletarian and nonproletarian elements. It cannot direct its economic policy along the lines of the consistently and clearly expressed interests of the working class.[25]

[22] Lenin, "Draft Resolution on Measures to Overcome Economic Chaos," *Collected Works,* Vol. 20 (New York, 1929), part 2, p. 136.
[23] *Pervyi Vserossiiskii S"ezd Professional'nykh Soiuzov, Polnyi Stenograficheski Otchet* (Moscow, 1918), p. 364.
[24] *Ibid.,* p. 97 (Lozovski).
[25] *Ibid.,* p. 80.

So the working class, through the trade unions, must be able to protect itself against such a government. Zinov'ev, for the Bolsheviks, insisted, on the contrary, that the workers could have no interests as against the workers' state and that the unions, therefore, had no need for independence.

By March the government, on the insistence of Lenin, had gone to great lengths to restore production, including labor discipline, incentive wage schemes such as piece rates, the use of "bourgeois specialists" at high salaries, one-man management instead of committees, and even negotiations with former tycoons to organize joint monopolies with state and private capital.

These measures stimulated pained protests within the Party (see p. 191), but such dissident voices were stilled by the outbreak of the civil war. The policy of "War Communism" was instituted: contribution by all, according to ability, to fulfill the needs of the defense of the revolution. In the industrial sector of the economy the unions, closely collaborating with the government, assumed more and more administrative duties, including military recruitment and supply services. The Second Congress of Trade Unions (January, 1919) approved a Bolshevik resolution on the "statization" of the unions—their integration into the state machinery. On the one hand, strikes in nationalized industries were ruled out, and on the other, the unions regulated wages and conditions of work and chose the Commissar of Labor, who defined his role as, "to give obligatory effect to recommendations and plans worked out by the trade unions." In March, with Lenin's approval, the Eighth Party Congress drew up a new program, to replace that of 1903, which said, in its economic section, ". . . the trade unions ought to come actually to concentrate in their hands all the administration of the entire national economy as an economic unit. . . . The participation of the trade unions in economic management . . . is, moreover, the principal means of the struggle against bureaucracy in the economic apparatus." The phrase "to come to" referred to no definite future time, but the tenor of the program was clearly toward an increasing role for the unions in economic life.

In the agricultural sector, however, contribution according to ability meant, in practice, confiscation of surpluses, since there were no industrial consumers' goods to trade to the peasants. The peasants soon responded, as might have been foreseen, by restricting acreage to their own needs. Shortages of food in the cities sapped industrial production, blackmarketing was rife, and the proletariat itself melted back to the land.

Faced thus with the disintegration not only of the economy but also of the class on which the revolution was supposed to be based, Lenin called for a retreat, the N.E.P., and a resort to the free market incentives of capitalism. Only then did the mangled economy begin to revive. The retreat was to be temporary, but Lenin set no time limit and he died without starting another advance toward socialism. Had he lived he might have done so, but, in spite of his emphasis on the primacy of politics, Lenin proved unable to bend the economics of the country to his will. Until 1928, when Stalin violently turned the rudder toward the left, it seemed that the Russian revolution, like all others before it in history, had moved unsteadily toward the right.

[ON ORGANIZATION]

Lenin, *What Is To Be Done?* (1902), in his *Selected Works,* Vol. 1 (Moscow, 1952), Part 1, pp. 322-323, 336-338, 354.

The political struggle of Social-Democracy is far more extensive and complex than the economic struggle of the workers against the employers and the government. Similarly (and indeed for that reason), the organization of a revolutionary Social-Democratic party must inevitably be of a *different* kind than the organizations of the workers designed for this struggle. A workers' organization must in the first place be a trade organization; secondly, it must be as broad as possible; and thirdly, it must be as little clandestine as possible (here, and further on, of course, I have only autocratic Russia in mind). On the other hand, the organizations of revolutionaries must consist first, foremost and mainly of people who make revolutionary activity their profession (that is why I speak of organizations of *revolutionaries*, meaning revolutionary Social-Democrats). In view of this common feature of the members of such an organization, *all distinctions as between workers and intellectuals*, and certainly distinctions of trade and profession, must be *utterly obliterated*. Such an organization must of necessity be not too extensive and as secret as possible. . . .

I assert: 1) that no revolutionary movement can endure without a stable organization of leaders that maintains continuity; 2) that the wider the masses spontaneously drawn into the struggle, forming the basis of the movement and participating in it, the more urgent the need of such an organization, and the more solid this organization must be (for it is much easier for demagogues to sidetrack the more backward sections of the masses); 3) that such an organization must consist chiefly of people professionally engaged in revolutionary activity; 4) that in an autocratic state, the more we *confine* the membership of such an organization to people who are professionally engaged in revolutionary activity and who have been professionally trained in the art of combating the political police, the more difficult will it be to wipe out such an organization, and 5) the *greater* will be the number of people of the working class and of the other classes of society who will be able to join the movement and perform active work in it.

We can never give a mass organization that degree of secrecy without which there can be no question of persistent and continuous struggle against the government. But to concentrate all secret functions in the hands of as small a number of professional revolutionaries as possible does not mean that the latter will "do the thinking for all" and that the crowd will not take an active part in the *movement*. On the contrary, the crowd will advance from its ranks increasing numbers of professional revolutionaries; for it will know that it is not enough for a few students and for a few workingmen waging the economic struggle, to gather together and form a "committee," but that it takes years to train oneself to be a professional revolutionary; the crowd will "think" not of amateurish methods alone but of such training. The centralization of the secret functions of the *organization* by no means implies the centralization of all the functions of the *movement*. The active participation of the widest mass in the illegal press will not diminish because a "dozen" professional revolutionaries centralize the secret functions connected with this work; on the contrary, it will *increase* tenfold. In this way, and in this way alone, will we ensure that reading of illegal literature, writing for it, and to some extent even distributing it, will *almost cease to be secret work*, for the police will soon come to realize the folly and futility of setting the whole judicial and administrative machine into motion to intercept every copy of publication that is being broadcast in thousands. This applies not only to the press, but to every function of the movement, even to demonstrations. The active and widespread participation of the masses will not suffer; on the contrary, it will benefit by the fact that a "dozen" experienced revolutionaries, trained professionally no less than the police, will centralize all the secret aspects of the work—drawing up leaflets, working out approximate plans and appointing bodies of leaders for each urban district, for each factory district and for each educational institution, etc. (I know that exception will be taken to my "undemocratic" views, but I shall reply fully to this anything but intelligent objection later on.) The centralization of the most secret functions in an organization of revolutionaries will not diminish, but rather increase the extent and quality of the activity of a large number of other organizations which are intended for a broad public and are therefore as loose and as non-secret as possible, such as workers' trade unions, workers' self-education circles and circles for reading illegal literature, socialist and also democratic circles among *all* other sections of the population, etc., etc. We must have such circles, trade unions and organizations everywhere in *as large a number as possible* and with the widest variety of functions; but it would be absurd and dangerous to *confuse* them with the organization of *revolutionaries*, to obliterate the border line between them, to dim still more the masses' already incredibly hazy appreciation of the fact that in order to "serve" the mass movement we must have people who will devote themselves exclusively to Social-Democratic activities, and that such people must *train* themselves patiently and steadfastly to be professional revolutionaries. . . .

The only serious organizational principle for the active workers of our movement should be the strictest secrecy, the strictest selection of members and the training of professional revolutionaries. Given these qualities, something even more than "democracy" would be guaranteed to us, namely, complete, comradely, mutual confidence among revolutionaries. And this is absolutely essential for us because there can be no question of replacing it by universal democratic control in Russia. And it would be a great mistake to believe that the fact that it is impossible to establish real "democratic" control renders the members of the revolutionary organization beyond control altogether. They have not the time to think about the toy forms of democracy (democracy within a close and compact body of comrades in which complete, mutual confidence prevails), but they have a lively sense of their *responsibility*, knowing as they do from experience that an organization of real revolutionaries will stop at nothing to rid itself of an undesirable member.

[ON THE PARTY (AGAINST THE MENSHEVIKS)]

Lenin, *One Step Forward, Two Steps Back* (1904), *Selected Works*, Vol. 1 (Moscow, 1952), Part 1; brackets in the text indicate pages of this edition.

Depending on degree of organization in general and degree of secrecy of organization in particular, roughly the following categories may be distinguished: 1) organizations of revolutionaries; 2) organizations of workers as broad and as varied as possible. (I confine myself to the working class, taking it as self-evident that, under certain conditions, certain elements

of other classes will also be included here.) These two categories constitute the Party. Further, 3) organizations of workers
which are associated with the Party; 4) organizations of workers
which are not associated with the Party but actually submit
to its control and direction; 5) unorganized elements of the
working class who also come partly under the direction of the
Social-Democratic Party, at any rate during the big manifestations of the class struggle. That, approximately, is how the matter
presents itself to me. From the point of view of Comrade Martov,
on the contrary, the border line of the Party remains absolutely
vague, for "every striker" may "proclaim himself a Party member." What is the use of this vagueness? A widespread "title." Its
harm is that it introduces a *disorganizing* idea, the confusing
of class and Party. . . . [478]

Aristocratic anarchism cannot understand that formal rules
are needed precisely in order to replace the narrow circle ties
by the broad Party tie. It was unnecessary and impossible to give
formal shape to the internal ties of a circle or the ties between
circles, for these ties rested on friendship or on a "confidence"
for which no reason or motive had to be given. The Party tie
cannot and must not rest on either of these; it must be founded
on *formal*, "bureaucratically" worded rules (bureaucratic from
the standpoint of the undisciplined intellectual), strict adherence
to which can alone safeguard us from the wilfulness and caprices
characteristic of the circles, from the circle methods of scrapping
that goes by the name of the free "process" of the ideological
struggle. . . . [620]

Bureaucracy versus democracy is precisely the same thing as
centralism versus autonomism; it is the organizational principle
of revolutionary Social-Democracy as opposed to the organizational principle of opportunist Social-Democracy. The latter strive
to proceed from the bottom upward, and, therefore, wherever
possible and as far as possible, uphold autonomism, a "democracy" which is carried (by the overzealous) to the point of
anarchism. The former strive to proceed from the top down-
ward, and uphold an extension of the rights and powers of the
centre in respect to the parts. In the period of disunity and the
circles, this top from which revolutionary Social-Democracy

strove to proceed organizationally was inevitably one of the circles, the one which was most influential because of its activity and its revolutionary consistency (in our case, the *Iskra* organization). In the period of restoration of real Party unity and dissolution of the obsolete circles in this unity, this top is inevitably the *Party Congress*, as the supreme organ of the Party; the Congress as far as possible includes representatives of all the active organizations, and, by appointing the central bodies (often with a membership which satisfies the advanced elements of the Party more than the backward elements, and which is more to the taste of its revolutionary wing than its opportunist wing), makes them the top until the next Congress. Such, at any rate, is the case among the Social-Democratic Europeans, although this custom, which is so detested in principle by the anarchists, is gradually beginning, not without difficulty and not without conflicts and squabbles, to spread to the Social-Democratic Asiatics. . . . [624-625]

In its struggle for power the proletariat has no other weapon but organization. Disunited by the rule of anarchic competition in the bourgeois world, . . . the proletariat can become, and inevitably will become, an invincible force only when its ideological unification by the principles of Marxism is consolidated by the material unity of an organization which will weld millions of toilers into an army of the working class. [644-645]

[ON REVOLUTIONARY TACTICS, 1905]

Lenin, "Two Tactics of Social-Democracy in the Democratic Revolution," *Selected Works*, Vol. 1 (Moscow, 1952), Part 2; brackets in the text indicate pages of this edition.

Marxism teaches that a society which is based on commodity production, and which has commercial intercourse with civilized capitalist nations, at a certain stage of its development, itself, inevitably takes the road of capitalism. Marxism has ir-

revocably broken with the ravings of the Narodniks and the
anarchists to the effect that Russia, for instance, can avoid
capitalist development, jump out of capitalism, or skip over it
and proceed along some path other than the path of the class
struggle on the basis and within the framework of this same
capitalism. . . . And from these principles it follows that the
idea of seeking salvation for the working class in anything save
the further development of capitalism is *reactionary*. . . . [48]

Marxism teaches the proletarian not to keep aloof from the
bourgeois revolution, not to be indifferent to it, not to allow the
leadership of the revolution to be assumed by the bourgeoisie
but, on the contrary, to take a most energetic part in it, to fight
most resolutely for consistent proletarian democracy, for carrying the revolution to its conclusion. We cannot jump out of the
bourgeois-democratic boundaries of the Russian revolution, but
we can vastly extend these boundaries, and within these boundaries we can and must fight for the interests of the proletariat. . . . [51]

The degree of economic development of Russia (an objective
condition) and the degree of class consciousness and organization
of the broad masses of the proletariat (a subjective condition in-
separably connected with the objective condition) make the immediate complete emancipation of the working class impossible. . . . A socialist revolution is out of the question unless the
masses become class conscious and organized, trained and educated in open class struggle against the entire bourgeoisie. . . .
Whoever wants to reach Socialism by a different road, other than
that of political democracy, will inevitably arrive at conclusions
that are absurd and reactionary both in the economic and the
political sense. . . . [24-25]

The only force capable of gaining "a decisive victory over
tsarism," is the *people,* i.e., the proletariat and the peasantry. . . .
And such a victory will be precisely a dictatorship, i.e., it must
inevitably rely on military force, on the arming of the masses,
on an insurrection, and not on institutions of one kind or another,
established in a "lawful" or "peaceful" way. It can be only a
dictatorship, for the proletariat and the peasantry will call forth
the desperate resistance of the landlords, of the big bourgeoisie

and of tsardom. Without a dictatorship it is impossible to break down that resistance and to repel the counterrevolutionary attempts. But of course it will be a democratic, not a socialist dictatorship. It will not be able (without a series of intermediary stages of revolutionary development) to affect the foundations of capitalism. At best it may bring about a radical redistribution of landed property in favour of the peasantry, establish consistent and full democracy including the formation of a republic, eradicate all the oppressive features of Asiatic bondage, not only in village but also in factory life, lay the foundation for a thorough improvement in the position of the workers and for a rise in their standard of living, and—last but not least—carry the revolutionary conflagration into Europe. Such a victory will by no means as yet transform our bourgeois revolution into a socialist revolution; the democratic revolution will not directly overstep the bounds of bourgeois social and economic relationships. . . . [56-57]

The bourgeoisie, in the mass, will inevitably turn towards counterrevolution, towards the autocracy, against the revolution and against the people, immediately its narrow, selfish interests are met. . . . The peasantry includes a great number of semi-proletarians as well as petty-bourgeois elements. This causes it also to be unstable and compels the proletariat to unite in a strictly class party. But the instability of the peasantry differs radically from the instability of the bourgeoisie, for at the present time the peasantry is interested not so much in the absolute preservation of private property as in the confiscation of the landed estates, one of the principal forms of private property. While this does not make the peasantry become socialist or cease to be petty-bourgeois, it is capable of becoming a wholehearted and most radical adherent of the democratic revolution. . . . Moreover, the peasantry is attached to the revolution not only by the prospect of radical agrarian reform but by its general and permanent interests. Even in fighting the proletariat the peasantry stands in need of democracy, for only a democratic system is capable of giving exact expression to its interests and of ensuring its predominance as the mass, as the majority. The more enlightened the peasantry becomes . . . the more consistently and determinedly will it favour a thoroughgoing democratic revolution; for, unlike the bourgeoisie, it has nothing to fear from the supremacy of the people. . . . [104-105]

Indeed, what is revolution from the Marxist point of view? The violent break-up of the obsolete political superstructure, the contradiction between which and the new relations of production caused its collapse at a certain moment. The contradiction between the autocracy and the entire structure of capitalist Russia, all the requirements of her bourgeois-democratic development, has now caused its collapse, all the more severe owing to the lengthy period in which this contradiction was artificially sustained. The superstructure is cracking at every joint, it is yielding to pressure, it is growing weaker. The people, through the representatives of the most diverse classes and groups, must now, by its own efforts, build a new superstructure for itself. At a certain stage of development the uselessness of the old superstructure becomes obvious to all. The revolution is recognized by all. The task now is to define *which* classes must build the new superstructure, and *how* they are to build it. . . . This definition is given in the slogan: the democratic dictatorship of the proletariat and the peasantry. This slogan defines the classes upon which the new "builders" of the new superstructure can and must rely, the character of the new superstructure (a "democratic" as distinct from a socialist dictatorship), and how it is to be built (dictatorship, i.e., the violent suppression of violent resistance, arming the revolutionary classes of the people). . . .

The complete victory of the present revolution [1905] will mark the end of the democratic revolution and the beginning of a determined struggle for a socialist revolution. The satisfaction of the demands of the present-day peasantry, the utter rout of reaction, and the winning of a democratic republic will mark the complete end of the revolutionism of the bourgeoisie and even of the petty bourgeoisie—will mark the beginning of the real struggle of the proletariat for Socialism. The more complete the democratic revolution, the sooner, the more widespread, the purer and the more determined will be the development of this new struggle. The slogan of a "democratic" dictatorship expresses the historically limited nature of the present revolution and the necessity of a new struggle on the basis of the new order

for the complete emancipation of the working class from all oppression and all exploitation. [137-139]

["THE LAW OF UNEVEN DEVELOPMENT"]

Lenin, "The United States of Europe Slogan" (1915), *Selected
Works,* Vol. 1 (Moscow, 1952), Part 2, pp. 416-417.

A United States of the World (not of Europe alone) is
the state form of the union and freedom of nations which we
associate with Socialism—until the complete victory of Communism brings about the total disappearance of the state, including the democratic state. As a separate slogan, however, the
slogan of a United States of the World would hardly be a correct
one, first, because it merges with Socialism; second, because it
may be wrongly interpreted to mean that the victory of Socialism
in a single country is impossible, and it may also create miscon-
ceptions as to the relations of such a country to the others.
    Uneven economic and political development is an absolute
law of capitalism. Hence, the victory of Socialism is possible first
in several or even in one capitalist country, taken singly. The
victorious proletariat of that country, having expropriated the
capitalists and organized its own socialist production, would
stand up *against* the rest of the world, the capitalist world, attracting to its cause the oppressed classes of other countries,
raising revolts in those countries against the capitalists, and in
the event of necessity coming out even with armed force against
the exploiting classes and their states. The political form of society in which the proletariat is victorious by overthrowing the
bourgeoisie, will be a democratic republic, which will more and
more centralize the forces of the proletariat of the given nation,
or nations, in the struggle against the states that have not yet
gone over to Socialism. The abolition of classes is impossible without the dictatorship of the oppressed class, the proletariat. The
free union of nations in Socialism is impossible without a more

or less prolonged and stubborn struggle of the socialist republics against the backward states.

IMPERIALISM AS A SPECIAL
STAGE OF CAPITALISM

Lenin, *Imperialism, the Highest Stage of Capitalism* (1916), *Selected Works,* Vol. I (Moscow, 1952), Part 2; brackets in the text refer to pages of this edition.

We must now try to sum up, put together, what has been said above on the subject of imperialism. Imperialism emerged as the development and direct continuation of the fundamental characteristics of capitalism in general. But capitalism only became capitalist imperialism at a definite and very high stage of its development, when certain of its fundamental characteristics began to change into their opposites, when the features of the epoch of transition from capitalism to a higher social and economic system had taken shape and revealed themselves all along the line. Economically, the main thing in this process is the displacement of capitalist free competition by capitalist monopoly. Free competition is the fundamental characteristic of capitalism, and of commodity production generally; monopoly is the exact opposite of free competition, but we have seen the latter being transformed into monopoly before our eyes, creating large-scale industry and forcing out small industry, replacing large-scale by still larger-scale industry, and carrying concentration of production and capital to the point where out of it has grown and is growing monopoly: cartels, syndicates and trusts, and merging with them, the capital of a dozen or so banks, which manipulate thousands of millions. At the same time the monopolies, which have grown out of free competition, do not eliminate the latter, but exist over it and alongside of it, and thereby give rise to a number of very acute, intense antagonisms, frictions and conflicts. Monopoly is the transition from capitalism to a higher system.

If it were necessary to give the briefest possible definition of imperialism we should have to say that imperialism is the monopoly stage of capitalism. Such a definition would include what is most important, for, on the one hand, finance capital is the bank capital of a few very big monopolist banks, merged with the capital of the monopolist combines of industrialists; and, on the other hand, the division of the world is the transition from a colonial policy which has extended without hindrance to territories unseized by any capitalist power, to a colonial policy of monopolistic possession of the territory of the world which has been completely divided up.

But very brief definitions, although convenient, for they sum up the main points, are nevertheless inadequate, since very important features of the phenomenon that has to be defined have to be especially deduced. And so, without forgetting the conditional and relative value of all definitions in general, which can never embrace all the concatenations of a phenomenon in its complete development, we must give a definition of imperialism that will include the following five of its basic features: 1) the concentration of production and capital has developed to such a high stage that it has created monopolies which play a decisive role in economic life; 2) the merging of bank capital with industrial capital, and the creation, on the basis of this "finance capital," of a financial oligarchy; 3) the export of capital as distinguished from the export of commodities acquires exceptional importance; 4) the formation of international monopolist capitalist combines which share the world among themselves, and 5) the territorial division of the whole world among the biggest capitalist powers is completed. Imperialism is capitalism in that stage of development in which the dominance of monopolies and finance capital has established itself; in which the export of capital has acquired pronounced importance; in which the division of the world among the international trusts has begun; in which the division of all territories of the globe among the biggest capitalist powers has been completed. [523-525]

Imperialism has the tendency to create privileged sections

also among the workers, and to detach them from the broad masses of the proletariat. [544-545]

The receipt of high monopoly profits by the capitalists in one of the numerous branches of industry, in one of the numerous countries, etc., makes it economically possible for them to bribe certain sections of the workers, and for a time a fairly considerable minority of them, and win them to the side of the bourgeoisie of a given industry or given nation against all the others. The intensification of antagonisms between imperialist nations for the division of the world increases this striving. And so there is created that bond between imperialism and opportunism, which revealed itself first and most clearly in England, owing to the fact that certain features of imperialist development were observable there much earlier than in other countries. [565]

Imperialism is the epoch of finance capital and of monopolies, which introduce everywhere the striving for domination, not for freedom. The result of these tendencies is reaction all along the line, whatever the political system, and an extreme intensification of existing antagonisms in this domain also. Particularly intensified become the yoke of national oppression and the striving for annexations, i.e., the violation of national independence (for annexation is nothing but the violation of the right of nations to self-determination). [560]

Monopolies, oligarchy, the striving for domination instead of striving for liberty, the exploitation of an increasing number of small or weak nations by a handful of the richest or most powerful nations—all these have given birth to those distinctive characteristics of imperialism which compel us to define it as parasitic or decaying capitalism. More and more prominently there emerges, as one of the tendencies of imperialism, the creation of the "rentier state," the usurer state, in which the bourgeoisie to an ever increasing degree lives on the proceeds of capital exports and by "clipping coupons." It would be a mistake to believe that this tendency to decay precludes the rapid growth of capitalism. It does not. In the epoch of imperialism, certain branches of industry, certain strata of the bourgeoisie and certain countries betray, to a greater or lesser degree, now one and now another of these tendencies. On the whole, capitalism is growing far more rapidly than before; but this growth is not only becoming more and more uneven in general, its unevenness also manifests itself, in particular, in the decay of the countries which are richest in capital (England). [564]

Any other basis under capitalism for the division of spheres of influence, of interests, of colonies, etc., than a calculation of the *strength* of the participants in the division, their general economic, financial, military strength, etc., is *in*conceivable. And the strength of these participants in the division does not change to an equal degree, for the *even* development of different undertakings, trusts, branches of industry, or countries is impossible under capitalism. Half a century ago Germany was a miserable, insignificant country, as far as her capitalist strength was concerned, compared with the strength of England at that time; Japan was the same compared with Russia. Is it "conceivable" that in ten or twenty years' time the relative strength of the imperialist powers will have remained *un*changed? Absolutely inconceivable.

Therefore, in the realities of the capitalist system, and not in the banal philistine fantasies of English parsons, or of the German "Marxist," Kautsky, "interimperialist" or "ultraimperialist" alliances, no matter what form they may assume, whether of one imperialist coalition against another, or of a general alliance embracing *all* the imperialist powers, are *in*evitably nothing more than a "truce" in periods between wars. Peaceful alliances prepare the ground for wars, and in their turn grow out of wars; the one conditions the other, giving rise to alternating forms of peaceful and non-peaceful struggle out of *one and the same* basis of imperialist connections and relations within world economics and world politics. [558-559]

[ON REVOLUTIONARY
TACTICS, APRIL, 1917]

Lenin, a) "Letters on Tactics," in his *The April Theses* (Moscow, 1951), b) " 'April Theses' On the Tasks of the Proletariat in the Present Revolution," and c) "On the Dual Power," *Selected Works*, Vol. 2 (Moscow, 1951), Part 1, as indicated in following notes.

Comrade Kamenev draws a contrast between "party of the masses" and "group of propagandists." But precisely at this moment the "masses" have yielded to the intoxication of "revolutionary" defencism. Would it not be more seemly also for internationalists in such a situation to be able to stand up against "mass" intoxication than to "want to remain" with the masses, i.e., to yield to the general epidemic? Have we not seen how in all the belligerent European countries the chauvinists justified themselves with the plea that they wanted "to remain with the masses"? Is it not our duty to be able for a certain time to be in the minority against "mass" intoxication? Is not the work of propagandists, precisely at the present time, the pivot of the task of *liberating* the proletarian line from "mass" defencist and petty-bourgeois intoxication? [26]

1. In our attitude towards the war, which also under the new government of Lvov and Co. unquestionably remains on Russia's part a predatory imperialist war owing to the capitalist nature of that government, not the slightest concession to "revolutionary defencism" is permissible. . . .

2. The specific feature of the present situation in Russia is that it represents a *transition* from the first stage of the revolution—which, owing to the insufficient class consciousness and organization of the proletariat, placed the power in the hands of the bourgeoisie—*to the second* stage, which must place the power

[26] a), p. 37.

in the hands of the proletariat and the poorest strata of the peasantry. . . .

3. No support for the Provisional Government. . . .

4. . . . It must be explained to the masses that the Soviets of Workers' Deputies are the *only possible* form of the revolutionary government, and that therefore our task is, as long as *this* government yields to the influence of the bourgeoisie, to present a patient, systematic, and persistent *explanation* of the errors of their tactics, an explanation especially adapted to the practical needs of the masses.

As long as we are in the minority we carry on the work of criticizing and exposing errors and at the same time we preach the necessity of transferring the entire power of state to the Soviets of Workers' Deputies, so that the masses may by experience overcome their mistakes.

5. Not a parliamentary republic—to return to a parliamentary republic from the Soviets of Workers' Deputies would be a retrograde step—but a republic of Soviets of Workers', Agricultural Labourers' and Peasants' Deputies throughout the country, from top to bottom.

Abolition of the police, the army and the bureaucracy.

The salaries of all officials, all of whom are to be elected and to be subject to recall at any time, not to exceed the average wage of a competent worker.

6. . . . Confiscation of all landed estates.

Nationalization of *all* lands in the country, the disposal of the land to be put in the charge of the local Soviets. . . .

7. The immediate amalgamation of all banks in the country into a single bank, and the institution of control over it by the Soviets of Workers' Deputies.

8. It isn't our *immediate* task to "introduce" Socialism, but only to bring social production and distribution of products at once under the *control* of the Soviets of Workers' Deputies.

9. Party tasks:

   a) Immediate convocation of a Party congress;

   b) Alteration of the Party program, mainly:

      1) On the question of imperialism and the imperialist war;

> 2) On our attitude towards the state and *our* demand
> for a "commune state";
>
> 3) Amendment of our antiquated minimum program.
>
> c) Change of the Party's name. [Lenin suggested "Com-
> munist Party."]
>
> 10. A new International.[27]

"The revolutionary-democratic dictatorship of the proletariat
and the peasantry" has *already* become a reality in the Russian
revolution; for this "formula" envisages only a *relation of classes,*
and not *a concrete political institution giving effect* to this relation, to this cooperation. The "Soviet of Workers' and Soldiers'
Deputies"—there you have the "revolutionary-democratic dictatorship of the proletariat and the peasantry" already accomplished in reality.

This formula is already antiquated. . . .

He who continues to regard the "completion" of the bourgeois revolution *in the old way,* sacrifices living Marxism to the
dead letter.

According to the old conception, the rule of the proletariat and
the peasantry, their dictatorship, can and must come *after* the
rule of the bourgeoisie.

But in actual fact, it has *already* turned out *differently:* an
extremely original, novel and unprecedented *interlacing of the
one with the other* has taken place.[28]

The highly remarkable specific feature of our revolution is
that it has brought about a *dual power.* This fact must be grasped
first and foremost: unless it is understood, we cannot advance.
We must know how to supplement and amend old "formulas".
. . . *Nobody* previously thought, or could have thought, of a
dual power.

In what does this dual power consist? In the fact that side
by side with the Provisional Government, the government of the
bourgeoisie, there has arisen *another government,* weak and
incipient as yet, but undoubtedly an actually existing and growing
government—the Soviets of Workers' and Soldiers' Deputies.[29]

[27] b), pp. 13-17.
[28] a), pp. 20-22.
[29] c), p. 20

[ON THE STATE]

Lenin, "The Tasks of the Proletariat in Our Revolution," and "On the Dual Power," *Selected Works*, Vol. 2 (Moscow, 1951), Part 1, pp. 36-38, 20-21.

The Soviets of Workers', Soldiers', Peasants' and other Deputies are not understood; not only in the sense that their class character, their part in the *Russian* revolution, is not clear to the majority. They are not understood also in the sense that they constitute a new form, or rather a new *type of state.*

The most perfect, the most advanced type of bourgeois state is the *parliamentary democratic republic:* power is vested in the parliament; the state machine, the apparatus and organ of administration, is of the customary kind: the standing army, the police and the bureaucracy—which in practice is never replaced, is privileged and stands *above* the people.

But since the end of the nineteenth century, revolutionary epochs have advanced a *higher* type of democratic state, a state which in certain respects, as Engels put it, ceases to be a state, is "no longer a state in the proper sense of the word." . . .

It is extremely easy (as history proves) to revert from a parliamentary bourgeois republic to a monarchy, for all the machinery of repression—the army, the police, and the bureaucracy—is left intact. The Commune and the Soviets of Workers', Soldiers', Peasants' and other Deputies *smash* and eliminate that machinery.

The parliamentary bourgeois republic hampers and stifles the independent political life of the *masses,* their direct participation in the *democratic* organization of the life of the state from top to bottom. The contrary is the case with the Soviets of Workers' and Soldiers' Deputies.

The Soviets are a power entirely different from that generally existing in the parliamentary bourgeois-democratic republics of the usual type still prevailing in the advanced countries of Europe and America. This circumstance is often forgotten, often not reflected on, yet it is the crux of the matter. *This* power is of *the same type* as the Paris Commune of 1871. The fundamental characteristics of this type are: 1) the source of power is not a law previously discussed and enacted by parliament, but the direct initiative of the people's masses from below, in their localities—direct "seizure" to use a current expression; 2) the replacement of the police and the army, which are institutions separated from the people and set against the people, by the direct arming of the whole people; order in the state under such a power is maintained by the armed workers and peasants *themselves,* by the armed people *themselves;* 3) officialdom, the bureaucracy are either similarly replaced by the direct rule of the people themselves or at least placed under special control; they not only become elected officials, but are also *subject to recall* at the first demand of the people; they are reduced to the position of simple agents; from a privileged stratum holding "jobs" remunerated on a high, bourgeois scale, they become workers of a special "branch," whose remuneration *does not exceed* the ordinary pay of a competent worker.

This, and this *alone,* constitutes the *essence* of the Paris Commune as a special type of state.

[THE "WITHERING" OF THE STATE]

Lenin, *The State and Revolution* (1917), *Selected Works,* Vol. 2 (Moscow, 1951), Part 1; brackets in the text indicate pages of this edition.

The supersession of the bourgeois state by the proletarian state is impossible without a violent revolution. The abolition of the proletarian state, i.e., of the state in general, is impossible except through the process of "withering away."
. . . [220]

Engels' words regarding the "withering away" of the state
are so widely known, they are so often quoted, and so clearly
reveal the essence of the customary adulteration of Marxism to
look like opportunism that we must deal with them in detail.
. . . [213]

In the first place, at the very outset of his argument Engels
says that, in seizing state power, the proletariat thereby "abolishes
the state as state." It is not "good form" to ponder over the
meaning of this. Generally, it is either ignored altogether, or
is considered to be something in the nature of "Hegelian weakness" on Engels' part. As a matter of fact, however, these words
briefly express the experience of one of the greatest proletarian
revolutions, the Paris Commune of 1871, of which we shall speak
in greater detail in its proper place. As a matter of fact, Engels
speaks here of the proletarian revolution "abolishing" the *bourgeois* state, while the words about the state withering away
refer to the remnants of the *proletarian* state *after* the socialist
revolution. According to Engels the bourgeois state does not
"wither away," but is "*abolished*" by the proletariat in the course
of the revolution. What withers away after this revolution is
the proletarian state or semistate.

Secondly, the state is a "special repressive force." Engels gives
this splendid and extremely profound definition here with the
utmost lucidity. And from it follows that the "special repressive
force" for the suppression of the proletariat by the bourgeoisie,
of millions of toilers by handfuls of the rich, must be replaced
by a "special repressive force" for the suppression of the bourgeoisie by the proletariat (the dictatorship of the proletariat).
This is precisely what is meant by "abolition of the state as
state." This is precisely the "act" of taking possession of the
means of production in the name of society. And it is self-evident
that *such* a replacement of one (bourgeois) "special force" by
another (proletarian) "special force" cannot possibly take place
in the form of "withering away."

Thirdly, in speaking of the state "withering away," and the
even more graphic and colourful "ceasing of itself," Engels
refers quite clearly and definitely to the period *after* "the state
has taken possession of the means of production in the name

of the whole society," that is, *after* the socialist revolution. We all know that the political form of the "state" at that time is the most complete democracy. But it never enters the head of any of the opportunists who shamelessly distort Marxism that Engels is consequently speaking here of *democracy* "ceasing of itself," or "withering away." This seems very strange at first sight; but it is "incomprehensible" only to those who have not pondered over the fact that democracy is *also* a state and that, consequently, democracy will also disappear when the state disappears. Revolution alone can "abolish" the bourgeois state. The state in general, i.e., the most complete democracy, can only "wither away." [215-216]

Someone may . . . fear that we are expecting the advent of an order of society in which the principle of the subordination of the minority to the majority will not be observed—for democracy means the recognition of just this principle?

No, democracy is *not* identical with the subordination of the minority to the majority. Democracy is a *state* which recognizes the subordination of the minority to the majority, i.e., an organization for the systematic use of *violence* by one class against the other, by one section of the population against another. . . . [284]

Engels expressed this splendidly in his letter to Bebel when he said, as the reader will remember, that "the proletariat uses the state not in the interests of freedom but in order to hold down its adversaries, and as soon as it becomes possible to speak of freedom the state as such ceases to exist."

Democracy for the vast majority of the people, and suppression by force, i.e., exclusion from democracy, of the exploiters and oppressors of the people—this is the change democracy undergoes during the *transition* from capitalism to Communism.

Only in communist society, when the resistance of the capitalists has been completely crushed, when the capitalists have disappeared, when there are no classes (i.e., when there is no difference between the members of society as regards their relation to the social means of production), *only* then "the state . . . ceases to exist," and it "*becomes possible to speak of freedom.*" Only then will there become possible and be realized a

truly complete democracy, democracy without any exceptions
whatever. And only then will democracy begin to *wither away*,
owing to the simple fact that, freed from capitalist slavery, from
the untold horrors, savagery, absurdities and infamies of capitalist exploitation, people will gradually *become accustomed* to
observing the elementary rules of social intercourse that have
been known for centuries and repeated for thousands of years
in all copybook maxims; they will become accustomed to observing them without force, without compulsion, without subordination, *without the special apparatus* for compulsion which
is called the state. [291-292]

THE HIGHER PHASE
OF COMMUNIST SOCIETY

Lenin, *The State and Revolution* (1917), *Selected Works*, Vol. 2
(Moscow, 1951), Part 1; brackets in the text indicate pages of
this edition.

The economic basis for the complete withering away
of the state is such a high stage of development of Communism
that the antithesis between mental and physical labour disappears when there, consequently, disappears one of the principal
sources of modern *social* inequality—a source, moreover, which
cannot on any account be removed immediately by the mere
conversion of the means of production into public property,
by the mere expropriation of the capitalists. . . .
    It will become possible for the state to wither away com-
pletely when society adopts the rule: "From each according to
his ability, to each according to his needs," i.e., when people
have become so accustomed to observing the fundamental rules
of social intercourse and when their labour becomes so productive that they will voluntarily work *according to their ability*.
"The narrow horizon of bourgeois right," which compels one to

calculate with the coldheartedness of a Shylock whether one has not worked half an hour more than somebody else, whether one is not getting less pay than somebody else—this narrow horizon will then be crossed. There will then be no need for society to regulate the quantity of products to be received by each; each will take freely "according to his needs." . . . [299-300]

We are not utopians, we do not indulge in "dreams" of dispensing *at once* with all administration, with all subordination; these anarchist dreams, based upon a lack of understanding of the tasks of the proletarian dictatorship, are totally alien to Marxism, and, as a matter of fact, serve only to postpone the socialist revolution until people are different. No, we want the socialist revolution with people as they are now, with people who cannot dispense with subordination, control and "foremen and bookkeepers." . . . [249]

The workers, having conquered political power, will smash the old bureaucratic apparatus, they will shatter it to its very foundations, they will destroy it to the very roots; and they will replace it by a new one, consisting of the very same workers and office employees, *against* whose transformation into bureaucrats the measures will at once be taken which were specified in detail by Marx and Engels: 1) not only election, but also recall at any time; 2) pay not exceeding that of a workman; 3) immediate introduction of control and supervision by *all*, so that *all* shall become "bureaucrats" for a time and that, therefore, *nobody* may be able to become a "bureaucrat." . . . [313-314]

Accounting and control—that is the *main* thing required for "arranging" the smooth working, the correct functioning of the *first phase* of communist society. All citizens are transformed here into hired employees of the state, which consists of the armed workers. All citizens become employees and workers of a *single* nation-wide state "syndicate." All that is required is that they should work equally, do their proper share of work, and get equally paid. The accounting and control necessary for this have been *simplified* by capitalism to the extreme and reduced to the extraordinarily simple operations—which any liter-

ate person can perform—of supervising and recording, knowledge of the four rules of arithmetic, and issuing appropriate
receipts. [304-305]

THE IMMEDIATE TASKS

OF THE SOVIET GOVERNMENT

Lenin, "The Immediate Tasks of the Soviet Government" (1918),
Selected Works, Vol. 2 (Moscow, 1951), Part 1; brackets in the
text indicate pages of this edition.

This is a peculiar epoch, or rather stage of development,
and in order to utterly defeat capital, we must be able to adapt
the forms of our struggle to the peculiar conditions of this stage.
. . . Owing to the considerable "delay" in introducing accounting and control . . . we have to resort to the old bourgeois method and to agree to pay a very high price for the
"services" of the biggest bourgeois specialists. All those who are
familiar with the subject appreciate this, but not all ponder
over the significance of this measure being adopted by the
proletarian state. Clearly, such a measure is a compromise, a
departure from the principles of the Paris Commune and of
every proletarian power, which call for the reduction of all
salaries to the level of the wages of the average worker, which
call for fighting careerism, not with words, but with deeds. . . .
[458-459]
The struggle that was developing around the recent decree on
the management of the railways, the decree which grants individual executives dictatorial powers (or "unlimited" powers) is
characteristic. . . . The question has become one of really enormous significance: firstly, the question of principle, viz., is the
appointment of individual persons, dictators with unlimited powers, in general compatible with the fundamental principles of
Soviet government? Secondly, what relation has this case—this
precedent, if you will—to the special tasks of the government

in the present concrete situation? We must deal very thoroughly
with both these questions.

. . . If we are not anarchists, we must admit that the state,
that is, compulsion, is necessary for the transition from capitalism to Socialism. The form of compulsion is determined by the
degree of development of the given revolutionary class, and
also by special circumstances, such as, for example, the heritage
of a long and reactionary war and the forms of resistance put
up by the bourgeoisie and the petty bourgeoisie. Hence, there
is absolutely *no* contradiction in principle between Soviet (*that
is,* socialist) democracy and the exercise of dictatorial powers by
individuals. The difference between proletarian dictatorship and
bourgeois dictatorship is that the former strikes at the exploiting
minority in the interests of the exploited majority, and that it is
exercised—*also through individuals*—not only by the toiling and
exploited masses, but also by organizations which are built in
such a way as to rouse these masses to the work of history-
making. (The Soviet organizations are organizations of this
kind).

In regard to the second question concerning the significance
of precisely individual dictatorial powers from the point of view
of the specific tasks of the present moment, it must be said
that large-scale machine industry—which is precisely the material source, the productive source, the foundation of Socialism—
calls for absolute and strict *unity of will,* which directs the
joint labours of hundreds, thousands and tens of thousands of
people. The technical, economic and historical necessity of this
is obvious, and all those who have thought about Socialism
have always regarded it as one of the conditions of Socialism.
But how can strict unity of will be secured?—By thousands subordinating their will to the will of one. . . . [480-482]

The fight against the bureaucratic distortion of the Soviet
form of organization is assured by the firmness of the connection
between the Soviets and the "people," meaning by that the
toilers and exploited, and by the flexibility and elasticity of this
connection. . . .

It is precisely the closeness of the Soviets to the "people,"
to the toilers, that creates the special forms of recall and other

means of control from below which must be most zealously developed now. . . . Nothing could be sillier than to transform the Soviets into something congealed and self-contained. The more resolutely we now have to stand for a ruthlessly firm government, for the dictatorship of individuals *in definite processes of work*, in definite aspects of *purely executive* functions, the more varied must be the form and methods of control from below in order to counteract every shadow of possibility of distorting the principles of Soviet government, in order repeatedly and tirelessly to weed out bureaucracy. . . . [488-489]

BIBLIOGRAPHY

Works by Lenin

Collected Works (Moscow, 1960-   ). The Moscow and New York, 1927-1945, edition in seven scattered volumes was not completed; the German edition, also uncompleted, added seven other volumes.
Selected Works, 12 volumes (Moscow, 1934-1938). The New York, undated, and London, 1936-1939, editions are generally identical with this as to pagination.
The Immediate Tasks of the Soviet Government (1918).
Imperialism, the Highest Stage of Capitalism (1916).
"Left Wing" Communism, an Infantile Disorder (1920).
Materialism and Empirio-Criticism (1908).
The Proletarian Revolution and the Renegade Kautsky (1918).
The State and Revolution (1917).
The Tasks of the Proletariat in Our Revolution (1917).
The Tax In Kind (1921). On the New Economic Policy.
Two Tactics of Social Democracy in the Democratic Revolution (1905).
What the "Friends of the People" Are and How They Fight the Social Democrats (1894).
"Will the Bolsheviks Retain State Power?" (1917).

Biography

Walter, Gérard, *Lénine* (Paris, 1950).
Wolfe, Bertram D., *Three Who Made a Revolution* (New York, 1948). Includes Stalin and Trotsky.

Exposition

Bentley, W., "The Contribution of Lenin and Stalin to Communist Theory," *Cahiers Bruges*, Vol. 2 (July, 1952), pp. 84-107.

Carr, Edward H., "Lenin's Theory of the State," in his *The Bolshevik Revolution*, Vol. 1 (London, 1950), pp. 233-249.

Choron, Jacques, *La doctrine bolcheviste* (Paris, 1935).

Choronshitzky, Jakob, *Lenins ökonomische Anschauungen* (Berlin, 1928).

Collinet, Michel, *Du bolchevisme* (Paris, 1957).

Daniels, Robert V., "The State and Revolution: A Case Study in the Genesis and Transformation of Communist Ideology," *American Slavic and East European Review*, Vol. 12 (February, 1953), pp. 22-43.

Deborin, Abram M., "Lenin als revolutionärer Dialektiker," *Unter dem Banner des Marxismus*, Vol. 1 (July, 1925), pp. 201-230.

Freymond, Jacques, *Lénine et l'imperialisme* (Lausanne, 1951).

Haimson, Leopold H., *The Russian Marxists and the Origins of Bolshevism* (Cambridge, Mass., 1955).

Harper, J., *Lenin als Philosoph; Kritische Betrachtung der philosophischen Grundlagen des Leninismus* (Amsterdam, 1938).

Kautsky, Karl, *The Dictatorship of the Proletariat* (1918; London, 1919).

————, *Terrorism and Communism* (1919; London, 1920).

Klein, Matthäus, and Kosing, Alfred, eds., *Philosophie im Klassenkampf: fünfzig Jahre W. I. Lenin: Materialismus und Empiriokritizismus* (Berlin, 1959).

Lazić, Branko M., *Lénine et la IIIe Internationale* (Nauchatel, 1951). Preface by Raymond Aron.

Leont'ev, Lev A., *Ueber das Werk W. I. Lenins 'Der Imperialismus als höchstes Stadium des Kapitalismus'* (Berlin, 1951).

Limon, Didier L., "Lénine et le contrôle ouvrier," *Revue internationale*, Vol. 1 (April-May, 1946), pp. 366-379, 455-470.

Luppol, Ivan K., *Lenin und die Philosophie* (Vienna, 1929). A thorough Marxist study.

Luxemburg, Rosa, *Leninism or Marxism* (Glasgow, 1935). In French as —*Marxisme, réformisme et Léninisme* (Paris, 1934).

————, *The Russian Revolution*, trans. by Bertram D. Wolfe (New York, 1940).

Machers, Gerd, *Bakunin und Lenin* (Offenbach a. M., 1932).

Meyer, Alfred G., *Leninism* (Cambridge, Mass., 1957).

Mignot, John, *Le Léninisme* (Louvain and Paris, 1933).

Page, Stanley W., "The Russian Proletariat and World Revolution: Lenin's Views to 1914," *American Slavic and East European Review*, Vol. 10 (February, 1951), pp. 1-13.

Pannekoek, Anton, *Lenin as Philosopher* (1938; New York, 1948).

Pastore, Annibale, *La filosofia di Lenin* (Milan, 1946).

–Pipes, Richard, *Social Democracy and the St. Petersburg Labor Movement, 1885-1897* (Cambridge, Mass., 1963).

Sarel, Benno, "Lénine, Trotski, Staline et le problème du parti revolutionnaire," *Temps modern*, Vol. 7 (November, 1951), pp. 848-879.

Smith, David G., "Lenin's 'Imperialism': A Study in the Unity of Theory and Practice," *Journal of Politics*, Vol. 17 (November, 1955), pp. 546-569.

Spalcke, Karl, *Die Diktatur des Proletariats bei Kautsky und Lenin* (Tübingen, 1930).

Stalin, Joseph, *The Foundations of Leninism* (1924). Several editions.

–Thompson, Ronald Bettes, *Lenin's Theory of the State, 1914-1916* (Chicago, 1954?). University of Chicago Library microfilm.

Treadgold, Donald W., *Lenin and His Rivals* (London, 1955).

4

Martov:

Marxism Means Mass Support

For twenty years Martov (Iuri O. Tsederbaum, 1873-1923) was Lenin's most consistent opponent. A study of his ideas leads one to the suspicion that, had the Russian Marxists adhered to his position and rejected the innovations of Lenin, they would have been as ineffectual as their Western comrades. Yet such a study leads also to enhanced respect for the clarity and cogency of Martov's thought.

The pattern of Martov's life was like that of the other émigrés, although conditioned by his being Jewish. His background was secular, middle-class, and intellectual, and he very early absorbed *narodnik* ideals. Arrested during his first year at the University of St. Petersburg, he was exiled to Vilna, where he participated in Marxist educational activities among the Jewish textile workers. Back in St. Petersburg in 1895, his group joined with Lenin's to form the "Union of Struggle for the Liberation of Labor." Both were shortly arrested, and the "Union" thereafter turned to "Economism." In 1900, after the planning of *Iskra* with Lenin and Potresov, Martov traveled widely in Russia promoting the project among Marxist circles, and rejoined Lenin in Munich after the paper was started.

A loyal member of the *Iskra* team, Martov helped to plan the Second Congress and helped to drive the Bund out of the Party by his attack upon its federal concept of organization. He differed with Lenin on the requirements of Party membership (Point 1 of the Rules), and carried the Congress for his less stringent position. Then, when Lenin undertook to exclude Axelrod, Potresov, and Zasulich from the editorial board of *Iskra*, Martov rose in fury against him. The Congress and the Party were thus divided into Bolsheviks and Mensheviks, a schism that was never healed.

Soon joined by Plekhanov, Martov maneuvered to isolate Lenin and to gain control of the central organs of the Party. They tried to rebuild party unity while resisting undue influence by the former Economists who had joined them. In spite of grassroots cooperation, and two joint congresses, the chasm between the two factions grew deeper as the polemics uncovered more and more fundamental points of difference. With the exception of the Fifth Congress in 1907, it appears that the Mensheviks usually had the support of a majority of the Russian Marxists until September, 1917, when their continued connection with Kerensky's Provisional Government cost them their control of the Petrograd soviet.

During the First World War Martov led the left, the internationalist wing of the Mensheviks, resisting the social patriotism of Plekhanov and working with Lenin at the Zimmerwald and Kienthal conferences for the restoration of international socialist unity. Being thus opposed to participation in the War, he was in the minority among the Mensheviks and was unable after his return to Russia in May, 1917, either to influence his faction or to join the Bolsheviks. Even after the revolution of October he continued to advocate ineffectually a coalition government of all socialist parties. Keenly aware of the undemocratic features of Lenin's new government, he combined, until his death in 1923, a very prescient criticism of Bolshevism with a staunch defense of the Bolsheviks against all bourgeois attacks.

With his first publication Martov penetrated to the heart of the problems facing Russian Marxism. In a preface to a translated pamphlet (1893) he faced the major issue of the relation of the Marxist intellectuals to the vigorous union movement among illiterate workmen. The former were armed, he said, with an understanding of history, with "consciousness" of the mission of the proletariat; the latter, lacking this knowledge, were reacting spontaneously to the oppressions of capitalism without under-

standing the broad ramifications of the class struggle. To show
that neither could succeed alone Martov drew a parallel from
recent history. The *narodniks* of the 1870's had believed in
"spontaneity": the masses, with a little stimulation, would arise
and shake off their rulers. The People's Will of 1879-1881, on
the contrary, had believed in "consciousness": a handful of dedicated conspirators would remove the despots and liberate the
people. Both had failed, but they had bequeathed the lesson
that spontaneity and consciousness must be combined.[1] But how?

During his exile in Vilna Martov found a partial answer. Some
years of study circles among factory workers had led the Jewish
Social Democrats to the conclusion that education served only
to elevate the most capable workers into the middle class—to
enable them to desert the class they were supposed to lead—and
that a new and different approach must be used. This approach,
as drawn up by Arkadie Kremer and edited by Martov in a
hectographed pamphlet *On Agitation* (1894), called for the
gradual development of consciousness among the workers by
the active participation of the Marxist intellectuals in the spontaneous workers' movement. Propaganda should be based on
actual factory conditions and should not attempt to remove the
worker too far from his own experiences. The intellectuals should
then combine their propaganda with "agitation"—the leadership
of mass meetings, demonstrations, and strikes—whenever objective conditions made this possible. By stimulating and helping
in the pursuit of short-range economic goals and by interpreting
the experience gained, the intellectuals would lead the workers
to understand the necessity for long-range political goals. They
would then be using arguments that were clear and significant

[1] In this preface Martov seems also to have anticipated the Parvus-Trotsky
theory (see p. 121) that the workers would hold power after leading
the bourgeois revolution, although he missed its significance. He wrote,
"The nearest goal of social democracy is the attainment of political freedom; the main task is the organization of a workers' party. Whether this
is accomplished before a Russian revolution, or after, is all the same.
If not, we shall participate in the revolution side by side with the other
progressive parties; if so, the organized social democratic party will be able
to retain the fruits of victory in the hands of the working class." Preface
to Jules Guesde's *Le Collectivisme*, quoted in Martov, *Zapiski Sotsial-Demo-
krata* (Moscow, 1924), pp. 151-152.

to the workers. Like children in a progressive school, the workers would "learn by doing," would learn that behind their specific employer lay the whole bourgeois class and behind it the government. And the Marxists, by organizing and leading the ordinary conflicts over wages and working conditions, would earn a position of leadership in the later political struggle.[2]

Martov clearly regarded the tactics advocated in *On Agitation* as means toward a revolutionary political end, and the formation of the Union of Struggle for the Liberation of Labor indicates Lenin's agreement on this approach. The pamphlet, however, had been so optimistic about the learning capacities of the workers as to disparage the function of Social Democratic teachers. Soon there appeared young men who argued that the Marxists should themselves be guided by the workers, that they should not try to turn the economic struggle into preconceived political channels. These were the Economists, and (as noted earlier, p. 28) the plan for calling a Second Party Congress was based on their systematic exclusion, as far as possible. All of the *Iskra* editors participated in these planning procedures, which were hardly compatible with Axelrod's and Martov's later ideas of a mass party. It seems, therefore, that the Congress itself was an important element in the development of Martov's attitude toward majority rule.

Lenin is usually seen as an élitist conspirator and Martov as an advocate of a mass movement and Marxism by majority vote.[3] This interpretation, however, while basically correct, requires refinement. In the planning of the Second Congress both men were quite conscious of the necessity to build a majority for the "*Iskra* line." To gain a dependable victory over the Economists they deliberately narrowed the constituent bases of the Congress. On Point 1 of the Rules Martov used a simple majority to defeat Lenin, and Lenin accepted his defeat, not reopening the question when, toward the end of the Congress, he controlled a majority. Yet when Martov saw the ways in which Lenin was

[2] Kremer, *Ob Agitatsii* (Geneva, 1896), especially pp. 20-24.
[3] Martov's close friend, Fedor Dan, later saw the two wings of the Russian party as the forerunners of the international split between socialism and Communism. Dan, "Aus dem Nachlass J. Martows," *Der Kampf*, Vol. 18 (May, 1925), p. 169.

determined to use his contrived Congress majority—expelling his colleagues from the *Iskra* board and disbanding strong Marxist organizations that disagreed with him—he drew back in horror. He seemed suddenly to have realized the merits of consensus as against majority rule. It appears that, although Lenin had published his ideas on party organization in *What Is To Be Done?*, Martov had not understood that, in Lenin's mind, the Congress was intended to establish centralized control over all Russian Marxism. Knowing that a substantial majority, including the organizations that had not been invited to the Congress and those that had walked out, would not accept such control, Martov rejected the Congress majority in favor of a search for consensus and cooperation on a broader scale. Lenin, on the contrary, was unable to "imagine any other way of avoiding a split in a party that is at all organized except by the submission of the minority to the majority."[4] For Lenin a majority was always a means for control. He insisted tenaciously on the name Majority, Bolshevik, for his faction; he preferred a small organization in which he could command a majority to a large one where he could not; and even in 1917 he delayed the seizure of power until he had a majority in the Petrograd soviet. Martov, on the other hand, doubted the efficacy of majorities and looked to the broad support promised by the Marxist reading of history.[5]

Their differences on party organization also can easily be exaggerated. At the Congress Lenin said, "I by no means consider our difference [over Point 1] so substantial as to be a matter of life or death to the Party. We shall certainly not perish because of a bad clause in the Rules!"[6] Both men wanted both an open and an underground party, Martov stressing the former and Lenin the latter. At the Congress Martov denied that he was afraid of a conspiratorial organization, but insisted that, "For

[4] Lenin, *Selected Works,* Vol. 2 (London, 1936), p. 465.

[5] At the Menshevik Conference of April, 1905, a "workers' opposition" tried to secure democratic election of all Party committees, but the intellectuals preferred coöptation and the attempt failed. Martov, *Geschichte der russischen Sozialdemokratie,* trans. by A. Stein (Berlin, 1926), p. 136.

[6] *Vtoroi Ocherednoi S"ezd RSDRP, Polnyi Tekst Protokolov* (Geneva, 1903), p. 250.

me a conspiratorial organization has meaning only in so far as it is enveloped by a broad Social Democratic Labor Party." [7] In practice Martov soon came to stand, partly through Axelrod's influence, for the broadest party possible. During the revolution of 1905, when open activity seemed so promising, Axelrod projected expansion of the Social Democrats into an open labor party, a party that would reach beyond Marxist orthodoxy to marshal and coordinate the revolutionary efforts of all the lower strata of the population. In support of that conception Martov reexamined Marx's writings on the Paris commune and discovered that the dictatorship of the proletariat was really a form of social structure rather than a form of government, one in which all the "healthy elements" of society, all except the class enemy, the "rich capitalists," are "welded to the proletariat," not by force but by conscious agreement with its program. Such agreement was possible only under democracy; democracy, therefore, was the governmental form necessary for the dictatorship of the proletariat.

For Lenin, on the contrary, such a labor party seemed worthless, even dangerous. The proletariat should be converted to Marxism, not exposed to bourgeois influence in a labor party. The other classes should be destroyed, not amalgamated into the workers' party. And the dictatorship of the proletariat is the weapon for their destruction—although he continued to view it as democratic.[8]

Only gradually, through years of polemics, did the two sides in this controversy come to understand the nature and the magnitude of their differences. In the meantime each distorted the position of the other, seeing in its ideas and actions, if not desertion from the proletarian ranks, at least objective aid and comfort for the bourgeoisie. In Lenin's tight, illegal party Martov saw conspiracy, Blanquism, and profound distrust of economic influences, of democracy, and of the proletariat—a distrust more

[7] *Ibid.*, p. 239.
[8] The Chinese Communist theory of New Democracy, with its bloc of four classes and its ideas of class conversion, may be closer to Lenin in methods, but it appears to be closer to Martov in objective.

appropriate for a *narodnik* or a Socialist-Revolutionary than for a Marxist. In Martov's association with former Economists, his support for the bourgeois liberals, and his desire for a mass party, Lenin saw a disguised abandonment of the cause of revolution in favor of a hopeless and non-Marxian reformism.

Yet Martov's relation to the liberals was not reformist. It was always based on revolutionary Marxist analysis. Like the other comrades, he believed that capitalism was growing in Russia and that the autocracy would be overthrown by a bourgeois revolution. Like the others, he believed that the weakness of the liberals required the proletariat to assume an active role in this revolution. But he denied that, in the absence of adequate economic development, the proletariat could assume power alone or even participate in power with the bourgeois parties without being compromised. The task, therefore, was to help the liberals in their historic mission of overthrowing the tsar, pushing them as far as possible toward political democracy, toward the "objective limits" of the revolution, while at the same time maintaining complete independence of action. Thereafter, under a bourgeois republic, the Social Democrats would still be the party of extreme left opposition, while the capitalistic development of the country would prepare the conditions necessary for a second, a socialist, revolution.

In the practical application of these ideas also the Mensheviks saw the situation differently from the Bolsheviks. For the latter, the liberals' acceptance of the First Duma marked their desertion to the ranks of reaction. For the Mensheviks, on the contrary, the lack of any real power in the Duma meant that the overthrow of the feudal régime remained to be accomplished, and the liberals remained revolutionary. As early as 1906 Martov argued that "New strife between the bourgeoisie and the proletariat . . . would strengthen the position of the autocracy and thus would retard the progress of the emancipation of the people." [9] While Lenin continued to refer to the government, even after the revision of the election law in 1907, as a "bourgeois monarchy," Martov saw the Stolypin régime as a backward step

[9] Martov (*pseud.* El'mar), *Narod i Gosudarstvennaia Duma* (St. Petersburg, 1906), p. 20.

in feudalism, making the bourgeoisie still more revolutionary. At the Party Congress of 1907, therefore, the Mensheviks proposed two conciliatory resolutions on relations with other parties:

1. To influence, by its independent policy, the liberal and democratic parties, relentlessly fighting both against their conciliatory tendencies, now displayed especially by the Cadets, and against the agrarian utopias and superficial revolutionism of the *narodniks*, and at the same time supporting the manifestations of their struggle against the present régime.

2. To enter into agreements with these parties in separate, definite cases, guided by the demands that the task of strengthening the attack on the autocracy places upon Social Democracy, in order to use them in the interests of broadening the current of the revolution and of the attainment by the proletariat of its own great goal.[10]

These were rejected by the Bolshevik majority.

The difference of view is sometimes stated as Lenin's preference for the petty-bourgeois peasants and suspicion of the urban bourgeoisie, and Martov's opposite attitude. This difference hinged on a distinction that Lenin made, but Martov did not, between economic development in the cities and in the Russian countryside. In formulating his demand for a "dictatorship of the proletariat and the peasantry," Lenin considered the peasants to be revolutionary—ready to overthrow the feudal landlords, while the urban liberals had turned reactionary in support of the "bourgeois monarchy." In rejecting this demand, Martov saw the feudal régime intact, both at the center and in the hinterland. The resolutions above, therefore, display parallel attitudes toward urban and rural parties. Martov argued that the peasants had not yet gone to "the school of the capitalist bourgeoisie," and could not be integrated into a Marxist party. He recognized the importance of agitation among them, none the less, and the Menshevik resolution of 1905 called for support for all forcible seizures of land and for "revolutionary local government in the villages and a revolutionary league of village selfgoverning societies" to organize a general peasant uprising.[11]

---

[10] *Piatyi S"ezd RSDRP, Protokoly* (Moscow, 1935), p. 715.
[11] Quoted in Lenin, *Selected Works*, Vol. 3 (London, 1936), p. 543, from the resolution, "Work among the Peasants," of the Menshevik Conference.

The years of polemics and of attempts at unity led finally, in 1911 and 1912, to the abandonment on both sides of all hope that the divided Party could be reunited. Yet in October, 1914, when international socialism had collapsed in ruins, Lenin had kind words for Martov and his stand against "social-patriotism" and the War.[12] At the conferences of the internationalists at Zimmerwald (1915) and Kienthal (1916) Martov took with the majority a centrist position for peace without victory, as distinguished from Lenin's left position for converting the War into a civil war. A manifesto he prepared with Axelrod for the Kienthal conference presented his program in a brief passage: "The complete economic and political union of all civilized nations will be one of the primary tasks of the socialist transformation of the present economic system." This he thought possible only through direct class struggle for state power, and the consequent democratization of the armed forces (militia), of the economy, and of the state itself. Any other peace program of the "bourgeois socialists" was only seduction of the workers.[13]

After the February revolution in Russia it was Martov who proposed the return of the émigrés by way of Germany. Back in Petrograd, convinced that "If the revolution does not kill the war, the war will destroy the revolution," he found himself at odds with his own faction, most of whom now supported the war "in defense of the revolution." He opposed the Provisional Government and its Menshevik ministers because they continued the war and because he was convinced that the bourgeois parties in the coalition would never support the radical parts of the Social Democratic program. At the same time he opposed the Bolsheviks because he believed the economic conditions were not ripe for socialism, the proletariat was too weak to rule, and the attempt would be a great defeat for socialism. "We must not substitute for the conquest of power by a majority of the revolutionary democracy, the conquest of power in a struggle with that majority and against it." [14] Instead he called for a new coali-

[12] See Lenin, *Collected Works*, Vol. 18 (New York, 1930), p. 70.

[13] P. Axelrod, S. Lapinski, and L. Martoff, *Kriegs- und Friedensprobleme der Arbeiterklasse* (Zurich, 1916), pp. 8, 15-16.

[14] Quoted in Trotsky, *The History of the Russian Revolution*, trans. by Max Eastman, Vol. 2 (London, 1933), p. 313.

tion ministry of all socialist parties, an idea widely supported in the Democratic Conference in September and in the Preparliament in October. In the Second Congress of Soviets, on the evening following the Bolshevik coup, which, he believed, "threatens to bring about bloodshed and civil war and the triumph of a counterrevolution which would suppress in blood the whole movement of the proletariat and, at the same time, destroy the gains of the revolution," Martov again proposed a coalition.[15] The Bolsheviks at least tactically accepted, but the right wing Mensheviks and Socialist Revolutionaries refused.

Martov thus had little or no influence on the course of the revolution. His remaining years went largely into criticism of Bolshevism and reconstruction of the socialist international. The Bolsheviks, he believed, had deserted Marxism for mysticism—thinking that a socialist revolution could be accomplished without the prerequisite economic development and without socialist consciousness among the masses. This "revolutionary romanticism" lay behind the Communist International, which was gaining ground because the workers, having lost faith in the old organizations during the war, were victims of "spiritual atavism," and were reviving early, simple illusions and prejudices.

Thus has the moment arrived that Mikhail Bakunin, the precursor of the present Moscow saviors, predicted a half-century ago—the moment when the eyes of the whole proletariat of Europe would be turned toward the east, and when they would believe that the carriers of the Russian peasant revolution would also be the leaders of the revolution in western Europe. Now the moment has arrived when the apostles of the messiah promised by Bakunin can go forth to all countries to preach the Bakuninist evangel in all languages and to destroy the results (so hated by Bakunin) of scientific Marxian socialism.[16]

In his grimmer moments he thought Lenin and Trotsky personally guilty of a "violent Bonapartist imperialism," but at other times he saw Marxism itself subject to its own laws of the "supremacy of matter over consciousness," so that the primitive

[15] Robert P. Browder and Alexander F. Kerensky, eds., The Russian Provisional Government, 1917, Vol. 3 (Stanford, 1961), p. 1797.
[16] Martov, Das Problem der Internationale und die russische Revolution, trans. by A. Stein (Magdeburg, 1920), p. 15.

conditions of Russia worked themselves into different perversions of Marxism such as a "primitive, anarcho-jacobin 'communism'."

He saw no constructive solution save through world proletarian solidarity. For a time he hoped to bring the Bolsheviks, for their own good as well as for that of international socialism, into a new international over which the Western Marxists would exercise decisive influence. Giving this up, he helped in 1921 to form the "Two-and-a-Half International" between the reformist Second and the "Bonapartist" Third. In considering the amalgamation of this with the Second, he insisted that a mechanical combination was not enough and that a commitment must be made to the class struggle and to the dictatorship of the proletariat. Further, to prevent recurrence of the debacle that overtook socialism in 1914 and of such distortions as Bolshevism, he formulated two additional requirements:

1. The International continues its activities also during war.
2. In conflicts over questions of national policy the International is the final tribunal.[17]

The statutes of the revived Second International, drawn up after his death, contained these two "Martov points," somewhat weakened.[18]

[17] Martov, "Das Problem der Internationale," *Der Kampf*, Vol. 16 (January, 1923), p. 8. This article was Martov's last testament for the movement.
[18] The second point was limited to "conflicts between nations." *Protokoll des Internationalen Sozialistischen Arbeiterkongresses in Hamburg* (Berlin, 1923), p. 97.

[ON PARTY ORGANIZATION]

Martov, "Vpered ili Nazad? II Proletarii i Intelligenty v Russkoi
Sotsial'demokratii," *Iskra*, No. 69, supplement (July 10, 1904),
trans. by Theodore Denno.

The organization that at the Second Congress enacted
its rules, which are being interpreted in a strict sense by the
"Majority," is, by European standards, nothing more than an organization *of leaders* of the proletarian struggle, but not an
organization of struggling proletarians. Of the worker parties,
our party has appeared in idea only, but not in the main composition of its organization (committees), among the members of
which the percentage of workers is quite insignificant. From
their inception these organizations took various measures to
change the ratio between proletarian and intellectual elements
to one more favorable for the former. But up to now they have
not been successful because the process of class development of
the Russian proletariat . . . was continuously outrun by the
process of the revolutionizing of the democratic intelligentsia. . . .
Particularly sharply was this chiefly intellectual character
sketched in the *"Iskra"* period, when, in the struggle for revolutionary proletarian *principles* of the movement and for the forms
of organization corresponding to them, we ran into a collision
with the naturally-growing "pure worker" organizations opposing our committees and acting as a brake on the development
of the movement toward revolutionary class struggle. Those
"broad workers' organizations," backward relative to the committees in their organizational methods and in the content of
their work, would have to give way to the committees and—
leave the scene. *According to the notion* of most *"Iskra*-ists" of
that time, this elimination of the "broad workers' organizations"

in no way demonstrated an enhancing of the predominantly
intellectual character of the party organization. . . . On the
contrary, in the period of struggle with the "democratic" organizations, it was presumed that the looseness of these latter would
tear down all the artificial barriers between the "intellectual"
committees and the irresponsible agitator and propagandist circles of workers, and, thereby, permit the former to erect "from
the top down" a permanent and sufficiently broad organization
in which all conscious and revolutionary elements of the proletariat would find a place and in which would automatically be
completed "from the bottom up" the process of "conquest" by
the proletariat of that position in the party which is determined
by its proletarian program. . . .

[Our] committees and unions were essentially constituted by
a voluntary union of the single-minded, a collective of "professional revolutionaries," believing in their own initiative *to bring
order* into the chaos of the local movement and to unite the
activities of the numerous circles, groups and units set apart by
this movement. Thus arose our committees and the rôle they
played up to the time of the Congress. It was one of the organizational problems of the latter to regulate the mutual relations
between the separate committees and the coordinate organizations in order to introduce planning and unity. . . .

How did the building of the party "from the top down," starting from the Party Congress and the organs created by it, have
to proceed? The "Minority" answered this question *after the
Congress* when it showed that the problems of *organization*
standing before us could not be solved except by the resolution
of the questions of *tactics* brought up by the development of
our party. This means the following. The work of the recent past
was, in essence, a work of attracting the broad masses of the
proletariat into the struggle against the autocracy, that "general-
national" enemy of Russia. For the prosecution of this work it
was enough for us to have single-minded committees that allowed themselves, in the eyes of the mass, enough revolutionary
authority periodically to mobilize it for all kinds of political
"demonstrations" and that were connected to the mass by means

of different groups and circles. . . . Political leadership of such
a kind cannot be accounted by the proletariat as real Social
Democratic leadership. For it to become such, our party had
to reform itself essentially so that development and growth of a
self-sufficient *class party of the proletariat,* in which "committees" would appear acknowledged by it as its *political representatives,* corresponded to a further broadening and revolutionizing
of the mass movement. . . . The conscious stratum of the proletariat must, therefore, assume active participation in all aspects
of party life, in the process of the party working out its program,
its tactical principles and methods of organization. When this
actually comes to pass, we will be able with full right to call
ourselves the *avant garde* of the Russian proletariat; then and
only then will we be able to hope that the inevitably impending
moment for the liquidation of tsarism will, also, be the moment
for the incursion of the Russian proletariat, *as a conscious class,*
into those spheres of open political life that the Russian bourgeoisie is trying to grab for itself. . . .

But we well know that for us a central party organization is
necessary. Not contesting the "willful" organizations created by
the workers, we, however, are not thinking of completely subordinating to *these* organizations our fighting, secret organization
built from the top down; we are not "building a party from the
bottom up." [19] We testify to the right of our secret organization,
sanctioned by the Congress and the "public opinion" of the conscious proletariat, to subordinate to its revolutionary control the
activity of these "willful" workers' organizations—for the purpose
of maintaining unity of political action and for the purpose of
"secret selection." And the more comprehensive . . . our agitation becomes, the greater will be the development of political
life in all these worker organizations, and the less the danger
that the "organization of professional revolutionaries," central-
izing the leadership activity, would be ideologically and mate-
rially "torn from the mass," and the less the danger that it would
turn itself into a *conspiratorial* circle. . . .

[19] Lenin had accused Martov of this in *One Step Forward, Two Steps
Back,* section Q.

Indeed, if we ask the question, in what relationship does "proletarian discipline" stand to the organizational utopia of Lenin, which we have subjected to criticism, there will be but one answer: what Lenin idealizes in his system, as a higher manifestation of native proletarian discipline, is nothing other than the political passivity and comparative party immaturity of the majority of the conscious proletarians, passivity and immaturity on which is supported the artless edifice of the "colonies" of our party organization.

MATERIALISM:

METAPHYSICAL AND DIALECTIC

Martov, *Mirovoi Bol'shevizm* (Berlin, 1923), as translated in *International Review*, Vol. 2 (June, 1937), pp. 74-76.

The working class is a product of capitalist society. Its mind is subjected to the influence of capitalist society. Its consciousness is developed under the pressure of the bourgeois masters. The school, the church, the barracks, the factory, the press, social life, all contribute to form the consciousness of the proletarian masses. They are all potent factors in the service of bourgeois ideas and tendencies. According to Charles Naine, it was on this observation of fact that the revolutionary socialists, at least in Switzerland, based their belief in the necessity of a dictatorship by a minority of conscious proletarians over the nation and even [over] the majority of the proletariat itself.

Emile Pouget, the prominent syndicalist leader, wrote:

. . . If democratic mechanism were applied in the labor organizations, the lack of will on the part of the unconscious majority would paralyze all action. The minority is not disposed to abdicate its claim and aspirations before the inertia of a mass that has not yet been quickened by the spirit of revolt. Therefore, the conscious minority has an obligation to act without considering the outlook of the refractory mass . . .[20]

. . .

This idea flows, without doubt, from a *materialist* conception. It is based on the observation that the thought of man depends on the material environment.

This idea characterized many socialists and communists, utopian and revolutionary, at the end of the 18th century and the beginning of the 19th.

We can discover its traces in Robert Owen, Cabet, Weitling, Blanqui. All recognized that the mental enslavement of the masses came from the material circumstances of their existence in the present society. And all deduced from this condition that only a radical modification of the material circumstances of their existence, only a radical transformation of society, would render the masses capable of directing their own destiny.

But by whom will this transformation be realized?

"The wise educators of humanity sprung from the privileged classes, that is to say, individuals freed from the material pressure weighing on the mind of the masses—they will do it!" That was the answer of the social utopians.

"A revolutionary minority composed of men whom a more or less accidental combination of circumstances has enabled to save their brains and will from this pressure, persons who constitute in our society an exception that proves the rule—they will do it!" This was the answer of revolutionary communists like Weitling and Blanqui, and the conception of their epigones of the anarchosyndicalist type, as Pouget and the late Gustave Hervé.

A benevolent dictatorship for some, a violent dictatorship for the others, such is the *deus ex machina* that was going to throw up a bridge between the social environment producing the mental enslavement of the masses and the social environment that would render possible their development as human beings. . . .

Whether pacifist or revolutionary, the utopians—we see—were only *half* materialist. They understood in a purely metaphysical

[20] From an article by Pouget: "L'organization et l'action de la Confédération Générale du Travail" ("The Organization and Action of the General Confederation of Labor") published in the collection *Le mouvement social dans la France contemporaine*, pages 34-36. [Martov]

manner the thesis that human psychology depends on the material environment. They were hardly aware of the *dynamics* of the social process. Their materialism was not *dialectical*.

The state of correlation binding a given aspect of the social consciousness to a given aspect of social life, which is the determining cause of the former, presented itself in the minds of those people as something congealed, as something immovable. That is why they stopped being materialists and became idealists of the first water as soon as they tried to find out how it was necessary to act practically in order to modify the social milieu and render possible the regeneration of the masses.

Quite a good while ago, in his theses on Feuerbach, Marx observed:

The materialist doctrine that men are the products of conditions and education, different men therefore the products of other conditions and changed education, forgets that circumstances may be altered by men and that the educator has himself to be educated. This doctrine leads inevitably to the idea of a society composed of two distinct portions, one of which is elevated above society (Robert Owen for example).

Applied to the class struggle of the propertyless, this means the following. Impelled by the same "circumstances" of capitalist society that determine their character as an enslaved class, the workers enter into a struggle against the society that enslaves them. The process of this struggle modifies the former "circumstances." It modifies the environment in which the working class moves. By this the working class modifies its own character. From a class reflecting passively the mental servitude in which they are held, the propertyless become a class which frees itself actively from all enslavement, including that of the mind.

This process is not at all rectilinear. It does not take in homogeneously all the layers of the proletariat, nor all the phases of its consciousness. It will be far from attaining its full development when the combination of historic circumstances permits, or obliges, the working class to tear from the hands of the bourgeoisie the apparatus of political power. The workers are condemned to penetrate into the realm of socialism when they still bear a good share of those "vices of the oppressed," the yoke of which Lassalle had so eloquently urged them to throw off. As a result of the struggle against capitalism, the proletariat modifies the material milieu surrounding it. It modifies in this way its own character and emancipates itself culturally. Exercising its conquered power, the proletariat frees itself completely from the intellectual influence of the old society—in the degree that it realizes a radical transformation of the material milieu, which in the last place determines its character. . . .

The conscious will of the revolutionary vanguard can appreciably accelerate and facilitate this process. It can never *avoid* it.

Some people presume that if a compact revolutionary minority, animated by the desire to establish socialism, seizes the machinery of government, and concentrates in its own hands the means of production and distribution and the control of the organization of the masses and their education,[21] it may—in pursuance of its socialist ideal—create an environment in which the popular mind will little by little be purged of its old heritage and filled with a new content. Only then will the people stand erect and be able to move by their own strength on the road to socialism.

If this utopia could be followed to the end, it would lead to a diametrically opposite result, though we considered it only from the angle of Marx's affirmation that the "educator has himself to be educated." For the practice of *such* a dictatorship, and the relations established between the dictatorial minority and the mass, "educate" the dictators, who may be everything we want them to be but who cannot direct social evolution toward the construction of a new society. That such an education can only corrupt the *masses*, that it can only debase them, does not need to be demonstrated. . . .

[21] The suppression of the entire press outside of the official has its partisans and has even been partially tried in Europe under the euphonious label of "socialization of the press." [Martov]

MARX AND THE STATE

Martov, *Mirovoi Bol'shevizm* (Berlin, 1923), as translated by Integer in *International Review*, Vol. 2 (September, 1937), pp. 109-111, 123-125.

The partisans of the "pure soviet system" (an expression current in Germany) do not, as a rule, realize that the fundamental question in the methods of contemporary Bolshevism is the organization of a minority dictatorship. On the contrary, they usually begin by sincerely looking around for political instruments that would best express the genuine will of the majority. They arrive at "sovietism" only after repudiating the instrument of universal suffrage because it does not appear to furnish the solution they are seeking.

Psychologically the most characteristic thing about the rush of the "extreme leftists" toward "sovietism" is their desire to jump over the historic inertia of the masses. Dominating their *logic,* however, is the idea that Soviets constitute a new, "finally discovered" political mode that is said to be the specific instrument of the class rule of the proletariat just as the democratic republic is called the specific instrument of the rule of the bourgeoisie. . . .

Basing itself largely on the experience of the revolutionary labor movement in England, the 1848 communism—scientific socialism—of Marx and Engels, identified the problem of the conquest of State power by the proletariat with that of the organization of a rational democracy.

The *Communist Manifesto* declared: "We have already seen that the first step in the working-class revolution is raising the proletariat to the position of a ruling class, the conquest of democracy."

According to Lenin the *Manifesto* poses the question of the State "still extremely in the abstract and employing ideas and

expressions that are quite general" (*State and Revolution*, page
29, Russian ed.). The problem of the conquest of State power
is presented more concretely in *The Eighteenth Brumaire*. Its
concretecization is completed in *Civil War in France*, written
after the experience of the Paris Commune. Lenin is of the
opinion that, in the course of this development, Marx has been
led precisely to that conception of the dictatorship of the proletariat which forms today the basis of Bolshevism.

In 1852, in *Eighteenth Brumaire*, Marx wrote:

"Every previous revolution has brought the machinery of State
to a greater perfection instead of breaking it up."

On the 12th of April, 1871, in a letter to Kugelmann, he formulated his viewpoint on the problem of revolution as follows:

If you look at the last chapter of my *Eighteenth Brumaire*, you will
see that I declare the next attempt of the French Revolution to be not
merely to hand over, from one set to another, the bureaucratic and
military machine, as was the case up to now, but to shatter it. That
is precisely the preliminary condition of any real people's revolution
on the Continent. It is exactly this that constitutes the attempt of our
heroic Parisian comrades. (*Neue Zeit*, XX, i, 1901-2, p. 709.)

In this spirit, Marx declared (*Civil War in France*) that the
Commune was: "a republic that was not merely to suppress the
monarchic form of class domination but the class State itself."

What was then the Commune?

It was an attempt to bring about the effective and rational
establishment of a democratic State by destroying the military
and bureaucratic State apparatus. It was an attempt to establish
a State based entirely on the power of the people.

As long as he speaks of the destruction of the bureaucracy, the
police and permanent army, as long as he speaks of the electiveness and recall of all officials, of the broadest autonomy possible
in local administration, of the centralization of all power in the
hands of the people's representatives (thus doing away with the
gap between the legislative and executive departments of the
government, and replacing the "talking" parliament with a "working institution"); as long as he speaks of all of this in his defence
of the Commune, Marx remains faithful to the conception of

the social revolution he presented in the *Communist Manifesto,* where the dictatorship of the proletariat is identified with the "conquest of democracy." He therefore remains quite logical with himself when in his letter to Kugelmann, quoted above, he stresses that the destruction of the "bureaucratic and military machine" is the "preliminary condition of any real people's revolution *on the Continent*" (*our emphasis.*) . . .

Commenting on Marx's idea, Lenin observed quite correctly (*State and Revolution,* page 36, Russian ed.):

> This could be conceived in 1871, when England was still the pattern of a purely capitalist country, without a military machine and, in a large measure, without a bureaucracy. That is why Marx excluded England, where a revolution, even a people's revolution, could be imagined, and was then possible, without the preliminary condition of the destruction of the State machine since the latter was available, all ready, for it.

Unfortunately, Lenin hurried to pass over this point without reflecting on all the questions posed to us by Marx's restrictions.

According to Lenin, Marx admitted a situation in which the people's revolution would not need to shatter the available ready State machinery. This was the case when the State machinery did not have the military and bureaucratic character typical of the Continent and could therefore be utilized by a real people's revolution. The existence, within the framework of capitalism and in spite of the latter, of a *democratic apparatus of self-administration,* which the military and bureaucratic machine had not succeeded in crushing, was evidently exceptional. In that case, according to Marx, the people's revolution should simply take possession of that apparatus and perfect it, thus realizing the State form that the revolution could best use for its creative purposes.

It is not for nothing that Marx and Engels admitted theoretically the possibility of a *pacific* socialist revolution in England. This theoretic possibility rested precisely on the democratic character that the British State seemed to show at that time.

Much water has flowed under the bridges since then. In England, as in the United States, imperialism has forged the "military and bureaucratic State machine" the absence of which had constituted, as a general feature, the difference between the political evolution of the Anglo-Saxon countries and the general type of capitalist State. At the present time, it is permissible to doubt if these particular traits have been preserved even in the youngest Anglo-Saxon republics: Australia and New Zealand. "Today," remarks Lenin with justification, "both in England and in America the 'preliminary condition of any real people's revolution' is the break-up, the shattering of the 'available ready machinery of the State.'"

The theoretic possibility has not revealed itself in reality. But the sole fact that he admitted such a possibility shows us clearly Marx's opinion, leaving no room for arbitrary interpretation. What Marx designated as the "destruction of the State machine" in *Eighteenth Brumaire* and in his letter to Kugelmann was the destruction of the *military and bureaucratic apparatus* that the bourgeois democracy had inherited from the monarchy and perfected in the process of consolidating the rule of the bourgeois class. There is nothing in Marx's reasoning that even suggests the destruction of the *State organization as such* and the replacement of the State during the revolutionary period, that is during the dictatorship of the proletariat, with a social bond formed on a *principle opposed to that of the State*. Marx and Engels foresaw such a substitution only in conclusion of a process of "a progressive withering away" of the State and all the functions of social *coercion*. They foresaw this atrophy of the State and the functions of social coercion as the result of the prolonged existence of the socialist régime.

It is not for nothing that Engels wrote in 1891, in his preface to *Civil War in France*:

"In reality, however, the State is nothing more than a machine for the oppression of one class by another, and indeed in the democratic republic no less than in the monarchy; and at best an evil inherited by the proletariat after its victorious struggle for class supremacy whose *worse sides* the proletariat, just like the Commune, will have at the earliest possible moment to lop off, until such time as a new generation, reared under new and free social conditions, will be able to throw on the scrap-heap all the useless lumber of the State."

Isn't this clear enough? The proletariat lops off "the worst sides" of the democratic State (for example: the police, permanent army, the bureaucracy forming a separate entity, exaggerated centralization, etc.) But it does not suppress the democratic State as such. On the contrary, it creates the democratic State in order to have it replace the "military and bureaucratic State," which must be shattered.

"If there is anything about which there can be no doubt it is that our party and the working class can only gain supremacy under a political régime like the democratic republic. *The latter is, indeed, the specific form of the dictatorship of the proletariat, as has been demonstrated by the French revolution.*"

That is how Engels expresses himself in his critique of the draft of the Erfurt program. . . .

This is so clear, so explicit, that when Lenin quotes these words, he finds it necessary to obscure their meaning.

Engels, he says, repeats here in a particularly emphatic form the fundamental idea which, like a red thread, runs throughout all Marx's work, viz., that the Democratic Republic *comes nearest* the dictatorship of the proletariat. For such a republic, without in the least setting aside the domination of capital, and, therefore, the oppression of the masses and the class struggle, inevitably leads to such an extension, intensification and development of that struggle that, as soon as the chance arises for satisfying the fundamental interests of the oppressed masses, this chance is realized inevitably and solely in the form of the dictatorship of the proletariat, of the guidance of these masses by the proletariat.[22]

However, Engels does not speak of a political form that "comes nearest the dictatorship," as is interpreted by Lenin in his commentaries. He speaks of the only "specific" political form in which the *dictatorship can be realized.* According to Engels, the dictatorship is forged in the *democratic republic.* Lenin, on the other hand, sees democracy *merely* as the means of sharp-

[22] *State and Revolution,* page 66, Chapter IV. [Martov]

ening the class struggle, thus confronting the proletariat with the problem of the dictatorship. For Lenin, the democratic republic finds its conclusion in the dictatorship of the proletariat, giving birth to the latter but destroying itself in the delivery. Engels, on the contrary, is of the opinion that when the proletariat has gained supremacy in the democratic republic and thus realized its dictatorship, *within the democratic republic,* it will consolidate the latter through that very act and invest it, for the first time, with a character that is genuinely, fundamentally and completely democratic. That is why, in 1848, Engels and Marx identified "raising the proletariat to a ruling class" with "the conquest of democracy." That is why, in *The Civil War,* Marx celebrated in the experience of the Commune the total triumph of the principles of people's power: universal franchise, electiveness and recall of all officials. . . .

We are, therefore, obliged to arrive at the following conclusion when we consider the opinions of Marx and Engels on the dictatorship of the proletariat, on the democratic republic and on the "State that is an evil."

To Marx and Engels, the problem of the taking of political power by the proletariat is linked to the destruction of the bureaucratic-military machine, which rules the bourgeois State in spite of the existence of democratic parliamentarism.

To Marx and Engels, the problem of the dictatorship of the proletariat is linked to the establishment of a State based on sincere and total democracy, on universal suffrage, on the widest local self-administration, and has, as its corollary, the existence of the effective hegemony of the proletariat over the majority of the population. . . .

It is true, however, that it is possible to discover in the works of Marx and Engels the traces of other ideas, which appear to offer ground to theses in which the *forms,* and even the *institutions,* that embody the political power of the proletariat take on an essentially new character, opposed in principle to the forms and institutions that embody the political power of the bourgeoisie, and opposed in principle to the *State* as such.

These ideas belong to a special cycle and merit a separate study. We shall deal with them in the following chapter.

THE COMMUNE OF 1871

Martov, *Mirovoi Bol'shevizm* (Berlin, 1923), as translated in *International Review*, Vol. 2, No. 9 (October [?], 1937), pp. 138-141, and Vol. 3, No. 1 (1938), pp. 11-14.

When he considered the Commune in his writings, Marx could not merely present his views on the dictatorship of the proletariat. The uprising had many enemies. The first thing to be done was to defend the Commune against their calumny. It was natural for this circumstance to influence Marx's manner of dealing with the slogans and ideas of the movement of March 1871. . . .

Thus, the "destruction of the bureaucratic and military machine" of the State, dealt with in Marx's letter to Kugelmann, changed imperceptibly and came to stand for the suppression of all State power, of *any* apparatus of compulsion in the service of the social administration. The destruction of the "power of the modern State," the Continental type of State, became the destruction of the State as such.

Are we in the presence of an intentional lack of precision, enabling Marx to gloss over, in silence, the weak points of the Paris Commune at a moment when the Commune was being trampled by triumphant reaction? Or did the mighty surge of the revolutionary proletariat of Paris, set in motion under the flag of the Commune, render acceptable to Marx certain ideas of Proudhonian órigin? No matter what is the case, it is true that Bakounin and his friends concluded that in his *Civil War in France*, Marx approved of the social revolutionary path traced by them. . . . And Bakounin announced triumphantly: "The Communalist revolution had so mighty an effect that despite their logic and real inclinations, the Marxists—with all their ideas overthrown by the Commune—were obliged to bow before the insurrection and appropriate its aims and program." Such statements are not free from exaggeration. But they contain a grain of truth.

It is these, not very precise, opinions of Marx on the destruction of the State by a proletarian insurrection and the creation of the Commune that Lenin recognizes as the basis of the new social-revolutionary doctrine he presumes to reveal. On the top of these opinions of Marx, Lenin raises the Anarcho-Syndicalist canvas, picturing the destruction of the State *as the immediate result of the conquest of the dictatorship by the proletariat, and replacing the State* with that "finally discovered political form," which in 1871 was embodied in the Commune and is represented today by the "soviets." . . .

Mehring is of the opinion that Marx and Engels clearly saw the contradiction existing between the theses presented in the *Civil War* and their previous way of posing the question as that of the conquest of State power. Mehring writes: "Thus, when, after Marx's death, Engels had the occasion to combat the Anarchist tendencies, he, for his part at least, repudiated these reservations and resumed integrally the old conceptions found in the Manifesto."

What are the "old conceptions found in the Manifesto"? They are the following:

The working class seizes the State machinery forged by the bourgeoisie.

It *democratizes* this machinery from top to bottom. . . .

MARX AND THE DICTATORSHIP

OF THE PROLETARIAT

Martov, *Mirovoi Bol'shevizm* (Berlin, 1923), as translated in *International Review*, Vol. 3 (May-June, 1938), pp. 22-25.

. . . .

But no matter what was the error in Marx's evaluation, he succeeded in outlining very clearly the problems of the dictatorship of the proletariat. "The Commune," he said, "was the true representative of all the healthy elements of French society, and therefore the truly *national government*. (*Civil War*, page 38, emphasis by Martov.)

According to Marx, the dictatorship of the proletariat does not consist in the crushing by the proletariat of all non-proletarian classes in society. On the contrary, it is, according to Marx, the welding to the proletariat of all the "healthy elements" of society —all except the "rich capitalists," all except the class against which the historic struggle of the proletariat is directed. Both in its composition and in its tendencies, the government of the Commune was a working men's government. But this government was an expression of the dictatorship of the proletariat not because it was *imposed* by violence on a non-proletarian majority. It did not come into being that way. On the contrary, the government of the Commune was a proletarian dictatorship because those workers and those "acknowledged representatives of the working class" had *received the power from the majority itself*. Marx stressed the fact that "the Commune was formed of municipal councillors, chosen by universal suffrage in various wards of the city . . . By suppressing those organs of the old governmental power which merely served to oppress the people, the Commune divested of its legal functions an authority that claims to be above society itself, and put those functions in the hands of the responsible servants of the people . . . The people organized in Communes (outside of Paris) was called on to use universal suffrage just as any employer uses his individual right to choose workers, managers, accountants in his business."

The completely democratic constitution of the Paris Commune, based on universal suffrage, on the immediate recall of every office-holder by the simple decision of his electors, on the suppression of bureaucracy and the armed force as opposed to the people, on the electiveness of all offices—that is what constitutes, according to Marx, the essence of the dictatorship of the proletariat. He never thinks of opposing such a dictatorship to democracy. Already in 1847, in his first draft of the Communist Manifesto, Engels wrote:

It (the proletarian revolution) will establish first of all the democratic administration of the State and will thus install, directly or indirectly, the political domination of the proletariat. Directly—in England, where the proletariat forms the majority of the population. Indirectly—in France and in Germany, where the majority of the population is not composed only of proletarians but also of small peasants and small bourgeois, who are only now beginning to pass into the proletariat and whose political interests fall more and more under the influence of the proletariat. (*The Principles of Communism*, Russian translation under the editorship of Zinoviev, p. 22.)

"The first step in the revolution," by the working class, declares the Manifesto, "is to raise the proletariat to the position of a ruling class, to win the battle of democracy."

Between the elevation of the proletariat to the position of a ruling class and the conquest of democracy, Marx and Engels put an equals sign. They understood the application of this political power by the proletariat only in the form of a total democracy.

In the measure that Marx and Engels became convinced that the socialist revolution could only be accomplished with the support of the *majority* of the population accepting *knowingly* the positive program of socialism—so their conception of a class dictatorship lost its Jacobin content. But what is the positive substance of the notion of the dictatorship once it has been modified in this manner? Exactly that which is formulated with great precision in the program of our Party (Russian Social-Democratic Labor Party), a program drafted at a time when the theoretic discussion provoked by "Bernsteinism" led Marxists to polish and determine with care certain expressions which had obviously lost their exact meaning with long usage in the daily political struggle.

The program of the Social-Democratic Labor Party of Russia was the only official program of a Labor Party that defined the idea of the conquest of political power by the proletariat in the terms of a "class dictatorship." Since Bernstein, Jaures and other critics of Marxism insisted on giving the expression "dictatorship of the proletariat" the Blanquist definition of power held by an organized minority and resting on violence exercised by this minority over the majority, the authors of the Russian program were obliged to fix as narrowly as possible the limits of this political idea. They did that by declaring that the dictatorship of the proletariat is the power used by the proletariat to crush all resistance which the exploiting class might oppose to the realization of the socialist and revolutionary transformation. Simply that.

An effective force concentrated in the State, which can thus realize the *conscious will of the majority* despite the resistance of an economically powerful minority—that is the dictatorship of the proletariat. It can be nothing else than that in light of the teachings of Marx. Not only must such a dictatorship adapt itself to a democratic régime, but it can only exist in the framework of democracy, that is, under conditions where there is full exercise of absolute political equality on the part of all citizens. Such a dictatorship can only be conceived in a situation where the proletariat has effectively united about itself "all the healthy elements" of the nation, that is, all those who cannot but profit by the revolutionary transformation inscribed in the program of the proletariat. It can only be established when historic development will have brought all the healthy elements to recognize the advantage to them of this transformation. The government embodying such a dictatorship will be, in the full sense of the term, a "national government."

BIBLIOGRAPHY

Works by Martov

–*Die Arbeitersache in Russland* (Geneva, 1903).
À bas la peine de mort! (Paris, 1919).
Le bolchevisme mondial, trans. by V. Mayer (Paris, 1934). Chapter,
  "Marx et le problème de la dictature du prolétariat" also in Fedor
  Dan and Julius Martov, *La dictature du prolétariat* (Paris, 1947).
Geschichte der russischen Sozialdemokratie, trans. by Alexander Stein
  (Berlin, 1926). Continued after 1908 by Fedor Dan.
"Die preussische Diskussion und die russische Erfahrung," *Die Neue
  Zeit*, Vol. 28, No. 2 (September 16, 1910), pp. 907-919.
Das Problem der Internationale und die russische Revolution, trans.
  by A. Stein (Magdeburg, 1920).
"Das Problem der Internationale," *Der Kampf*, Vol. 16 (January,
  1923), pp. 1-9.
The State and the Socialist Revolution, trans. by Integer (New York,
  1938). Chapters from *Le bolchevisme mondial*.

Exposition

–Abramovitch, Raphael, and others, *Julius Martow. Sein Werk und
  seine Bedeutung für den Sozialismus* (Berlin, 1924).
———, "Julius Martow und das russische Proletariat," *Der Kampf*,
  Vol. 16 (June, 1923), pp. 180-188.
———, *The Soviet Revolution 1917-1939* (New York, 1962).
Bystrianski, V. A. (Bystranski, W.), *Die Menschewiki und die Sozial-
  Revolutionäre in der russischen Revolution* (Hamburg, 1922).
Dan, Fedor, "Aus dem Nachlass J. Martows," *Der Kampf*, Vol. 18
  (May, 1925), pp. 166-170.
Lenin, V. I., *One Step Forward, Two Steps Back* (1904).
———, *Two Tactics of Social Democracy in the Democratic Revo-
  lution* (1905).
–Pipes, Richard, *Social Democracy and the St. Petersburg Labor
  Movement, 1885-1897* (Cambridge, Mass., 1963).
Vardin (Wardin), I. V., *Die Partei der Menschewiki in der russischen
  Revolution* (Hamburg, 1922).

5

Trotsky:
A Minority Can Take Power

THE MOST COLORFUL and original of all the Russian revolutionaries, Trotsky was, both in theory and in practice, much more important in the October revolution and in the subsequent development of the Soviet Union than the Russians have recently been ready to admit. After some fourteen years of opposition to the Bolsheviks, more in the interest of party unity than in support of the Mensheviks, and after disagreeing with Lenin on many important points (although not always those stressed by the Stalinists), he was brought by his own analysis of events, by Lenin's influence on him, and by his influence upon Lenin, to a position so close to that of the Bolsheviks that, in 1917, he in the Petrograd soviet and Lenin in the Social Democratic Party jointly could prepare the uprising.

The son of an illiterate, irreligious, and very successful kulak of the southern Ukraine, Trotsky (Lev D. Bronshtein, 1879-1940) first met the proletariat in his father's mill and workshop, and the peasantry in large numbers as hired laborers on his father's farm. At sixteen he was exposed to arguments on socialism in the family in Nikolaev where he was boarding while finishing secondary school. Thus stimulated, he abandoned school and joined a circle that met in the suburbs to study illegal literature. He became in turn a disciple of Bentham and then of Chernyshevski, and argued the *narodnik* position against the only Marxist in the group (whom he married in prison four years later).

Within a year of joining the group, however, he was a convinced Marxist. To him ideas meant action. By early 1898 he had organized a labor union, ambitiously named the South Russian Workers Union, had written and painstakingly hectographed many leaflets, and had been arrested for his trouble. After two years in prisons, where he read, among other things, such legal Marxist works as the *Essays on Historical Materialism* of Labriola, Plekhanov's *Monistic Conception of History,* Lenin's *Development of Capitalism in Russia,* and Bernstein's *Premises of Socialism,* he was sent to central Siberia. There the *narodnik* exiles were publishing a legal journal, the *Eastern Review,* and by writing for it Trotsky developed such skill and renown as a propagandist that, when he escaped in 1902, he was called to London by Lenin to write for *Iskra.*

Brought thus, at twenty-three, into the circle of émigré leaders of Russian Marxism, Trotsky formed friendships with Axelrod, Martov, and Zasulich which drew him to their defense when Lenin tried to reorganize the board of editors at the Party Congress in 1903. He was, therefore, among the Mensheviks in the resulting split, even though he had advocated, while in Siberia, the same tight organization and party discipline for which he now criticized Lenin. In the subsequent polemics he made a remarkably prescient statement: "Lenin's methods lead to this: first the party organization supersedes the party as a whole; then the central committee supersedes the organization; and finally a single dictator supplants the central committee." [1]

Excluded from the new Menshevik *Iskra* by Plekhanov, who had early developed a definite dislike for him, he lived for a half year in Munich with Parvus (Alexander Helfand), another maverick émigré then highly respected as a Marxist theoretician. Out of their intellectual exchange came the idea that, the proletariat having assumed the leadership in the approaching revolution, it would also assume the power, and, therefore, the new government would be not bourgeois but Social Democratic, proletarian. This idea was first expressed early in 1905 in an

[1] Leon Trotsky, *Nashi politicheskye zadachi* (Geneva, 1904), p. 54; quoted in Isaac Deutscher, *The Prophet Armed* (New York, Oxford University Press, 1954), p. 90.

introduction by Parvus to one of Trotsky's pamphlets. On reading it, Lenin, who was then using his formula "revolutionary-democratic dictatorship of the proletariat and the peasantry" in the sense of a majority movement, exploded: "This *cannot be!* . . . This cannot be, because only a revolutionary dictatorship relying on the overwhelming majority of the people can be at all durable. . . . The Russian proletariat, however, at present constitutes a minority." [2] With such expectations of majority rule, then universal among the Marxists, the new theory was not yet reconciled, but from this embryo Parvus and Trotsky soon gave birth to the doctrine of "permanent revolution," [3] the doctrine that, under the imperious drive of the proletarian dictatorship, "feudal" Russia would be carried without a pause across the period of "bourgeois" democracy and into socialism.

In the early stages of the revolution Trotsky expected support from the peasantry, whose seizures of land it would sanction. In this sense the revolution would have mass support and there was no need to wait for the growth of capitalism and its proletariat. In the later stages, however, he, like other Marxists, expected the peasants to desert; but he did not, as did the Mensheviks, deduce from this a necessity to avoid the responsibilities of power until great strength had been developed in the proletariat itself. Already an internationalist, he looked instead for support to come from revolution in western Europe, which he expected the Russian sparks to ignite. This expectation, based though it was on the assurance, then general among Marxists, that the West was ripe for revolution, Stalin would later use as evidence that Trotsky lacked confidence in both the peasantry and the proletariat of Russia.

This doctrine was the first Russian attempt to escape from the

[2] V. I. Lenin, "Social-Democracy and the Provisional Revolutionary Government," in his *Selected Works*, Vol. 3 (London, 1936), p. 35.

[3] They borrowed this somewhat undescriptive phrase from the Marx of 1850, who had it from Babeuf, perhaps by way of Blanqui. It had been in the air of Paris since 1796, and was, in its early form, a response to the Thermidorian reaction, a demand that the French revolution be carried through to its objective (to equality, Babeuf thought) and protected permanently against any reaction. For an excellent analytical summary of Trotsky's doctrine see Isaac Deutscher, *The Prophet Armed* (New York, 1954), pp. 150-162.

two phases of Marx's historical schema, the first rejection by a
Marxist of the idea that a long period of capitalistic development
would have to produce a preponderance of industrial workers
before the proletarian revolution could succeed. It was also the
first consistent claim that the revolution could be, and would be,
carried through to socialism by a minority. On both counts it
was then unacceptable to both Mensheviks and Bolsheviks.
Lenin objected to the "absurd, semi-anarchist" idea that the
proletariat, which admittedly would lead the bourgeois revolution, could retain power for a socialist revolution in the existing
economic conditions of Russia and without much more class
consciousness and organization among the masses.[4] His argument was almost identical with that which Martov was to use
against Lenin himself in 1917 (see p. 98f).

Even in answering Parvus and Trotsky, however, Lenin spoke
of "making the Russian revolution . . . a movement of many
years," which, in spite of its bourgeois character, would touch
off the socialist revolution in western Europe. "And if we succeed
in doing that, . . . the revolutionary conflagration will spread
all over Europe; . . . the revolutionary wave in Europe will
sweep back again into Russia and will convert an epoch of a few
revolutionary years into an era of several revolutionary decades." [5]
By September, 1905, moreover, he recognized that some socialist
measures might soon be taken, "for, from the democratic revolution we shall at once, according to the degree of our strength,
the strength of the class conscious and organized proletariat,
begin to pass over to the socialist revolution. We stand for continuous revolution. We shall not stop half way." [6] His difference
with Trotsky was, nevertheless, substantial. Lenin, conspirator
though he was, did not believe that a minority could achieve
socialism. He was still convinced that much time and mass education were needed. Trotsky, the orator and improvisor, was convinced that enough strength could be mustered temporarily to

---

[4] Lenin, *Two Tactics of Social-Democracy in the Democratic Revolution*,
in his *Selected Works*, Vol. 3, p. 52.

[5] Lenin, "Social-Democracy and the Provisional Revolutionary Government," in *ibid.*, p. 31.

[6] Lenin, "The Attitude of Social-Democracy toward the Peasant Movement," in *ibid.*, p. 145.

take and to hold Russia until the workers of Europe would arise.
These theories were put to the test even as they were being
formulated. In January, 1905, the tsar began the revolution by
firing into crowds of unarmed petitioners. In October the most
complete of all general strikes [7] spread over Russia, as Trotsky
had predicted, and soviets were organized in many cities. The
Mensheviks, already oriented toward such broadly based, spontaneous organs, embraced them immediately. Trotsky rose rapidly
to the leadership in the Petersburg soviet. In December, however,
the soviet, not yet adequately supported by arms, was arrested.
Its brief life span was hardly a conclusive test, but, as a silent
warning, no answering revolutions appeared in the West. Trotsky
did not heed this warning, but he did accumulate much practical experience and prestige that were to be useful in 1917.

Trotsky used his trial to tell the public, from the dock, the
meaning of the revolution, and after an escape from Siberia he
continued his propaganda efforts in Europe and in America. In
polemics with other Marxists he frequently tried to stand apart
from the Mensheviks, with the idea of bringing them closer to
the Bolsheviks, but personally he stood on most issues further
to the left than either.

In spite of the invectives exchanged since 1903, Lenin and
Trotsky had arrived at substantial agreement by the spring of
1917. Trotsky saw that Lenin, in his "April Theses," did not want
to halt the revolution, even temporarily, at the bourgeois-democratic stage; and Lenin saw a now-or-never opportunity in the
Russian and the international situations that convinced him, im-
plicitly if not expressly, that Trotsky's formula of "permanent
revolution" could succeed. Undoubtedly each respected and had
influenced the other, although their rapprochement was more a
pragmatic union in a determined and concentrated struggle
toward the same goal.[8]

[7] "No strike in history in any land has ever been as 'general' as this one."
Bertram Wolfe, *Three Who Made a Revolution* (Boston, 1955), p. 321.

[8] It appears that Lenin did not read until 1919 Trotsky's principal work
as an interpreter of Marxism, the *Itogi i Perspektivy* (*Results and Perspectives,* an unfortunate title for a major effort) written in the Peter-Paul
fortress in 1906, which set forth the complete theory of the permanent
revolution.

Trotsky returned from New York in May, 1917, to his position of leadership in the Petrograd soviet, which was again in the control of the Mensheviks, while Lenin wielded his influence through the Central Committee of the Bolshevik Party. In September, the Bolsheviks, as the most resolute defenders of Petrograd against the assault of the tsarist general Kornilov, obtained a majority in the soviet. Lenin, in hiding since July, concluded that, with this majority, the time had come for an armed seizure of power. Appearing in disguise (to avoid Kerensky's police), he persuaded the Central Committee of this, over determined opposition from Kamenev and Zinev'ev. The soviet appointed a Military Revolutionary Committee, and, as its chairman, Trotsky arranged the details of the seizure, which was accomplished almost without bloodshed. This he did in the name of the soviet, thus giving the October revolution a broader basis of support than Lenin's plan for action in the name of the Bolshevik Party would have done. The nationwide Congress of Soviets, which met in Petrograd the following day, represented some twenty million voters and proved to contain a Bolshevik majority of almost two-thirds. It sanctioned the transfer of "all power to the soviets."

The Bolsheviks believed that their majority at this Congress would justify their one-party rule, but they did invite the Left Socialist Revolutionaries, as representatives of the peasants, to join the government. The Socialist Revolutionaries at first refused, then acceded, taking commissariats, only shortly to withdraw. Standing thus alone, the Bolsheviks were in the position that Trotsky had envisioned since 1905: they were a minority in the nation and they felt themselves dependent upon revolution in the West. They were confident that it would come quickly, especially in Germany. This confidence was the keynote of Trotsky's policy as Foreign Commissar; it accounted for his delaying tactics in the peace negotiations with Germany, and for his "no war, no peace" formula in breaking them off. This hope died hard in Trotsky, yet when Bukharin proposed to reject the German ultimatum, and thus to stake the future of the Russian revolution on a possible revolt in Germany (see p. 191), Trotsky, by withholding his vote, permitted Lenin to carry the Central

Committee in favor of the ultimatum and peace, even with great losses of territory. Even then the hope of support from revolution in the West was not abandoned, although the Bolsheviks had faced and accepted temporarily their position as a minority government in an isolated country. They were convinced that their peace and land policies, if not their Party, enjoyed majority approval.

Made War Commissar in March, 1918, Trotsky, by his administrative ability and seemingly endless energy, built a new army in an exhausted and war-weary land, an army which by 1920 defeated the tsarist generals and repelled invasions by the British, French, Poles, Czechs, Japanese, and Americans. Although hardly full scale efforts, these invasions confirmed the Marxist expectations and instilled in the Russians a lasting fear of the capitalist countries.

As soon as victory in the civil war was achieved and the invaders repulsed, new problems arose. Transition to a peace-time economy seemed to call for a relaxation of the incentive and disciplinary measures of War Communism, but, with production still declining and many former soldiers turning to blackmarketing and brigandage, an opposite course was chosen. At the Third Congress of Economic Soviets Trotsky collaborated with M. P. Tomski, the trade union leader, to push through a resolution calling for the use of army recruiting machinery for the mobilization and transfer of labor. On January 15 the Third Red Army, then in the Urals, was converted into the First Red Army of Labor and put to work. Trotsky became the most outspoken advocate of the militarization of labor and an unabashed defender of compulsory methods.

In March he was placed in charge of the almost paralyzed railways, and a decree mobilized all rail workers for labor service. He established a five-year plan for the locomotive industry, secured the dismissal of the leaders of the rail union, and appointed new ones. He succeeded in repairing a rapidly deteriorating transport system, and for his results he was acclaimed, but his popularity was tarnished by his advocacy of compulsory labor and his attacks on union autonomy. Since his relations with the unions thus undermined his public support and provoked some sharp attacks by Lenin, later to be used by Stalin, they were a strong contributing factor in his ultimate defeat. They should, therefore, be examined in some detail.

Trotsky's measures were supported at the Ninth Party Congress in March, where he proclaimed, "Militarization is unthinkable without the militarization of the trade unions as such, without the establishment of a régime in which every worker feels himself a soldier of labor." [9] Trotsky himself had proposed that War Communism be replaced by something resembling the later N.E.P., but the Central Committee had rejected this proposal and the Congress adopted instead militarization of labor and one-man management in industry. Against militarization, which meant more extreme "statization," there was no open dissent, although Shliapnikov, then abroad, had circulated contrary theses restating the old distinction between economic and political power and naming the unions as "the only responsible organizer of the national economy." [10] Against individual management feeling was stronger and more vocal. Tomski defended "the presently existing principle of collegial management of industry" as being "the only one able to insure the participation of the broad non-party working masses through the trade unions." [11] The group called Democratic Centralists termed committee management "indispensable" to the Party's system of democratic centralism and "the strongest weapon against the renascence of departmentalism and bureaucratic deadening of the soviet apparatus." [12]

Thus was touched off the unrest that led to the great trade union debate of 1920-1921. The Mensheviks, not present at the Party Congress, were vocal at the Third Trade Union Congress in April and argued cogently that compulsion would reduce, not increase, production. Wage labor under capitalism had been more productive than slave or serf labor because it was more free; labor under socialism should be still more free, and therefore would be still more productive. Trotsky replied with his

[9] *Deviatyi S"ezd RKP(B), Protokoly* (Moscow, 1960), p. 94.

[10] *Deviatyi S"ezd RKP(B), Protokoly* (Moscow, 1934), p. 564; quoted in an editorial note omitted from the 1960 edition.

[11] *Deviatyi S"ezd RKP(B), Protokoly* (Moscow, 1960), pp. 562-563.

[12] *Ibid.*, p. 566 (N. Osinski, T. V. Sapronov, V. N. Maksimovski).

famous, or infamous, defense of compulsion, which consisted of
the quibble that, under any economic system, "man must work
in order not to die," and of the argument that discipline must
be imposed in proportion as ideological backwardness prevented
the workers and the labor unions from seeing the necessity for
voluntary cooperation. The Party having decided to continue
War Communism, he drew the logical conclusion: the economy
must be centrally planned and managed. The defensive role of
separate trade unions, guarding by wage and hour claims their
members' shares of goods and leisure against other claimants,
must be abandoned. They must become "production unions"
with a new positive role, working cooperatively to increase the
national product, which would automatically increase consumers'
goods for all. Bukharin soon elaborated this position, defending
compulsory labor service as "the self-organization of the working class." [13]

Through the summer the dissension mounted. In August came
the removal of the rail union leaders, and early in November,
wearing the laurels of his rehabilitation of the railways, Trotsky
spoke of the need for a similar "shake-up" of union leadership in
general. This angered Tomski and brought the Party Central
Committee into the dispute. The Committee itself was so deeply
divided on the several issues involved that a public discussion
was authorized, with delegates to the Tenth Party Congress to
be elected on the basis of the various platforms.

This debate, which served as a stalking horse for the more
important and controversial adoption of the N.E.P., seemed to
turn on the role of the trade unions, but it brought to the surface
all the latent dissatisfactions with the course of events since
the October revolution. The Party was divided three ways, with
the main bodies of opinion behind Lenin, Zinov'ev, and Tomski,
on the one hand, and Trotsky and Bukharin on the other, with
some support for the "Workers' Opposition" (for the latter's
views see pp. 169ff and 179ff).

Lenin was then planning the "retreat" into the N.E.P., and thus
saw the intra-Party struggle in extra-Party context. For him
the main problem was how to govern a peasant nation; and,

[13] Bukharin, *Ekonomika Perekhodnogo Perioda* (Moscow, 1920), p. 119.

true to his old party proclivities, he held any proposals, such as those of the Workers' Opposition, to vest real power in organs not controlled by the Party to be tantamount to abandoning the government and the revolution. The dictatorship of the proletariat could not be exercised by the class as a whole, organized in trade unions, because the class was "still so split up." The dictatorship must be exercised by the vanguard absorbed into the Party, and the unions must serve as "transmission belts" between the vanguard and the masses of workers and peasants, winning their support for the régime. "But the trade unions are not state organizations, not organizations for coercion, they are educational organizations, organizations that enlist, that train; they are schools, schools of administration, schools of management, schools of Communism." [14] He denied, contradicting both Trotsky and the Workers' Opposition, that the Party program imposed on the trade unions the problem of managing production. This was impossible, he believed, "until the number of small producers in industry and agriculture has been reduced to less than half the population and of national economy." [15] Since, as he saw it, the workers' state was in fact a "workers' and peasants' state" [16] with "bureaucratic distortions," and since it would be more so under N.E.P., it followed that the unions must protect their members against the state as employer. Martov had been partially right in 1918 (see p. 60f) and the unions still needed independence.

Trotsky and Bukharin, on the other hand, followed by the leading economists of the Party, were still committed to the decision of the Ninth Party Congress to continue War Communism with the militarization of labor, individual management, and incentive wages. The solution to the problems of relations with the peasants, they thought, lay in providing them with goods by increasing industrial production. This required central planning

[14] Lenin, "The Trade Unions, the Present Situation and the Mistakes of Comrade Trotsky," *Selected Works*, Vol. 9, pp. 4-5.

[15] Lenin, "Once Again on the Trade Unions, the Present Situation and the Mistakes of Comrades Trotsky and Bukharin," *ibid.*, Vol. 9, p. 74.

[16] Bukharin objected to this characterization, and Lenin later corrected it, calling it a workers' state with a predominantly peasant population. Lenin, "The Party Crisis," *ibid.*, Vol. 9, p. 33.

and administration, tighter discipline, and the subordination of democracy to efficiency. For this Bukharin proposed the slogan "industrial democracy," which meant that

> All elections, nomination of candidates, supporting candidates, etc., must proceed not only from the point of view of political consistency, but also from the point of view of *business ability, administrative experience, organizing qualities* and actually tested concern for the material and spiritual interests of the toiling masses.[17]

The trade unions, not yet capable of shouldering the burden of management, must be transformed into "apparatuses of the workers' state" by closer links with the economic soviets through joint sessions and members in common in the state and union organs. Bukharin denied that this meant the absorption of the unions into the state. If on the one hand it called for the "statization" of the unions, he argued dialectically, on the other it required the "unionization of the state."

> Its logical and historical termination will be, not the absorption of the unions by the proletarian state, but the disappearance of both categories—of the state as well as of the unions, and the creation of a third—communistically organized society.[18]

In the course of these debates the extreme quality of Trotsky's opinions was clearly revealed and he never recovered the popularity he lost thereby. An energetic administrator, he emphatically demanded productive efficiency at the expense of union autonomy. The Workers' Opposition challenged him on grounds of democracy: his proposals violated the right of the workers to choose their own leaders. At the Tenth Party Congress (March, 1921) he answered them sharply:

> The Workers' Opposition has come out with dangerous slogans. They have made a fetish of democratic principles. They have placed the workers' right to elect representatives above the party, as it were, as if the party were not entitled to assert its dictatorship even if that

[17] Quoted in Lenin, "Once Again . . ." *ibid.*, Vol. 9, p. 52. Lenin objected on the grounds, among others, that this might be misinterpreted as repudiating, on the one hand, "dictatorship and individual management," and on the other, "ordinary democracy."

[18] *Deviatyi S"ezd RKP(B), Protokoly* (Moscow, 1933), p. 802.

dictatorship temporarily clashed with the passing moods of the workers' democracy. . . . It is necessary to create among us the awareness of the revolutionary historical birthright of the party.[19]

Trotsky thus gave strong support to the suppression of democracy within the Party, for which this Congress laid the foundation. He and Bukharin joined with Lenin to outlaw the organization of factions and groups within the Party. This rule, which departed from earlier successful practice, was aimed at the Workers' Opposition, but it marked the end of intra-Party democracy.

Trotsky bore the brunt of popular dissatisfaction with War Communism throughout 1920 and 1921 and was, perhaps for that reason, the first of the Bolsheviks to recognize its limitations. He proposed two divergent lines of departure from it, both of which were later tried: one, the restoration of the free market, and a second, centralized planning in industry. The first he thought would stimulate initiative among the people, and in February, 1920, he asked that the peasant, after paying a tax in kind, be given freedom to sell his surplus. The Central Committee refused to agree, but this idea formed the basis of the N.E.P. adopted a year later. In August, 1921, to implement the second line, which he thought even more necessary under N.E.P. than before and which was more in accord with his temperament, he asked that the state planning commission, Gosplan, be given autonomy and power to plan heavy industry. Again the Central Committee disagreed, and, although by December, 1922, Lenin also asked that Gosplan be given legislative authority, central planning was not accepted in practice until the Stalin era.

As the eventful years slipped by and the few flames of revolution that did arise in Europe were stamped out, the Russian leaders lived reluctantly in their isolation. The actuality they could accept, but the corresponding revision of the international aspects of the Marxist theory they hesitated to make. When the invading armies of the Polish Marshal Pilsudski were being pushed back from Kiev in 1920, Lenin and Stalin, over the

[19] Quoted in Isaac Deutscher, *The Prophet Armed* (New York, Oxford University Press, 1954), pp. 508-509.

opposition of Trotsky, insisted upon pursuing the Poles to
Warsaw, thinking that the Red Army would be greeted as a
liberator and that the Bolshevik dilemma could be solved by
exporting revolution by force. Again in 1923, when revolution
looked possible in Germany, Zinov'ev, as head of the International, planned an uprising—this time with Trotsky's support and
over the opposition of Stalin—only to have it cancelled at the last
moment. From this fiasco Stalin recoiled to attempt at last, with
the aid of Bukharin, a revision of Marxist theory, the doctrine
of socialism in one country (see p. 220ff). Placing this realistic
acceptance of the inevitable in contract to a stereotype of "permanent revolution" (distorted to emphasize its international
aspect), Stalin made Trotsky's die-hard hope of world revolution appear to be a disparagement of the Russians. Thus Trotsky,
the trouble-shooter for many of the difficult phases of the revolution, was converted into a trouble-maker in the eyes of official
Marxists and of non-Marxists as well, one satisfied with nothing
short of setting the whole world on fire.

Yet this argument was a result, not a cause, of the break
with the other leaders. Trotsky was the heir apparent to Lenin's
mantle, but for this very reason he, the ex-Menshevik, aroused
the jealousy of the old Bolsheviks. Their objective was to exclude
him from the succession, and his old disagreements with Lenin
on permanent revolution and other points were the best available weapons for that purpose. He found a coalition applying
against him the principles of strict discipline that Lenin had
favored but had not always enforced. His own arguments for
labor discipline and the "birth-right" of the Party, which had
reduced his popularity among the rank and file and thus made
him vulnerable, now came home.

Aside from these matters of power and personality, there were
issues of substance dividing the Politbureau and stemming from
the N.E.P. This anomaly of capitalism under socialist auspices
had gone too far, in Trotsky's opinion. Stalin, with Zinov'ev and
Kamenev, both timid conservatives by temperament, and then
with Bukharin and Rykov, who were psychologically committed
to N.E.P., was leading the Party and the country out of revolution and into capitalism. They were neglecting central planning

and industrialization, and were strengthening the kulaks. From the death of Lenin until Stalin's turn to the left in 1928 Trotsky saw danger on the right, the danger of a Thermidorian reaction.

All such disagreements exposed the minority to charges of violating the rule against factions in the Party. The issue of intra-Party democracy was always involved. Trotsky, who had helped to establish the rule and who, in both theory and practice, was one of the most dictatorial of the leaders, even Trotsky became an advocate of the restoration of Party democracy. But aside from the Democratic Centralists and the Workers' Opposition, who were not represented in the Politbureau, the opposition leaders thought of democracy only within the Central Committee and the Politbureau, not within the Party as a whole, until it was much too late.

The rule against factions made the organization of opposition a matter of conspiracy. When first Zinov'ev and Kamenev, and then Rykov and Bukharin, were ousted by Stalin, the question of collaboration with them arose; but to Trotsky and his followers they were all dangerous right-wingers with whom close cooperation was impossible. After 1927, it was apparent that Stalin had turned against the Thermidorians, and some of Trotsky's friends thought that he would be recalled from exile in Alma Ata. But Stalin had other plans. He would establish socialism, no matter what the cost. The new revolution that he had determined to carry out, unlike that of 1917, would have from the peasants not support or acquiescence but last-ditch class resistance. This project, as he conceived it, required dictatorship and obedience, not the old discussion and cooperation. In such a scheme no man as independent as Trotsky could fit.

Max Eastman, who was present at the Thirteenth Party Congress following Lenin's death, when Trotsky had his last real chance to check Stalin's incipient dictatorship, decided that, due to a personal diffidence to seize the scepter, Trotsky voluntarily stepped down.[20] The problem, however, was not primarily one of hesitation or modesty. The explanation involves the structure and psychology of Leninist party discipline, not only in the sense that Stalin controlled the Party through appointments, but

[20] Max Eastman, *Heroes I Have Known* (New York, 1942), pp. 239-259.

in the sense that Trotsky was sincerely committed to the system that was destroying him. His attitude and the quandary in which it placed him were best expressed in his defense at the Thirteenth Party Congress.

Comrades, none of us wishes to be or can be right against his party. In the final reckoning the party is always right, because the party is the only historic instrument that the proletariat possesses for the solution of its fundamental problems. I have already said that nothing would be easier than to say before the party, "All these criticisms, all declarations, warnings and protests—all these were entirely erroneous." I, comrades, cannot say that, however, because I do not think that. I know that to be right against the party is impossible. One can be right only with the party and through the party, since history has not created any other paths for the realization of one's rightness.[21]

Trotsky, in other words, held opinions that, by his own criterion, were wrong because they differed from those of the Party, yet he could not give them up.

The Party was supposed to be kept on the correct path by collective leadership, by debate and decision in the leading organs, and not by democratic appeals to the rank and file. As the opinions in the Politbureau and the Central Committee ceased to be independent, however, this process broke down, and Trotsky had no convincing alternative method to offer. He lacked the certainty of his own rightness that had inspired Lenin. The conciliatory propensity he had displayed in trying to unite the Bolsheviks and the Mensheviks before the First World War, and again in the conflict over the German ultimatum, prevented him from joining battle until it was too late.

In any event his underestimation of the abilities of Stalin cost him the position of leadership that his earlier activities and ideas had earned him, and cost Russia the services of its most versatile and most competent revolutionist. Yet, as Isaac Deutscher wrote, "There was hardly a single plank in Trotsky's programme of 1920-21 which Stalin did not use during the industrial revolution of the thirties." [22]

[21] *Trinadtsatyi S"ezd RKP(B), Stenograficheski Otchet* (Moscow, 1924), pp. 166-167.

[22] Deutscher, *The Prophet Armed* (New York, Oxford University Press, 1954), p. 515.

[THE PERMANENT REVOLUTION]

Trotsky, *Our Revolution* (New York, 1918), pp. 84-85, 98-101, 105, 109-110, 136-137, 143-144; his "Itogi i Perspektivy" (1906) translated as "Prospects of a Labor Dictatorship."

The proletariat grows and gains strength with the growth of capitalism. From this viewpoint, the development of capitalism is the development of the proletariat for dictatorship. The day and the hour, however, when political power should pass into the hands of the working class, is determined not directly by the degree of capitalistic development of economic forces, but by the relations of class struggle, by the international situation, by a number of subjective elements, such as tradition, initiative, readiness to fight. . . .

It is, therefore, not excluded that in a backward country with a lesser degree of capitalistic development, the proletariat should sooner reach political supremacy than in a highly developed capitalist state. Thus, in middle-class Paris, the proletariat consciously took into its hands the administration of public affairs in 1871. True it is, that the reign of the proletariat lasted only for two months, it is remarkable, however, that in far more advanced capitalist centers of England and the United States, the proletariat never was in power even for the duration of one day. To imagine that there is an automatic dependence between a dictatorship of the proletariat and the technical and productive resources of a country, is to understand economic determinism in a very primitive way. Such a conception would have nothing to do with Marxism.

It is our opinion that the Russian revolution creates conditions whereby political power can (and, in case of a victorious revolution, *must*) pass into the hands of the proletariat before the politicians of the liberal bourgeoisie would have occasion to give their political genius full swing. . . .

Once in power, the proletariat will appear before the peasantry as its liberator.

Proletarian rule will mean not only democratic equality, free self-government, shifting the burden of taxation on the propertied classes, dissolution of the army among the revolutionary people, abolition of compulsory payments for the Church, but also recognition of all revolutionary changes made by the peasants in agrarian relations (seizures of land). These changes will be taken by the proletariat as a starting point for further legislative measures in agriculture. Under such conditions, the Russian peasantry will be interested in upholding the proletarian rule ("labor democracy") at least in the first, most difficult period, not less so than were the French peasants interested in upholding the military rule of Napoleon Bonaparte who by force guaranteed to the new owners the integrity of their land shares.

But is it not possible that the peasants will remove the workingmen from their positions and take their place? No, this can never happen. This would be in contradiction to all historical experiences. History has convincingly shown that the peasantry is incapable of an independent political rôle. . . .

The Russian bourgeoisie yielded all revolutionary positions to the Russian proletariat. It will have to yield also the revolutionary hegemony over the peasants. Once the proletariat becomes master of the situation, conditions will impel the peasants to uphold the policies of a labor democracy. They may do it with no more political understanding than they uphold a bourgeois régime. The difference is that while each bourgeois party in possession of the peasants' vote uses its power to rob the peasants, to betray their confidence and to leave their expectations unfulfilled, in the worst case to give way to another capitalist party, the working class, backed by the peasantry, will put all forces into operation to raise the cultural level of the village and to broaden the political understanding of the peasants.

Our attitude towards the idea of a "dictatorship of the proletariat and the peasantry" is now quite clear. It is not a question whether we think it "admissible" or not, whether we "wish" or we "do not wish" this form of political coöperation. In our opinion, it simply cannot be realized, at least in its direct meaning.

Such a coöperation presupposes that either the peasantry has identified itself with one of the existing bourgeois parties, or it has formed a powerful party of its own. Neither is possible, as we have tried to point out. . . .

Two features of proletarian politics are bound particularly to meet with the opposition of labor's allies: *Collectivism* and *Internationalism*. The strong adherence of the peasants to private ownership, the primitiveness of their political conceptions, the limitations of the village horizon, its distance from world-wide political connections and interdependences, are terrific obstacles in the way of revolutionary proletarian rule. . . .

Social-Democracy can never assume power under a double obligation: to put the *entire* minimum program into operation for the sake of the proletariat, and to keep strictly *within the limits* of this program, for the sake of the bourgeoisie. Such a double obligation could never be fulfilled. Participating in the government, not as powerless hostages, but as a leading force, the representatives of labor *eo ipso* break the line between the minimum and maximum program. *Collectivism becomes the order of the day.* At which point the proletariat will be stopped on its march in this direction, depends upon the constellation of forces, not upon the original purpose of the proletarian Party.

It is, therefore, absurd to speak of a *specific* character of proletarian dictatorship (or a dictatorship of the proletariat *and* the peasantry) within a bourgeois revolution, viz., a *purely democratic* dictatorship. The working class can never secure the democratic character of its dictatorship without overstepping the limits of its democratic program. Illusions to the contrary may become a handicap. They would compromise Social-Democracy from the start.

Once the proletariat assumes power, it will fight for it to the end. One of the means to secure and solidify its power will be propaganda and organization, particularly in the village; another means will be a *policy of Collectivism.* Collectivism is not only dictated by the very position of the Social-Democratic Party as the party in power, but it becomes imperative as a means to secure this position through the active support of the working class. . . .

How far, however, can the Socialist policy of the working class advance in the economic environment of Russia? One thing we can say with perfect assurance: it will meet political obstacles long before it will be checked by the technical backwardness of the country. *Without direct political aid from the European proletariat the working class of Russia will not be able to retain its power and to turn its temporary supremacy into a permanent Socialist dictatorship.* We cannot doubt this for a moment. On the other hand, there is no doubt that a *Socialist revolution in the West would allow us to turn the temporary supremacy of the working class directly into a Socialist dictatorship.* . . . The Russian proletariat in power, even if this were only the result of a passing combination of forces in the Russian bourgeois revolution, would meet organized opposition on the part of the world's reaction, and readiness for organized support on the part of the world's proletariat. Left to its own resources, the Russian working class must necessarily be crushed the moment it loses the aid of the peasants. Nothing remains for it but to link the fate of its political supremacy and the fate of the Russian revolution with the fate of a Socialist revolution in Europe. All that momentous authority and political power which is given to the proletariat by a combination of forces in the Russian bourgeois revolution, it will thrust on the scale of class struggle in the entire capitalistic world. Equipped with governmental power, having a counter-revolution behind his back, having the European reaction in front of him, the Russian workingman will issue to all his brothers the world over his old battle-cry which will now become the call for the last attack: *Proletarians of all the world, unite!*

[THE PERMANENT REVOLUTION

IN RETROSPECT]

Trotsky, *The Permanent Revolution* (1928-1930), trans. by Max
Shachtman (New York, 1931), pp. xxxii-xxxv.

The permanent revolution, in the sense which Marx
attached to the conception, means a revolution which makes no
compromise with any form of class rule, which does not stop
at the democratic stage, which goes over to socialist measures
and to war against the reaction from without, that is, a revolution whose every next stage is anchored in the preceding one
and which can only end in the complete liquidation of all class
society.

To dispel the chaos that has been created around the theory
of the permanent revolution, it is necessary to distinguish three
lines of thought that are united in this theory.

First, it embraces the problem of the transition of the democratic revolution into the socialist. This is really the historical
origin of the theory. . . . In that lay the central idea of the
theory. If the traditional view was that the road to the dictatorship of the proletariat led through a long period of democracy,
the theory of permanent revolution established the fact that for
backward countries the road to democracy passed through the
dictatorship of the proletariat. By that alone, democracy does
not become a régime anchored within itself for decades, but
rather a direct introduction to the socialist revolution. Each is
bound to the other by an unbroken chain. In this way, there
arises between the democratic revolution and the socialist transformation of society a permanency of revolutionary development.

The second aspect of the "permanent" theory already char-
acterizes the socialist revolution as such. For an indefinitely
long time and in constant internal struggle, all social relations

are transformed. The process necessarily retains a political character, that is, it develops through collisions of various groups of society in transformation. Outbreaks of civil war and foreign wars alternate with periods of "peaceful" reforms. Revolutions in economy, technique, science, the family, morals and usages develop in complicated reciprocal action and do not allow society to reach equilibrium. Therein lies the permanent character of the socialist revolution as such.

The international character of the socialist revolution, which constitutes the third aspect of the theory of the permanent revolution, results from the present state of economy and the social structure of humanity. Internationalism is no abstract principle, but a theoretical and political reflection of the character of world economy, of the world development of productive forces, and the world scale of the class struggle.

THE ORGANIZATION OF LABOR

Trotsky, *Dictatorship vs. Democracy (Terrorism and Communism)* (1920; New York, 1922), pp. 133-137. Trotsky compiled this and the following two sections from his reports at the Third Congress of Trade Unions, the Ninth Party Congress, and the Third Congress of Economic Councils.

History is bringing us, along the whole line, to our fundamental problem—the organization of labor on new social foundations. The organization of labor is in its essence the organization of the new society: every historical form of society is in its foundation a form of organization of labor. While every previous form of society was an organization of labor in the interests of a minority, which organized its State apparatus for the oppression of the overwhelming majority of the workers, we are making the first attempt in world-history to organize labor in the interests of the laboring majority itself. This, however, does not exclude the element of compulsion in all its forms, both the most gentle

and the extremely severe. The element of State compulsion not
only does not disappear from the historical arena, but on the
contrary will still play, for a considerable period, an extremely
prominent part.

As a general rule, man strives to avoid labor. Love for work
is not at all an inborn characteristic: it is created by economic
pressure and social education. One may even say that man is
a fairly lazy animal. It is on this quality, in reality, that is founded
to a considerable extent all human progress; because if man
did not strive to expend his energy economically, did not seek
to receive the largest possible quantity of products in return
for a small quantity of energy, there would have been no technical development or social culture. It would appear, then, from
this point of view that human laziness is a progressive force.
Old Antonio Labriola, the Italian Marxist, even used to picture
the man of the future as a "happy and lazy genius." We must
not, however, draw the conclusion from this that the party and
the trade unions must propagate this quality in their agitation
as a moral duty. No, no! We have sufficient of it as it is. The
problem before the social organization is just to bring "laziness"
within a definite framework, to discipline it, and to pull mankind together with the help of methods and measures invented
by mankind itself. . . .

Capitalist industry utilizes auxiliary labor-power on a large
scale, in the shape of peasants employed on industry for only
part of the year. The village, throttled by the grip of landless-
ness, always threw a certain surplus of labor-power on to the
market. The State obliged it to do this by its demand for taxes.
The market offered the peasant manufactured goods. To-day,
we have none of this. The village has acquired more land; there
is not sufficient agricultural machinery; workers are required for
the land; industry can at present give practically nothing to the
village; and the market no longer has an attractive influence on
labor-power.

Yet labor-power is required—required more than at any time
before. Not only the worker, but the peasant also, must give
to the Soviet State his energy, in order to ensure that laboring
Russia, and with it the laboring masses, should not be crushed.

The only way to attract the labor-power necessary for our economic problems is to introduce *compulsory labor service.*

The very principle of compulsory labor service is for the Communist quite unquestionable. "He who works not, neither shall
he eat." And as all must eat, all are obliged to work. Compulsory
labor service is sketched in our Constitution and in our Labor
Code. But hitherto it has always remained a mere principle. Its
application has always had an accidental, impartial, episodic
character. Only now, when along the whole line we have reached
the question of the economic re-birth of the country, have problems of compulsory labor service arisen before us in the most
concrete way possible. The only solution of economic difficulties
that is correct from the point of view both of principle and of
practice is to treat the population of the whole country as the
reservoir of the necessary labor power—an almost inexhaustible
reservoir—and to introduce strict order into the work of its
registration, mobilization, and utilization.

How are we practically to begin the utilization of labor-power
on the basis of compulsory military service?

Hitherto only the War Department has had any experience
in the sphere of the registration, mobilization, formation, and
transference from one place to another of large masses. These
technical methods and principles were inherited by our War
Department, to a considerable extent, from the past.

In the economic sphere there is no such heritage; since in
that sphere there existed the principle of private property, and
labor-power entered each factory separately from the market.
It is consequently natural that we should be obliged, at any
rate during the first period, to make use of the apparatus of the
War Department on a large scale for labor mobilizations. . . .

If the organization of the new society can be reduced fundamentally to the reorganization of labor, the organization of labor
signifies in its turn the correct introduction of general labor service. This problem is in no way met by measures of a purely
departmental and administrative character. It touches the very
foundations of economic life and the social structure. It finds
itself in conflict with the most powerful psychological habits and
prejudices. The introduction of compulsory labor service pre-

supposes, on the one hand, a colossal work of education, and, on the other, the greatest possible care in the practical method adopted. . . .

We must see that the workers mobilized become convinced on the spot that their labor-power is being made use of cautiously and economically and is not being expended haphazard. . . . In a word, we have to complete, ameliorate, perfect, the system, methods, and organs for the mobilization of labor-power. But at the same time it is necessary once for all to make clear to ourselves that the principle itself of compulsory labor service has just so radically and permanently replaced the principle of free hiring as the socialization of the means of production has replaced capitalist property.

THE MILITARIZATION OF LABOR

Trotsky, *Dictatorship vs. Democracy (Terrorism and Communism)* (1920; New York, 1922), pp. 137-143.

The introduction of compulsory labor service is unthinkable without the application, to a greater or less degree, of the methods of militarization of labor. This term at once brings us into the region of the greatest possible superstitions and outcries from the opposition. . . .

Compulsory labor, we are told, is always unproductive. We ask what does compulsory labor mean here, that is, to what kind of labor is it opposed? Obviously, to free labor. What are we to understand, in that case, by free labor? That phrase was formulated by the progressive philosophers of the bourgeoisie, in the struggle against unfree, *i.e.*, against the serf labor of peasants, and against the standardized and regulated labor of the craft guilds. Free labor meant labor which might be "freely" bought in the market; freedom was reduced to a legal fiction, on the basis of freely-hired slavery. We know of no other form of free labor in history. Let the very few representatives of the

Mensheviks at this Congress explain to us what they mean by free, non-compulsory labor, if not the market of labor-power. History has known slave labor. History has known serf labor. History has known the regulated labor of the mediæval craft guilds. Throughout the world there now prevails hired labor, which the yellow journalists of all countries oppose, as the highest possible form of liberty, to Soviet "slavery." We, on the other hand, oppose capitalist slavery by socially-regulated labor on the basis of an economic plan, obligatory for the whole people and consequently compulsory for each worker in the country. Without this we cannot even dream of a transition to Socialism. The element of material, physical, compulsion may be greater or less; that depends on many conditions—on the degree of wealth or poverty of the country, on the heritage of the past, on the general level of culture, on the condition of transport, on the administrative apparatus, etc., etc. But obligation, and, consequently, compulsion, are essential conditions in order to bind down the bourgeois anarchy, to secure socialization of the means of production and labor, and to reconstruct economic life on the basis of a single plan.

For the Liberal, freedom in the long run means the market. Can or cannot the capitalist buy labor-power at a moderate price —that is for him the sole measure of the freedom of labor. That measure is false, not only in relation to the future but also in connection with the past.

It would be absurd to imagine that, during the time of bondage-right, work was carried entirely under the stick of physical compulsion, as if an overseer stood with a whip behind the back of every peasant. Mediæval forms of economic life grew up out of definite conditions of production, and created definite forms of social life, with which the peasant grew accustomed, and which he at certain periods considered just, or at any rate unalterable. Whenever he, under the influence of a change in material conditions, displayed hostility, the State descended upon him with its material force, thereby displaying the compulsory character of the organization of labor.

The foundations of the militarization of labor are those forms of State compulsion without which the replacement of capitalist economy by the Socialist will for ever remain an empty sound. Why do we speak of *militarization?* Of course, this is only an analogy—but an analogy very rich in content. No social organization except the army has ever considered itself justified in subordinating citizens to itself in such a measure, and to control them by its will on all sides to such a degree, as the State of the proletarian dictatorship considers itself justified in doing, and does. Only the army—just because in its way it used to decide questions of the life or death of nations, States, and ruling classes —was endowed with powers of demanding from each and all complete submission to its problems, aims, regulations, and orders. And it achieved this to the greater degree, the more the problems of military organization coincided with the requirements of social development.

The question of the life or death of Soviet Russia is at present being settled on the labor front; our economic, and together with them our professional and productive organizations, have the right to demand from their members all that devotion, discipline, and executive thoroughness, which hitherto only the army required.

On the other hand, the relation of the capitalist to the worker is not at all founded merely on the "free" contract but includes the very powerful elements of state regulation and material compulsion.

The competition of capitalist with capitalist imparted a certain very limited reality to the fiction of freedom of labor; but this competition, reduced to a minimum by trusts and syndicates, we have finally eliminated by destroying private property in the means of production. The transition to Socialism, verbally acknowledged by the Mensheviks, means the transition from anarchical distribution of labor-power—by means of the game of buying and selling, the movement of market prices and wages— to systematic distribution of the workers by the economic organizations of the county, the province, and the whole country. Such a form of planned distribution pre-supposes the subordination of those distributed to the economic plan of the State. And

this is the essence of *compulsory labor service,* which inevitably
enters into the programme of the Socialist organization of labor,
as its fundamental element.

If organized economic life is unthinkable without compulsory
labor service, the latter is not to be realized without the abolition
of fiction of the freedom of labor, and without the substitution
for it of the obligatory principle, which is supplemented by real
compulsion.

That free labor is more productive than compulsory labor is
quite true when it refers to the period of transition from feudal
society to bourgeois society. But one needs to be a Liberal or
—at the present day—a Kautskian, to make that truth permanent,
and to transfer its application to the period of transition from
the bourgeois to the Socialist order. If it were true that compulsory labor is unproductive always and under every condition,
as the Menshevik resolution says, all our constructive work
would be doomed to failure. For we can have no way to Socialism except by the authoritative regulation of the economic forces
and resources of the country, and the centralized distribution
of labor-power in harmony with the general State plan. The
Labor State considers itself empowered to send every worker
to the place where his work is necessary. And not one serious
Socialist will begin to deny to the labor State the right to lay
its hand upon the worker who refuses to execute his labor duty.
But the whole point is that the Menshevik path of transition
to "Socialism" is a milky way, without the bread monopoly,
without the abolition of the market, without the revolutionary
dictatorship, and without the militarization of labor.

Without general labor service, without the right to order and
demand fulfilment of orders, the trade unions will be transformed into a mere form without a reality; for the young Socialist
State requires trade unions, not for a struggle for better conditions of labor—that is the task of the social and State organizations as a whole—but to organize the working class for the ends
of production, to educate, discipline, distribute, group, retain
certain categories and certain workers at their posts for fixed
periods—in a word, hand in hand with the State to exercise their
authority in order to lead the workers into the framework of a

single economic plan. To defend, under such conditions, the "freedom" of labor means to defend fruitless, helpless, absolutely unregulated searches for better conditions, unsystematic, chaotic changes from factory to factory, in a hungry country, in conditions of terrible disorganization of the transport and food apparatus. . . . What except the complete collapse of the working-class and complete economic anarchy could be the result of the stupid attempt to reconcile bourgeois freedom of labor with proletarian socialization of the means of production?

Consequently, comrades, militarization of labor, in the root sense indicated by me, is not the invention of individual politicians or an invention of our War Department, but represents the inevitable method of organization and disciplining of labor-power during the period of transition from capitalism to Socialism. And if the compulsory distribution of labor-power, its brief or prolonged retention at particular industries and factories, its regulation within the framework of the general State economic plan—if these forms of compulsion lead always and everywhere, as the Menshevik resolution states, to the lowering of productivity, then you can erect a monument over the grave of Socialism. For we cannot build Socialism on decreased production. Every social organization is in its foundation an organization of labor, and if our new organization of labor leads to a lowering of its productivity, it thereby most fatally leads to the destruction of the Socialist society we are building, whichever way we twist and turn, whatever measures of salvation we invent. . . .

THE SINGLE ECONOMIC PLAN

Trotsky, *Dictatorship vs. Democracy (Terrorism and Communism)* (1920; New York, 1922), pp. 157-159.

The widest possible application of the principle of general labor service, together with measures for the militarization of labor, can play a decisive part only in case they are applied

on the basis of a single economic plan covering the whole country and all branches of productive activity. This plan must be
drawn up for a number of years, for the whole epoch that lies
before us. It is naturally broken up into separate periods or
stages, corresponding to the inevitable stages in the economic
rebirth of the country. We shall have to begin with the most
simple and at the same time most fundamental problems.

We have first of all to afford the working class the very possibility of living—though it be in the most difficult conditions—
and thereby to preserve our industrial centres and save the
towns. This is the point of departure. If we do not wish to melt
the town into agriculture, and transform the whole country into
a peasant State, we must support our transport, even at the
minimum level, and secure bread for the towns, fuel and raw
materials for industry, fodder for the cattle. Without this we
shall not make one step forward. . . .

This plan has great significance, not only as a general guide
for the practical work of our economic organs, but also as a
line along which propaganda amongst the laboring masses in
connection with our economic problems is to proceed. Our labor
mobilization will not enter into real life, will not take root, if
we do not excite the living interest of all that is honest, class-
conscious, and inspired in the working class. We must explain
to the masses the whole truth as to our situation and as to our
views for the future; we must tell them openly that our economic
plan, with the maximum of exertion on the part of the workers,
will neither to-morrow nor the day after give us a land flowing
with milk and honey: for during the first period our chief work
will consist in preparing the conditions for the production of
the means of production. Only after we have secured, though
on the smallest possible scale, the possibility of rebuilding the
means of transport and production, shall we pass on to the
production of articles for general consumption. In this way the
fruit of their labor, which is the direct object of the workers,
in the shape of articles for personal consumption, will arrive only
in the last, the fourth, stage of our economic plan; and only then
shall we have a serious improvement in our life. The masses,
who for a prolonged period will still bear all the weight of

labor and of privation, must realize to the full the inevitable internal logic of this economic plan if they are to prove capable of carrying it out. . . .

[RELATIONS WITH THE PEASANTS]

Trotsky, *The New Course* (1923), trans. by Max Shachtman (New York, 1943), pp. 62-70.

In March, 1919, in a report sent to the Central Committee from the Volga region . . . I wrote: "The temporary political situation—which may even last a long time—is nevertheless a much more profound social economic reality, for even if the proletarian revolution triumphs in the West, we shall have to base ourselves in large measure, in the construction of socialism, upon the middle peasant and to draw him into the socialist economy." . . .

There was a growing feeling of the necessity of changing the economic policy. Under the influence of my observations on the state of mind of the army and of my declarations during my economic inspection trip in the Urals, I wrote to the Central Committee in February, 1920:

"The seignioral and crown lands have been turned over to the peasantry. Our whole policy is directed against the peasants possessing a large area of land and a large number of horses (kulaks). On the other hand, our food policy is based upon the requisitioning of the surpluses of agricultural production (above consumer norms). This prompts the peasant not to cultivate his land except for his family needs. In particular, the decree on the requisitioning of every third cow (regarded as superfluous) leads in reality to the clandestine slaughter of cows, the secret sale of the meat at high prices and the disorganization of the dairy-products industry. At the same time, the semi-proletarian and even proletarian elements of the towns are settling in the villages, where they are starting their own farms. Industry is losing its hands, and in agriculture the number of self-sufficient farms tends to increase constantly. By that very fact, the basis of our food policy, established on the requisitioning of surpluses, is undermined. If in the current year the requisitioning yields a greater quantity of products, it must be attributed to the extension of Soviet territory and to a certain improvement in the provisioning apparatus. But in general, the food resources of the country are threatened with exhaustion and no improvement in the requisitioning apparatus will be able to remedy this fact. The tendency toward economic decay can be combatted by the following methods:

1. Replace the requisitioning of surpluses with a levy proportionate to the quantity of production (a sort of progressive tax on agricultural income), set up in such a way that it is nevertheless more profitable to increase the acreage sown or to cultivate it better;

2. Institute a more rigorous correlation between the delivery to the peasants of industrial products and the quantity of grain furnished by them, not only by cantons and towns, but by rural farms.

Have the local industrial enterprises participate in this task. Pay the peasants for the raw materials, the fuel and the food products supplied by them, in part in products of industrial enterprises.

"In any case, it is clear that the present policy of the requisition of food products according to norms of consumption, of joint responsibility for the delivery of these products and of the equal distribution of industrial products, is lowering agricultural production, bringing about the atomization of the industrial proletariat and threatens to disorganize completely the economic life of the country."

My text as a whole represented a fairly complete proposal to go over to the New Economic Policy in the country. To this proposal was linked another dealing with the new organization of industry, a less definitive and much more circumspect proposal, but directed on the whole against the regime of the "Centers" which was destroying all contact between industry and agriculture.

These proposals were at that time rejected by the Central Committee. . . . It is now possible to estimate variously the extent to which the adoption of the New Economic Policy was expedient in February, 1920. Opinion may be divided on this matter. Personally, I do not doubt that we would have gained from it.

[THE BUREAUCRACY]

Trotsky, *The New Course* (1923), trans. by Max Shachtman (New York, 1943), pp. 50-57.

It is clear that, as a conservative element, as the automatic pressure of yesterday upon today, tradition represents an extremely important force at the service of the conservative parties and deeply inimical to the revolutionary party. The whole strength of the latter lies precisely in its freedom from conservative traditionalism. Does this mean that it is free with regard to tradition in general? Not at all. But the tradition of a revolutionary party is of an entirely different nature.

If we now take our Bolshevik party in its revolutionary past and in the period following October, it will be recognized that its most precious fundamental tactical quality is its unequalled aptitude to orient itself rapidly, to change tactics quickly, to renew its armament and to apply new methods, in a word, to carry out abrupt turns. Tempestuous historical conditions have made this tactic necessary. Lenin's genius gave it a superior form. . . .

The more ingrown the party apparatus, the more imbued it is with the feeling of its own intrinsic importance, the slower it reacts to needs emanating from the ranks and the more inclined it is to set formal tradition against new needs and tasks. And if there is one thing likely to strike a mortal blow to the spiritual life of the party and to the doctrinal training of the youth, it is certainly the transformation of Leninism from a method demanding for its application initiative, critical thinking and ideological courage into a canon which demands nothing more than interpreters appointed for good and aye. . . .

Lenin cannot be chopped up into quotations suited for every possible case, because for Lenin the formula never stands higher than the reality; it is always the tool that makes it possible to grasp the reality and to dominate it. . . .

Since I am obliged to speak of myself for a moment, I will say that I do not consider the road by which I came to Leninism as less safe and reliable than the others. I came to Lenin fighting, but I came full and all the way. My actions in the service of the party are the only guarantee of this. . . .

Whatever the difficulties and the differences of opinion may be in the future, they can be victoriously overcome only by the collective work of the party's mind, checking up each time by itself and thereby maintaining the continuity of development.

[AGAINST SOCIALISM IN ONE COUNTRY]

Trotsky, *The Draft Program of the Communist International—A Criticism of Fundamentals* (1928), in his *The Third International After Lenin,* Max Shachtman, ed., trans. by John G. Wright (New York, 1936), pp. 3-4, 18-22, 51-61. Trotsky submitted this to the Sixth Congress of the Comintern from exile in Alma-Ata in opposition to the draft program written by Bukharin and Stalin, to which he refers.

In our epoch, which is the epoch of imperialism, i.e., of *world* economy and *world* politics under the hegemony of finance capital, not a single communist party can establish its program by proceeding solely or mainly from conditions and tendencies of developments in its own country. This also holds entirely for the party that wields the state power within the boundaries of the U.S.S.R. . . .

The draft, as we already know, seeks to proceed in its construction from the standpoint of world economy and its internal tendencies—an attempt which merits recognition. *Pravda* is absolutely correct in saying that herein lies the basic difference in principle between us and the national-patriotic social democracy. . . .

The draft refers time and again, and not always in the proper place, to the law of uneven development of capitalism as the main and almost all-determining law of that development. . . . In its first chapter the draft states that "the unevenness of economic and political development is an unconditional law of capitalism. This unevenness becomes still more accentuated and aggravated in the epoch of imperialism."

This is correct. . . . However, . . . what the draft says about the law of uneven development remains in essence one-sided and inadequate.

In the first place, it would have been more correct to say that the entire history of mankind is governed by the law of uneven development. Capitalism finds various sections of mankind at different stages of development, each with its profound internal contradictions. The extreme diversity in the levels attained, and the extraordinary unevenness in the rate of development of the different sections of mankind during the various epochs, serve as the *starting point* of capitalism. Capitalism gains mastery only gradually over the inherited unevenness, breaking and altering it, employing therein its own means and methods. In contrast to the economic systems which preceded it, capitalism inherently and constantly aims at economic expansion, at the penetration of new territories, the surmounting of economic differences, the conversion of self-sufficient provincial and national economies into a system of financial interrelationships. Thereby it brings about their *rapprochement* and equalizes the economic and cultural levels of the most progressive and the most backward countries. Without this main process, it would be impossible to conceive of the relative leveling out, first, of Europe with Great Britain, and then, of America with Europe; the industrialization of the colonies, the diminishing gap between India and Great Britain, and all the consequences arising from the enumerated processes upon which is based not only the program of the Communist International but also its very existence.

By drawing the countries economically closer to one another and leveling out their stages of development, capitalism, however, operates by methods of *its own*, that is to say, by anarchistic methods which constantly undermine its own work, set one country against another, and one branch of industry against another, developing some parts of world economy while hampering and throwing back the development of others. Only the correlation of these two fundamental tendencies—both of which arise from the nature of capitalism—explains to us the living texture of the historical process.

Imperialism, thanks to the universality, penetrability, and mobility and the break-neck speed of the formation of finance capital as the driving force of imperialism, lends vigor to *both these tendencies.* Imperialism links up incomparably more rapidly and more deeply the individual national and continental units into a single entity, bringing them into the closest and most vital dependence upon each other and rendering their economic methods, social forms, and levels of development more identical. At the same time, it attains this "goal" by such antagonistic methods, such tiger-leaps, and such raids upon backward countries and areas that the unification and leveling of world economy which it has effected, is upset by it even more violently and convulsively than in the preceding epochs. Only such a dialectical and not purely mechanical understanding of the law of uneven development can make possible the avoidance of the fundamental error which the draft program, submitted to the Sixth Congress, has failed to avoid.

Immediately after its one-sided characterization of the law of uneven development pointed out by us, the draft program says: "Hence it follows that the international proletarian revolution must not be regarded as a single, simultaneous, and universal act. Hence it follows that the victory of socialism is at first possible in a few, or even in one isolated capitalist country."

That the international revolution of the proletariat cannot be a simultaneous act, of this there can of course be no dispute at all among grown-up people after the experience of the October Revolution, achieved by the proletariat of a backward country under pressure of historical necessity, without waiting in the least for the proletariat of the advanced countries "to even out the front." Within these limits, the reference to the law of uneven development is absolutely correct and quite in place. But it is entirely otherwise with the second half of the conclusion—

TROTSKY   155

namely, the hollow assertion that the victory of socialism is possible "in one isolated capitalist country." To prove its point the draft program simply says: "Hence it follows. . . ." One gets the impression that this follows from the law of uneven development. But this does not follow at all. "Hence follows" something quite the contrary. If the historical process were such that some countries developed not only unevenly but even *independently of each other*, isolated from each other, then from the law of uneven development would indubitably follow the possibility of building socialism in one capitalist country—at first in the most advanced country and then, as they mature, in the more backward ones. Such was the customary and, so to speak, average idea of the transition to socialism within the ranks of the pre-war social democracy. This is precisely the idea that formed the theoretical basis of social-patriotism. Of course, the draft program does not hold this view. But it inclines towards it.

The theoretical error of the draft lies in the fact that it seeks to deduce from the law of uneven development something which the law does not and cannot imply. Uneven or sporadic development of various countries acts constantly to *upset* but in no case to *eliminate* the growing economic bonds and interdependence between those countries which the very next day, after four years of hellish slaughter, were compelled to exchange coal, bread, oil, powder, and suspenders with each other. On this point, the draft posits the question as if historical development proceeds only on the basis of sporadic leaps, while the economic basis which gives rise to those leaps, and upon which they occur, is either left entirely out of sight by the authors of the draft, or is forcibly eliminated by them. This they do with the sole object of defending the indefensible theory of socialism in one country.

After what has been said it is not difficult to understand that the only correct formulation of the question should read that Marx and Engels, even prior to the imperialist epoch, had arrived at the conclusion that on the one hand, unevenness, i.e., sporadic historical development, stretches the proletarian revolution through an entire epoch in the course of which nations will enter the revolutionary flood one after another; while, on the

other hand, the organic interdependence of the several countries, developing toward an international division of labor, excludes the possibility of building socialism in one country. This
means that the Marxian doctrine, which posits that the socialist
revolution can begin only on a national basis, while the building
of socialism in one country is impossible, has been rendered
doubly and trebly true, all the more so now, in the modern
epoch when imperialism has developed, deepened, and sharp-
ened *both* of these antagonistic tendencies. On this point, Lenin
merely developed and concretized Marx's own formulation and
Marx's own answer to this question. . . .

From the uneven sporadic development of capitalism flows
the non-simultaneous, uneven, and sporadic character of the
socialist revolution; from the extreme tensity of the interdependence of the various countries upon each other flows not only
the political but also the economic impossibility of building
socialism in one country.

Let us examine once again from this angle the text of the
program a little closer. We have already read in the introduction that:

"Imperialism . . . aggravates to an exceptional degree the
contradiction between the growth of the national productive
forces of world economy and national state barriers."

We have already stated that this proposition is, or rather was
meant to be, the keystone of the international program. But it is
precisely this proposition which excludes, rejects, and sweeps
away *a priori* the theory of socialism in one country as a reactionary theory because it is irreconcilably opposed not only to
the fundamental *tendency* of development of the productive
forces but also to the *material results* which have already been
attained by this development. The productive forces are incompatible with national boundaries. Hence flow not only foreign trade, the export of men and capital, the seizure of territories, the colonial policy, and the last imperialist war, but
also the economic impossibility of a self-sufficient socialist society.
The productive forces of *capitalist* countries have long since
broken through the national boundaries. Socialist society, however, can be built only on the most advanced productive forces,

on the application of electricity and chemistry to the processes
of production including agriculture; on combining, generalizing,
and bringing to maximum development the highest elements of
modern technology. . . . The question arises: how then can
socialism drive the productive forces back into the boundaries
of a national state which they have violently sought to break
through under capitalism? Or, perhaps, we ought to abandon
the idea of "unbridled" productive forces for which the national
boundaries, *and consequently also the boundaries of the theory
of socialism in one country,* are too narrow, and limit ourselves,
let us say, to the curbed and domesticated productive forces,
that is, to the technology of economic backwardness? . . .
   But this is not what the authors of the draft have in mind.
By a victory of socialism, they do not mean simply the capture
of power and nationalization of the means of production but
the building of a socialist society in one country. If we were to
accept this interpretation then we would obtain not a world
socialist economy based on an international division of labor but
a federation of self-sufficing socialist communes in the spirit of
blissful anarchism, the only difference being that these communes would be enlarged to the size of the present national
states. . . .
   As a matter of fact, world socialist economy will not at all
be a sum total of national socialist economies. It can take shape
in its fundamental aspects only on the soil of the world-wide
division of labor which has been created by the entire preceding
development of capitalism. In its essentials, it will be constituted
and built not after the building of "complete socialism" in a
number of individual countries, but in the storms and tempests
of the world proletarian revolution which will require a number
of decades. The economic successes of the first countries of the
proletarian dictatorship will be measured not by the degree of
their approximation to a self-sufficing "complete socialism" but
by the political stability of the dictatorship itself and by the
successes achieved in preparing the elements of the future world
socialist economy. . . .
   The new doctrine proclaims that socialism can be built on the
basis of a national state *if only there is no intervention.* From

this there can and must follow (notwithstanding all pompous
declarations in the draft program) a collaborationist policy towards the foreign bourgeoisie with the object of averting intervention, as this will guarantee the construction of socialism, that
is to say, will solve the main historical question. The task of the
parties in the Comintern assumes, therefore, an auxiliary character; their mission is to protect the U.S.S.R. from intervention
and not to fight for the conquest of power. It is, of course, not
a question of the subjective intentions but of the objective logic
of political thought.

[THE DICTATORSHIP IN RUSSIA]

Trotsky, *The Revolution Betrayed* (1936), trans. by Max Eastman
(New York, Doubleday, 1937), pp. 52-56. By permission of Pio-
neer Publishers.

The proletarian dictatorship is a bridge between the
bourgeois and the socialist society. In its very essence, therefore, it bears a temporary character. An incidental but very
essential task of the state which realizes the dictatorship consists
in preparing for its own dissolution. The degree of realization
of this "incidental" task is, to some extent, a measure of its success in the fulfillment of its fundamental mission: the construction of a society without classes and without material contradictions. Bureaucracy and social harmony are inversely proportional
to each other. . . .

In order that the state shall disappear, "class domination and
the struggle for individual existence" must disappear. Engels
joins these two conditions together, for in the perspective of
changing social regimes a few decades amount to nothing. But
the thing looks different to those generations who bear the weight
of a revolution. It is true that capitalist anarchy creates the
struggle of each against all, but the trouble is that a socialization
of the means of production does not yet automatically remove

the "struggle for individual existence." That is the nub of the
question!

A socialist state even in America, on the basis of the most
advanced capitalism, could not immediately provide everyone
with as much as he needs, and would therefore be compelled
to spur everyone to produce as much as possible. The duty of
stimulator in these circumstances naturally falls to the state,
which in its turn cannot but resort, with various changes and
mitigations, to the method of labor payment worked out by
capitalism. It was in this sense that Marx wrote in 1875: "Bourgeois law . . . is inevitable in the first phase of the communist
society, in that form in which it issues after long labor pains
from capitalist society. *Law can never be higher than the economic structure and the cultural development of society conditioned by that structure.*"

In explaining these remarkable lines, Lenin adds: "Bourgeois
law in relation to the distribution of the objects of consumption
assumes, of course, inevitably a *bourgeois state,* for law is nothing without an apparatus capable of compelling observance of
its norms. It follows (we are still quoting Lenin) that under
Communism not only will bourgeois law survive for a certain
time, but also even a bourgeois state without the bourgeoisie."
This highly significant conclusion, completely ignored by the
present official theoreticians, has a decisive significance for the
understanding of the nature of the Soviet state—or more ac-
curately, for a first approach to such understanding. Insofar as
the state which assumes the task of socialist transformation is
compelled to defend inequality—that is, the material privileges
of a minority—by methods of compulsion, insofar does it also
remain a "bourgeois" state, even though without a bourgeoisie.
These words contain neither praise nor blame; they merely
name things with their real names.

The bourgeois norms of distribution, by hastening the growth
of material power, ought to serve socialist aims—but only in the
last analysis. The state assumes directly and from the very beginning a dual character: socialistic, insofar as it defends social
property in the means of production; bourgeois, insofar as the
distribution of life's goods is carried out with a capitalistic meas-

ure of value and all the consequences ensuing therefrom. Such a contradictory characterization may horrify the dogmatists and scholastics; we can only offer them our condolences. . . .

We have thus taken the first step toward understanding the fundamental contradiction between Bolshevik program and Soviet reality. If the state does not die away, but grows more and more despotic, if the plenipotentiaries of the working class become bureaucratized, and the bureaucracy rises above the new society, this is not for some secondary reasons like the psychological relics of the past, etc., but is a result of the iron necessity to give birth to and support a privileged minority so long as it is impossible to guarantee genuine equality.

The tendencies of bureaucratism, which strangles the workers' movement in capitalist countries, would everywhere show themselves even after a proletarian revolution. But it is perfectly obvious that the poorer the society which issues from a revolution, the sterner and more naked would be the expression of this "law," the more crude would be the forms assumed by bureaucratism, and the more dangerous would it become for socialist development. The Soviet state is prevented not only from dying away, but even from freeing itself of the bureaucratic parasite, not by the "relics" of former ruling classes, as declares the naked police doctrine of Stalin, for these relics are powerless in themselves. It is prevented by immeasurably mightier factors, such as material want, cultural backwardness and the resulting dominance of "bourgeois law" in what most immediately and sharply touches every human being, the business of insuring his personal existence.

BIBLIOGRAPHY

Works by Trotsky

Communism and Syndicalism (1923-1931), trans. by Max Shachtman (New York, 1931).
Écrits 1928-1940, 3 Vols. (Paris, 1955-1959).
The First Five Years of the Communist International (1919-1924), trans. by John G. Wright (Vol. 1, New York, 1945, Vol. 2, London, 1953).

From October to Brest-Litovsk (1918; New York, 1919). Also known as *The October Revolution*.

In Defense of Marxism (1939-1940; New York, 1942).

The Lessons of October, 1917 (1924), trans. by Susan Lawrence and I. Olshan (London, 1925). Also trans. by John G. Wright (New York, 1937). Also edited by Paul Levi as *1917, Die Lehren der Revolution* (Berlin, 1925).

The New Course (1923), trans. by Max Shachtman (New York, 1943).

Russland in der Revolution (Dresden, [1910]). Also as *Die russische Revolution, 1905* (Berlin, 1923), in French as *1905* (Paris, 1923), and, in part, in Italian as *Mille novecento cinque* (Milan, 1948).

Our Revolution (1906), trans. by Moissaye J. Olgin (New York, 1918). Also in part as *–A Review and Some Perspectives*, trans. by J. Fineberg (Moscow, 1921).

The Permanent Revolution (1928-1930), trans. by Max Shachtman (New York, 1931).

Terrorism and Communism, A Reply to Karl Kautsky (1920; Ann Arbor, 1961). Also as *Dictatorship vs. Democracy* (New York, 1922). Also as *The Defence of Terrorism* (London, 1921).

The Third International After Lenin (1928), trans. by John G. Wright (New York, 1936).

Toward Socialism or Capitalism? (1925), trans. by R. S. Townsend and Z. Vengerova (London, 1926). Also known as *Whither Russia?*

Biography

Deutscher, Isaac, *The Prophet Armed, Trotsky: 1879-1921* (New York, 1954), and *The Prophet Unarmed Trotsky: 1921-1929* (New York, 1959).

Trotsky, Leon, *My Life* (New York, 1930).

Exposition

–Dan, Theodor, "Trotzkis Schicksal," *Klassenkampf*, Vol. 3 (No. 6, March 15, 1929), pp. 179-185.

Dewey, John, and others, *Not Guilty*. Report of the Commission of Inquiry into the charges made against Leon Trotsky in the Moscow trials (New York, 1938).

Dimitriev, Grigori, ed., *Die Tragödie Trotzki* (Berlin, 1925). Essays by leading Marxists.

Giusti, Wolfango, *Il pensiero di Trotzky* (Florence, 1949).

Johnson, J. R., "Trotsky's Place in History," *New International,* Vol. 6 (September, 1940), pp. 151-167.

Kagan, Naum Y. (Tasin, N.), *La dictadura del proletariado según Marx, Engels, Kautsky, Bernstein, Axelrod, Lenin, Trotzky, and Baüer* (Madrid, 1920).

Kautsky, Karl, *Von der Demokratie zur Staats-Sklaverei* (Berlin, 1921).

Martinet, Gilles, "Le socialisme et les société de transition (De Trotsky à Burnham)," *Revue internationale,* Vol. 4 (summer, 1947), pp. 12-30.

Murphy, John T., ed., *The Errors of Trotskyism* (London, 1925). Includes five items from *Um den Oktober.*

Novikov, S., "Trotsky's Travels (From 'Anti-Kautsky' to Kautsky)," *The Communist International* (London), Vol. 6 (May, 1929), pp. 478-487.

Parti communiste français, *La plate-form de l'opposition trotskiste* (Paris, 1928).

Pierre, A., "La disgrâce de Trotski," *Le monde slave,* N.S. Vol. 2 (No. 3; March, 1925), pp. 422-438.

Seydewitz, Max, *Stalin oder Trotzki, die UdSSR und der Trotzkismus* (London, 1938).

Shachtman, Max, *The Struggle for the New Course* (New York, 1943).

Stalin, Joseph, "The October Revolution and the Tactics of the Russian Communists" (1924), in his *Problems of Leninism* (Moscow, 1953).

Trotski et le trotskisme, textes et documents (Paris, 1937).

Trotsky, Leon, *et al., Um den Oktober* (Hamburg, 1925). Contains Trotsky's *Die Lehren des Oktober* and critiques by six leading Bolsheviks.

Zinoviev, Grigori E., and others, *Leninism or Trotskyism* (Chicago, 1925). Includes three items from *Um den Oktober.*

6

Kollontai:

Women and the Workers

FEW of the revolutionaries embodied so completely and consistently the idealism of the revolution as did Kollontai. The Social Democrats had few women among their leaders, in comparison with the nineteenth-century *narodnik* movement, but of these few she was the best orator, the most prolific writer, and the strongest theorist. Her work was of most significance in two areas, in the development of Marxist ideas regarding marriage and the family, and in the defense of the ideals of proletarian democracy against the growth of bureaucracy and the separation of the revolution from the working class.

Descended from a very old Ukrainian family of landed gentry (her mother was an energetic Finnish bourgeoise), Alexandra Kollontai (1872-1952) became subversive during the St. Petersburg textile strike of 1896. Her husband, Vladimir Kollontai, lacked both her intellectual and her revolutionary interests, so she left him, spent three years at the University of Zurich, joined the Social Democrats, and dashed in and out of Russia on various missions until 1908 when her partial immunity from arrest as the daughter of General Domontovich seemed to be wearing thin. Nominally a Menshevik, she stood close to Lenin on a number of issues, especially after the outbreak of war, and in 1915 she joined his faction.

Kollontai, arriving in March, was one of the first of the exiles to reach Russia after the February revolution and was soon elected to the executive committee of the Petrograd soviet.

163

Elected also to the Bolshevik Central Committee by the Sixth Party Congress in August, she was one of the nine who, in October, voted with Lenin for armed insurrection. In the new government she was appointed Commissar of Public Welfare, and John Reed has preserved the picture of her, with tears streaming down her cheeks, ordering the arrest of the striking employees of the commissariat who were withholding the funds with which she was supposed to help the needy.[1]

She did not, however, exercise power long enough to be corrupted by it. Her vigorous protests over the arrest of her current husband caused her removal from the commissariat and the Central Committee early in 1918, and she spent the next few years producing propaganda for the revolutionary movement among women. Her writings in this area made her the outstanding exponent of new views on sex, marriage, the family and related problems.

During this time she became increasingly dissatisfied with the course of the revolution away from its original ideals, away from proletarian democracy and toward bureaucracy and authoritarian methods. From 1920 to 1922, with A. G. Shliapnikov, the first Commissar of Labor, and others, she led the last strong protest movement against Lenin's leadership, the "Workers' Opposition," going so far as to appeal over the head of the Russian Party to the Communist International. Defeated both at home and abroad and condemned by the Eleventh Party Congress, she finally abandoned the struggle and turned to diplomatic work. From 1923 to 1945 she represented the USSR in Norway, Mexico, and Sweden, earning the distinction of the Order of Lenin and, more remarkably, of being the only major opposition leader to survive the purges of the 1930's.

Beginning with the *Manifesto* the Marxist movement had given special attention to the influences of economic conditions on the institutions of marriage, the home, and the family. Engels had emphasized the connection between monogamy and private property, and had insisted that equality for women could not be

[1] John Reed, *Ten Days that Shook the World* (New York, 1919), p. 262.

attained through law. Real emancipation of women would require "the re-introduction of the entire female sex into public industry," which in turn would require the abolition of the monogamous family as the economic unit of society.[2] August Bebel, in his widely read *Woman and Socialism* (1879), had accumulated statistics on the growth of factory employment of women, their discriminatory wages, and the deterioration of their health, morals, and home life. Among the proletariat, it appeared, the development of capitalism was destroying the family life prescribed by the bourgeois moral code. But with what was it to be replaced under socialism?

Kollontai's ardent nature was dissatisfied with Bebel's answer that all these evils would be swept away.[3] She went further than the economic and sociological studies, probing into the psychological changes that would flow from the new property relationships after the revolution. Just as, in Marxist theory, men's ideas are the result of their economic environment, so, she thought, women's ideas had been and would be molded by their material experiences. Capitalism had seen numerous advantages in holding women in a position of legal and educational inferiority, but socialism would find its advantages in equality—modified to accommodate the physiological differences of women. The revolution, therefore, would emancipate women both from the economic evils of capitalism and from the psychological ills of institutionalized inferiority. The effects upon the minds of women, and of men, would be radical.

The elimination of property would remove all economic considerations in the choice of mates; men and women would be free to love without such fears as the effects on social position or the costs of children. But would this freedom from economic

[2] Friedrich Engels, *The Origin of the Family, Private Property and the State* (1884; Moscow, 1954), pp. 102-123.

[3] She was even less satisfied with the contemporary feminist movement. The feminists, because they forgot the class struggle underlying the evils they attacked, saw the problem as a struggle between the sexes and erroneously opposed the interests of women to those of men. Moreover, in pursuit of "equal rights" they neglected the special needs and interests of women as mothers. Kollontai, *Trud Zhenshchiny v Evoliutsii Khoziaistva* (1921; 2nd ed., Moscow, 1928), pp. 96-97.

restraints and from "bourgeois morality" lead to free love or promiscuity? Would it, as Engels seemed to imply, remove the basis for monogamy? Kollontai's answer was complex, even ambiguous. To understand it a distinction is necessary between sexual relations on the one hand and the home and family on the other.

She denied that free love in its physical aspects (the "wingless Eros" as she called it) was the trend of proletarian morals. The civil war stimulated such relationships, but more peaceful conditions would revive the "winged Eros" of love in its psychological aspects. "Love in itself is a great creative force; it enlarges and enriches the souls of the one who feels it and the one to whom it is given." [4] Monogamy was, therefore, the natural form of union for the species and would continue under socialism. The great evil of monogamous marriage under capitalism, in her opinion, lay in its compulsory aspects, based on the difficulties attached to divorce. Remove these, make divorce readily available, and marriage would take on new dimensions of mutual fulfillment. "The ideal remains the monogamous union, resting on a great love, but not 'indissoluble' and congealed." [5]

The "new woman," however, would never permit her home and husband to absorb her completely. Love was never entirely private; it had a social aspect and social importance. It must be "love within comradeship," both toward the partner and toward the community. Kollontai's aim, in her fiction especially,[6] was "to teach women not to put all their hearts and souls into the love for a man, but into the essential thing—creative work. . . . Love must not crush the woman's individuality, not bind her wings. If love begins to enslave her, she must make herself free, she must step over all love tragedies, and go her own way." [7] Creative work, that is, social contribution, was a higher value than any individual relationship. Kollontai's ideal was monogamy

[4] Kollontai, *Novaia Moral' i Rabochii Klass* (Moscow, 1919), p. 45.

[5] *Ibid.*, p. 46.

[6] Four of her stories are in English, her "Vasilisa Malygina" translated as *Free Love* and as *Red Love*, and three others in *A Great Love*, including the revealing novelette, "The Love of Three Generations."

[7] Quoted in Isabel de Palencia, *Alexandra Kollontay* (New York, Longmans, Green, 1947), p. 137. Courtesy of the David McKay Co., Inc.

but, in both theory and practice, it was likely to be a series of monogamies.[8]

The "new woman" would thus find her happiness and fulfillment, as men long had done, outside the home, in contributing to social production and to the satisfaction of general public needs. This was not a temporary expedient, brought on by poverty or civil war, but a long-term part of the revolutionary emancipation of women. Even under capitalism the primitive home had been stripped of its creative and productive activities, leaving only the drudgery of cooking, cleaning, mending, and child care. Under socialism these too would be removed—by communal housing, inexpensive public restaurants, laundries, crèches, kindergartens, etc.—freeing the wife and mother for more productive work. As such institutions developed, the individual household, that "egotistically enclosed little world," would be unable to maintain itself. "As the private household is swallowed up by the public economy . . . the present tendency will gain strength in morals and habits, and the family, in its bourgeois sense, will die out." These new material conditions would bring new ideas. Marriage, as its material advantages diminished, would lose its stability. "In its place will grow up, be created, a new family— the family of the working collective, where not ties of blood, but community of work, unity of interests, aspirations and problems will firmly unite people, will train them to be true brothers in spirit." [9]

The political implications of Kollontai's domestic theories are apparent. As the individual economy of household consumption is replaced by collective consumption, the ties among family members are correspondingly weakened and their ties with larger social groups are strengthened. The separate family becomes a less complete and satisfying refuge for the individual vis-à-vis society. The significance of social life as against private life being thus enhanced, women became more important in society and less so in the home. The efficient allocation of the labor force is less hampered by marital and maternal ties. The ancient conservative role of the mother in early education is

8 Both she and her mother were divorcées.
9 Kollontai, *Trud Zhenshchiny v Evoliutsii Khoziaistva*, pp. 161-162.

diminished, and the minds of the coming generations are more completely available for molding by the society. The burden of inherited notions impeding social change is thus reduced, and the speed and flexibility of change is, to some extent, enhanced. Kollontai's desire to emancipate women was shared by Lenin. The new government, in December, 1917, issued decrees on civil marriage (only religious marriage had been possible) and on divorce by a simple procedure of notification. All births were made legitimate, and the wages of men and women were made equal for equal work. At the First Congress of Working and Peasant Women, held in November, 1918, under Kollontai's leadership, Lenin could say, "For the first time in history, our law has obliterated everything that made for the oppression of women." [10] Like her, however, he realized that new laws were not enough and repeatedly called for more public facilities to replace tasks usually performed in the home. "The real *emancipation of women,* real Communism, will begin only when a mass struggle . . . is started against this petty domestic economy, or rather when it is *transformed on a mass scale* into large-scale Socialist economy." [11] The food shortage encouraged the establishment of dining halls in connection with factories, and by 1921 Kollontai reported that some five million workers were taking their meals in such collectives.[12]

Lenin did not, however, share Kollontai's expectation of the withering away of the family. His sense of justice and of economic efficiency demanded the freeing of women from domestic drudgery, "the separation of the kitchen from marriage"; but, just as factory life had not made the workers socialist (see p. 47), so he did not expect the new material conditions of domestic life to have so great an impact as she expected on the minds of women. On the destruction of the family and on sexual relations, therefore, her views have remained in advance of public policy. In very conservative manner the Soviet leadership has perpetuated the monogamous family and neglected the poten-

[10] Lenin, *Collected Works,* Vol. 23 (New York, 1945), p. 300.

[11] Lenin, "A Great Beginning," *Selected Works,* Vol. 9 (London, 1937), p. 441. See also pp. 496 and 501 for later similar statements.

[12] Kollontai, *L'ouvrière et la paysanne dans la république sovietique* (Paris, 1921), p. 19.

tialities for rapid psychological change that Kollantai foresaw. Moreover, the leadership continues to supplant the economic functions of the home with public facilities for child care, eating, etc., and yet in a very nonmaterialistic manner it expects the bonds of family life to grow stronger.[13] Time (and the Chinese) may, however, reveal unexpected strength in Kollontai's position.

A second area in which Kollontai worked ardently, and even less successfully, was in the struggle to preserve the ideals of proletarian democracy, to head off or roll back the proliferation of bureaucracy and the development of a "new class." The culmination of this effort came in the great trade union controversy of 1920-1921 (see p. 127ff). In this debate she spoke for the Workers' Opposition.

Ever since the Bolsheviks had taken power some of them had felt a growing, gnawing anxiety about the course of the revolution. Many unforeseen problems had arisen and many expectations had been disappointed. In its necessary tacking and turning to meet new difficulties in these uncharted waters the Party might easily get off course. In the opinion of Kollontai this had happened most evidently and disastrously in relations with the proletariat.

Early in 1918 workers' control in industry had been abandoned as a failure, although the more idealistic Bolsheviks had retained faith in it because the chaos in industry was even more the result of other factors such as shortages of materials, war-time attrition and decay of machinery and rolling stock, inflation, and the disruption of normal channels of distribution. In its place, other quite capitalistic methods had been adopted to stimulate production. During the civil war these methods—one-man management, labor discipline, and the rest—could be tolerated as measures of desperation, but the failure of the Party,

---

[13] Cf. Khrushchev at the Twenty-second Party Congress, in *The Road to Communism, Documents of the 22nd Congress of the CPSU* (Moscow, [1962]), p. 266. Rudolf Schlesinger has made the shrewd suggestion that the retention of the private family in the Soviet Union is connected with the problem of incentives to work: the support of children in the home provides a powerful spur to the parents. Schlesinger, *The Family in the U.S.S.R.* (London, 1949), p. 405.

when the war was over, to bring the workers into active management seemed to Kollontai a betrayal of the aims of the revolution.

In the trade union controversy, she thought, the blindness of the Party leadership toward the working class became glaringly apparent. As the Workers' Opposition saw it, there were in this controversy three interrelated main issues: *first,* the class character of the régime—the effects of power, of the peasants, and of the bourgeois specialists upon the government and upon the Party—and the prospective impact upon this class character of the alternative solutions to the other issues; *second,* the uses of democracy in the Party, the government, the unions, and the proletariat in general—including (1) freedom of discussion within the Party, (2) election of officials versus appointment from above with its tendency toward bureaucracy, (3) committees versus one-man management in industry, including the problem of former capitalist managers, and (4) the militarization of labor; and *third,* how to increase production—which involved the problems of the relation of the unions to the government, their role in the economy, and the withering away of the state—and the subsidiary issue of wage policy: proletarian equality versus incentive wages.

On these issues, the Workers' Opposition held, the Party leaders had parted company with the proletariat. Neither Lenin, whose emphasis on discipline was discouraging freedom of thought, nor Trotsky, who saw efficient administration as the answer to everything, understood, in Kollontai's opinion, how their policies were carrying the Party away from the class it professed to lead. Rejecting both of their approaches, she took a more precise class position, but she identified the proletariat not with the Party but with the unions. Through the admission of ambitious intellectuals and the use of bourgeois experts, the Party had become permeated with non-proletarian elements and had come to display "bourgeois class hatred of the proletariat" as organized in the unions. Viewing the workers as helpless children who needed to spend years in "school," the Party had lost sight of the class content of the revolution, forgotten the words of Marx, and even those of its own program of 1919.

Our party not only reduces its speed but ever oftener "wisely" looks back and asks: "Have we not gone too far? Is this not the time to call a halt? Is it not wiser to be more cautious, and to avoid the daring experiments unseen in the whole of history?" . . . The workers demand a clear-cut, uncompromising policy, a rapid, forced advance toward communism.[14]

Seeking always to solve its problems by bureaucratic methods of administration and by coercion, the Party was alienating the very class it claimed to lead. The solutions were to be found, instead, in respect for the creativity of the workers, in a resurgence of the spontaneous enthusiasm of the early days of the revolution. The confidence of the proletariat could be recaptured only by increasing the democracy and the equality of the régime.

The Party interpretation of its program, relegating trade union control of industry to some indefinite future, was both sophistry and bad faith. Moreover, in Kollontai's opinion it was bad Marxism.

To debar the workers from the organization of industry, to deprive them, that is, their industrial organizations, of the opportunity to develop their powers in creating new forms of production in industry through their unions, to deny these expressions of the class organization of the proletariat, while placing full reliance on the "skill" of specialists trained and taught to carry on production under a quite different system of production,—is to jump off the rails of scientific Marxian thought. This is, however, just the thing that is being done by the leaders of our party at present.[15]

The Workers' Opposition, because of the accusation that they were anarcho-syndicalists, were not able to emphasize the connection of their position with the old Marxist expectation of the withering away of the state, but they believed that the building up of coercive state economic machinery subject to political control clearly violated that expectation. On the contrary, the economic machinery should be built up democratically from the factory committees, through the unions, to a non-political All-Russian Producers' Congress. The apparatus of the state, un-

[14] Kollontai, *The Workers' Opposition in Russia* (Chicago, n.d.), pp. 9, 13.
[15] *Ibid.*, p. 12.

encumbered with economic duties, would then be free to wither as soon as its political tasks were accomplished.

The objection that a producers' congress would not yield a Party majority was largely irrelevant, but Kollontai did not regard her proposals as being adverse to the Party's interests. On the contrary, she wanted the "purification of the party itself from the elements foreign to it," and "correction of the activity of the party by means of going back to democracy, freedom of opinion and criticism inside the party." [16] If the workers were now alienated and would send Mensheviks and Socialist-Revolutionaries to such a congress, this was the result of the undemocratic policies of the Party. "At present," stated Shliapnikov, another Opposition leader, "communists are being kicked out of the factory committees. The foundation of our unions, the factory committees, are becoming non-Party thanks to the fact, comrades, that the rights we grant to our union cells and Party cells are insignificant." [17] Show confidence in the proletariat, restore democracy—committee management, equality of wages, elections instead of appointments—and the Party would grow rapidly in strength and influence.

The attacks on the Workers' Opposition as a harmful faction pointed up the deterioration not only of democracy but also of intra-Party freedom of opinion. While accepting party discipline after decisions were made, Kollantai had to defend the principle of discussion prior to the decision.

Our "Workers' Opposition" firmly insists that it is necessary not only to reorganize the entire apparatus . . . but it is necessary to say, firmly and clearly, that a system of widely extended democracy and trust toward the masses, a guarantee of freedom of comrades' opinions, is needed, not only in times of respite but at all times, and not only on paper but in reality. For this we introduce the point about the freedom of discussion: we must recognize, owing to Party currents, the right to organize discussions, and must give an opportunity to the representatives of various currents to defend their views. . . .[18]

[16] *Ibid.*, p. 19.
[17] *Desiatyi S"ezd RKP(B), Protokoly* (Moscow, 1933), p. 392.
[18] *Ibid.*, p. 301.

So deeply committed was she to the Party and to the proletariat, however, that she had no thought of defending democracy
or freedom of opinion outside their ranks. She shared with
Trotsky the weakness of failing to see how easily the exclusion
of other parties and groups could be converted into the exclusion
of her own. The overwhelming rejection by the Tenth Party
Congress of the views of Trotsky and of Kollontai showed how
tight the central control of the Party already was and how little remained to be done to consolidate the dictatorship.

THE NEW WOMAN

Kollontai, *Novaia Moral' i Rabochii Klass* (Moscow, 1919), pp.
23-24, 27-33, trans. by Theodore Denno.

To the extent that the woman is more and more often
drawn into the cycle of society's life, she becomes a motive force
in the mechanism of the public economy, her horizon expands,
the walls of her home collapse, changing her world, and she
herself tries out and acquires interests previously completely
alien and incomprehensible to her.

Love ceases to be the mainstay of her life; love begins to take
the subordinate part it plays with the majority of men. Naturally
there are times in the life of the new woman when love and
passion occupy her soul, mind, heart and will, when all other
interests retreat into the background. At such times the modern
woman experiences sharp drama, enjoys herself, or suffers no
less than the woman of the past. But love and passion—they
are only parts of life. Its true content is that "sacred thing"
which the new woman serves—the social idea, science, profession, creativity—and this is the cause, the goal for her, for the
new woman, that is more important, valuable and sacred than
all the joys of the heart, all the delights of passion. . . .

There had to be an important revolution in the inner attitude of the woman; her internal life had to be intensely complicated; in her soul there had to be stored a rich capital of self-reliant values to prevent her from becoming bankrupt the moment her man took from her the values he had contributed. But precisely because the life of the new woman is not exhausted in love, because she has in her soul a store of curiosity and interests that make her a "man," we will become accustomed to employ new criteria in measuring the moral personality of a woman. For many centuries the merits of women were measured, not by their human qualities, not by their mental capabilities, not by their inner characteristics, but exclusively by the stock of womanly virtues that bourgeois property morality demanded of them. "Sexual purity," sexual virtue measured her worth. For the woman who transgressed the code of sexual rectitude there was no mercy. . . . But only in so far as woman stands on her own feet, ceases being dependent on father or husband, and participates side by side with men in the social struggle, will the old criteria become useless. . . .

The new woman does not renounce her "human nature," she does not run away from life, and does not dismiss those "earthly" joys that reality, sparing with its smiles, bestows. Such is the new woman: self-discipline instead of emotionality, the ability to value her freedom and independence instead of submissiveness and colorlessness, the enhancing of her individuality instead of a naive attempt to absorb and reflect the alien qualities of a "lover," the fulfilling of her right to "earthly" happiness instead of the hypocritical mask of chastity, and finally, the abolition of the degraded status of the experiences of love. There is before us not the female, the shadow of the male; there is a personality —a "Human Woman."

But who are these new single women? How has life produced them?

The new single woman is the child of the large scale capitalist system of economics. The single woman, who is not a rare phenomenon but a type produced on a massive scale, was born together with the hellish din of the factory machines and the summoning whistle of the factory workshops. Such a colossal change in the conditions of public economic activity . . . is forcing women, in the struggle for existence, to accommodate themselves to the conditions of the environment. The basic type of woman now finds herself caught up in the historic phase of economic development that mankind is now traversing. With changes in economic conditions, with the evolution of productive relations, the inner attitude of woman is also changing. The new woman as a type could only appear with the growth in the number of women wage workers. . . .

The new type of woman, inwardly self-confident, independent, free—answers to the morality that the working environment produces in the interests of its own class. The working class, for the fulfillment of its social mission, does not need a husband's servant or the housewife without personality who has only passive female virtues, but it does need "rebellious" personalities revolting against all enslavement—active, conscious members of the collective, of the class, with equal rights.

COMMUNISM AND THE FAMILY

Kollontai, *Communism and the Family* (San Francisco, n.d. [1920?]), pp. 12-15; slightly emended.

Let the working mothers be reassured. The communist society is not intending to take the children away from the parents, nor to tear the baby from its mother's breast; nor has it any intention of resorting to violence in order to destroy the family as such. No such thing! Such are not the aims of the communist society. What do we observe today? The old, former family is breaking up. It is gradually freeing itself from all the domestic labors which formerly were as so many pillars supporting the family as a social unit. Housekeeping? It also appears to have outlived its usefulness. The children? The parent-proletarians are already unable to take care of them; they can assure them neither subsistence nor education. This is the situation from which both parents and children suffer in equal measure.

The communist society therefore approaches the working woman and the working man and says to them: "You are young, you love each other. Everyone has the right to happiness. Therefore live your life. Do not flee happiness. Do not fear marriage, even though marriage was truly a chain for the working man and woman of capitalist society. Above all, do not fear, young and healthy as you are, to give to the workers' society new citizen-children. The society of the workers is in need of new working forces; it hails the arrival in the world of every newborn child. Nor should you be concerned because of the future of your child; your child will know neither hunger nor cold. It will not be unhappy nor abandoned to its fate as would have been the case in capitalist society. A subsistence ration and solicitous care are assured to the child and to the mother by the communist society, as soon as the child arrives in the world. The child will be fed, it will be brought up, it will be educated by society; but society will by no means tear the child away from such parents as may desire to participate in the education of their little ones. The society will take upon itself all material duties in the education of the child, but the paternal joys, the maternal satisfaction—these will not be taken away from those who show themselves capable of appreciating and understanding these joys." Can this be called a destruction of the family by means of violence?—or a forcible separation of child and mother?

There is no escaping the fact: the old type of family has seen its day. It is not the fault of the socialist state, it is the result of the changed conditions of life.

The family is ceasing to be a necessity of the state, as it was in the past; on the contrary, it is worse than useless, since it needlessly holds back the female workers from more productive and far more serious work. Nor is it any longer necessary to the members of the family themselves, since the task of bringing up the children, which was formerly that of the family, is passing more and more into the hands of the collectivity. But on the ruins of the former family we shall soon see rising a new form which will involve altogether different relations between men and women, and which will be *a union of affection and comradeship, a union of two equal members of the communist society,*

both of them free, both of them independent, both of them work-
ers. No more domestic "servitude" for women! No more inequality within the family! No more fear on the part of the woman
lest she remain without support or aid with little ones in her
arms if her husband should desert her. The woman in the communist state no longer depends on her husband but on her
work. It is not her husband but her robust arms which will
support her. There will be no more anxiety as to the fate of
her children. The state of the workers will assume responsibility
for these. Marriage will be purified of all its material elements,
of all money calculations, which constitute a hideous blemish
on family life in our days. Marriage is henceforth to be transformed into a sublime union of two souls in love with each other,
each having faith in the other; this union promises to each working man and to each working woman, simultaneously, the most
complete happiness, the maximum of satisfaction which can be
the lot of creatures who are conscious of themselves and of the
life which surrounds them. *This free union,* which is strong in
the comradeship with which it is inspired, *instead of the conjugal
slavery of the past—that is what the communist society of to-
morrow offers to both men and women.* Once the conditions of
labor have been transformed, and the material security of working women has been increased, and after marriage such as was
performed by the church—that so-called indissoluble marriage,
which was at bottom merely a fraud—after this marriage has
given place to the free and honest union of men and women
who are lovers and comrades, another shameful scourge will also
be seen to disappear, another frightful evil which is a stain on
humanity and which falls with all its weight on the hungry
working woman: prostitution.

This evil we owe to the commodity economy, to the institution of private property. Once the latter has been abolished,
the trade in women will automatically disappear.

Therefore let the women of the working class cease to worry
over the fact that the family as at present constituted is doomed
to disappear. They will do much better to hail with joy the dawn
of a new society which will liberate woman from domestic servitude, which will lighten the burden of motherhood for woman,

and in which we shall see disappear the most terrible curse, the scourge of prostitution.

The woman who is called upon to struggle in the great cause of the liberation of the workers—such a woman should know that in the new State there will be no more room for such petty divisions as were formerly understood: "These are my own children; to them I owe all my maternal solicitude, all my affection. Those are your children, my neighbor's children; I am not concerned with them. I have enough to do with my own." Henceforth the worker-mother, who is conscious of her social function, will rise to a point where she no longer differentiates between yours and mine; she must remember that there are henceforth only *our* children, children of communist, working Russia.

The worker's state has need of a new form of relation between the sexes. The narrow and exclusive affection of the mother for her own children must expand until it embraces all the children of the great proletarian family. In place of the indissoluble marriage based on the servitude of woman, we shall see rise the free union, fortified by the love and the mutual respect of the two members of the workers' state, equal in their rights and in their obligations. In place of the individual and egotistic family, there will arise a great universal family of workers, in which all the workers, men and women, will be, above all, workers, comrades. Such will be the relation between men and women in the communist society of tomorrow. This new relation will assure to humanity all the joys of so-called free love ennobled by a true social equality of the mates, joys which were unknown to the commercial society of the capitalist régime.

THE WORKERS' OPPOSITION

Kollontai, *The Workers' Opposition in Russia* (Chicago, n.d. [1921?]), pp. 5-7, 10-11, 20, 30-31, 36-40.

Behind the Workers' Opposition there stand the proletarian masses, or, to be more exact, the Workers' Opposition is the class-uniform, class-conscious and class-consistent part of our industrial proletariat—that part of it which considers it impossible to substitute the great creative power of the proletariat in the process of building communist economy by the formal label of the dictatorship of the working class.

The higher we go up the ladder of the Soviet and party hierarchy, the fewer adherents of the Opposition we find. The deeper we penetrate into the masses the more response do we find to the program of the Workers' Opposition. This is very significant, and very important. This must be taken into consideration by the directing centers of our party. If the masses go away from the "upper" elements; if there appears a break, a crack, between the directing centers and the "lower" elements, that means that there is something wrong with the "upper" elements, particularly when the masses are not silent, but think, act, move, and defend themselves and their own slogans. . . .

Before making clear what the cause is of the ever widening break between the "Workers' Opposition" and the official point of view held by our directing centers, it is necessary to call attention to two facts:

(1) The Workers' Opposition sprang from the depths of the industrial proletariat of Soviet Russia, and it is an outgrowth not only of the unbearable conditions of life and labor in which seven millions of the industrial workers find themselves, but is also a product of vacillation, inconsistencies, and outright deviations in our soviet policy from the clearly expressed class-consistent principles of the communist program.

(2) The Opposition did not originate in some particular center, was not a fruit of personal strife and controversy, but, on the contrary, covers the whole extent of Soviet Russia and meets with a resonant response.

At present there prevails an opinion that the whole root of the controversy arising between the Workers' Opposition and the numerous currents noticeable among the leaders consists exclusively in the difference of opinions regarding the problems that confront the trade unions. This, however, is not true. The break goes deeper. Representatives of the Opposition are not always able to clearly express and define it, but as soon as some vital question of the reconstruction of our republic is touched upon, controversies arise concerning a whole series of cardinal economic and political questions.

For the first time the two different points of view, as they are expressed by the leaders of our party and the representatives of our class-organized workers, found their reflection at the Ninth Congress of our party, when that body was discussing the question: "Collective versus personal management in the industry." At that time there was no opposition from a well formed group, but it is very significant that collective management was favored by all the representatives of the trade unions, while opposed to it were all the leaders of our party, who are accustomed to appraise all events from the institutional angle. They require a great deal of shrewdness and skill to placate the socially heterogeneous and the sometimes politically hostile aspirations of the different social groups of the population as expressed by proletarians, petty owners, peasantry, and bourgeoisie in the person of specialists, and pseudo-specialists of all kinds and degrees.

Why was it that none but the unions stubbornly defended the principle of collective management, even without being able to adduce scientific arguments in favor of it; and why was it that the specialists' supporters at the same time defended the "one man management"? The reason is that in this controversy, though both sides emphatically denied that there was a question of principle involved, two historically irreconcilable points of view had clashed. The "one man management" is a product of the individualist conception of the bourgeois class. The "one man management" is in principle an unrestricted, isolated, free will of one man, disconnected from the collective.

This idea finds its reflection in all spheres of human endeavor —beginning with the appointment of a sovereign for the state and ending with a sovereign director of the factory. This is the supreme wisdom of bourgeois thought. The bourgeoisie do not believe in the power of a collective body. They like only to whip the masses into an obedient flock, and drive them wherever their unrestricted will desires.

The working class and its spokesmen, on the contrary, realize that the new communist aspirations can be attained only through the collective creative efforts of the workers themselves. The more the masses are developed in the expression of their collective will and common thought the quicker and more complete will be the realization of working class aspirations, for it will create a new, homogeneous, unified, perfectly arranged communist industry. *Only those who are directly bound to industry can introduce into it animating innovations.*

Rejection of a principle—the principle of collective management in the control of industry—was a tactical compromise on behalf of our party, an act of adaptation; it was, moreover, an act of deviation from that class policy which we so zealously cultivated and defended during the first phase of the revolution.

Why did this happen? How did it happen that our party, matured and tempered in the struggle of the revolution, was permitted to be carried away from the direct road in order to journey along the round-about path of adaptation, formerly condemned severely and branded as "opportunism" [?] . . .

If we begin diligently to search for the cause of the arising controversy in our party, it becomes clear that the party is passing through a crisis which was brought about by *three fundamental causes.*

The first main basic cause is the distressful environment in which our party must work and act. The Russian Communist Party must build communism and carry into life its program: (1) In the environment of complete destruction and breakdown of the economic structure. (2) In the face of the never diminishing ruthless pressure of the imperialist states and white guards.

(3) To the working class of Russia has fallen the lot to realize communism, create new communist forms of economy in an economically backward country with a preponderant peasant population, where the necessary economic prerequisites for socialization of production and distribution are lacking, and where capitalism has not been able as yet to complete the full cycle of its development (from the unlimited struggle of competition of the first stages of capitalism to its highest form—to the regulation of production by capitalist unions—the trusts).

It is quite natural that all these factors hinder the practical realization of our program (particularly in its essential part—in the reconstruction of industries on the new basis) and inject into our soviet economic policy *diverse influences and a lack of uniformity.*

Out of this basic cause follow the two others. First of all, the economic backwardness of Russia and the domination of the peasantry within its boundaries create that diversity, and inevitably detract the practical policy of our party from the clear-cut *class direction, consistent in principle and theory.*

Any party standing at the head of a heterogeneous soviet state is compelled to consider the aspirations of peasants with their petty-bourgeois inclinations and resentments towards communism, as well as lend ear to the numerous petty bourgeois elements, remnants of the former capitalists in Russia, to all kinds of traders, middlemen, petty officials, etc., who have very rapidly adapted themselves to the soviet institutions and occupy responsible positions in the centers, appear in the capacity of agents of different commissariats, etc. No wonder that Zurupa, the People's Commissar of Supplies, at the Eighth Congress quoted figures which showed that in the service of the Commissariat of Supplies there were engaged 17 per cent of workers, 13 per cent of peasants, less than 20 per cent of specialists, and that of the remaining, more than 50 per cent were "tradesmen, salesmen, and similar people, in the majority even illiterate." (Zurupa's own words.) In Zurupa's opinion this is a proof of their democratic composition, even though they have nothing in common with the class proletarians, with the producers of all wealth, with the workers in factories and mills.

These are the elements—the elements of petty-bourgeois widely scattered through the soviet institutions, the elements of the middle class with their hostility toward communism, and with their predilections toward the immutable customs of the past, with resentments and fears toward revolutionary acts,—these are the elements that bring decay into our soviet institutions, breeding there an atmosphere *altogether repugnant to the working class.* They are two different worlds and hostile at that. And yet we in Soviet Russia are compelled to persuade both ourselves and the working class that the petty-bourgeoisie and middle classes (not speaking of well to do peasants) can quite comfortably exist under the common motto: "All power to the soviets," forgetful of the fact that in practical everyday life the interests of the workers and those of the middle classes and peasantry imbued with petty-bourgeois psychology must inevitably clash, rending the soviet policy asunder, and deforming its clear-cut class statutes.

Besides peasant-owners in the villages and burgher elements in the cities, our party in its soviet state policy is forced to reckon with the influence exerted by the representatives of wealthy bourgeoisie now appearing in the form of specialists, technicians, engineers, and former managers of financial and industrial affairs, who by all their past experience are bound to the capitalist system of production. They can not even imagine any other mode of production but only that one which lies *within the traditional bounds of capitalist economics.*

The more Soviet Russia finds itself in need of specialists in the sphere of technique and management of production, the stronger becomes the influence of these elements, foreign to the working class elements, on the development of our economy. Having been thrown aside during the first period of the revolution, and being compelled to take up an attitude of watchful waiting or sometimes even open hostility toward the soviet authorities, particularly during the most trying months (the historical sabotage by the intellectuals), this social group of brains in capitalist production, of servile, hired, well-paid servants of capital, acquire more and more influence and importance in politics with every day that passes. . . .

What does the statement of the Workers' Opposition stand for, and how does the latter understand the part that is to be played by the trade unions, or, to be more exact, by the industrial unions at the present moment? "We believe that the question of reconstruction and development of the productive forces of our country may be solved only if *the entire system of control over the people's economy* is changed." (From Shliapnikoff's report, Dec. 30th). Take notice, comrades,—"only if the entire system of control is changed." What does it mean? "The basis of the controversy,"—goes on the report,—"revolves around the question: by what means during this period of transformation can our Communist party carry out its economic policy—whether by means of workers organized into their class unions, or—over their heads—by bureaucratic means, through canonized functionaries of the state." The basis of the controversy is namely this: whether we shall realize communism through workers or over their heads, by the hands of soviet officials. And let us, comrades, ponder whether it is possible to attain and build a communist economy by the hands and creative abilities of the scions from the other class, who are imbued with their *routine of the past?* If we begin to think as Marxians, as men of science, we shall answer categorically and explicitly—no. . . .

It is well known to every Marxian that reconstruction of industry and development of creative forces of a country depend on two factors: on the development of technique, and the efficient organization of labor by means of increasing productivity and finding new incentives to work. This has been true during every period of transformation from a lower stage of economic development to one higher throughout all the history of human existence.

In a labor republic the development of productive forces by means of technique plays a secondary role in comparison with the second factor, that of the efficient organization of labor, and creation of a new system of economy. . . .

Who can, however, develop the necessary creativeness and keenness in this sphere? Whether bureaucratic elements, heads of the soviet institutions or the industrial unions whose members in their experience in regrouping workers in the shop come across creative, useful, practical methods that can be applied in the process of reorganizing the entire system of the people's economy? The Workers' Opposition asserts that administration of the people's economy is the trade unions' job, and, therefore, it is more Marxian in thought than the theoretically trained leaders.

The Workers' Opposition is not so ignorant as to wholly underestimate the great value of the technical progress or the usefulness of technically trained men. It does not, therefore, think that after electing its own body of control over the industry it may safely dismiss the Supreme Council of National Economy, the central industrial committees, economic centers, etc. Not at all. And yet the Workers' Opposition thinks that it must assert its own control over these technically valuable administrative centers, give them theoretical tasks, and use their services as the capitalists did when they hired the technicians in order to carry out their own schemes. Specialists indeed can do valuable work in developing the industries; they can make the workers' manual labor easier; they are necessary, indispensable, as science is indispensable to every rising and developing class, but the bourgeois specialists, even with the communist label pasted on, are powerless physically and too weak mentally to develop productive forces in a non-capitalist state; to find new methods of labor organization, and develop new incentives for intensification of labor. In this, the last word belongs to the working class—to the industrial unions. . . .

Bureaucracy, as it is, is a direct negation of mass self-activity, and, therefore, whoever accepts the principle of attracting the masses to an active participation in directing the affairs as a basis for the new system in the labor republic cannot look for good or bad sides in bureaucracy, but must openly and resolutely reject this useless system. Bureaucracy is not a product of our misery, as Comrade Zinovieff tries to convince, neither is it a reflex of "the blind subordination" to superiors generated by militarism, as others assert. This phenomenon has a deeper cause. It is a by-product of the same cause that explains our policy of double-dealing toward the trade unions: the growing influence in the soviet institutions of those elements which are hostile in spirit not only to communism, but to the elementary aspirations of the working masses as well. . . .

Fear of criticism and freedom of thought by combining together with bureaucracy quite often produce ridiculous forms.

There can be no self-activity without freedom of thought and
opinion, for self-activity manifests itself not only in initiative,
action, and work, but in *independent thought* as well. We are
afraid of mass-activity. We are afraid to give freedom to the
class activity, we are afraid of criticism, we have ceased to rely
on the masses, hence, *we have bureaucracy with us.* That is why
the Workers' Opposition considers that bureaucracy is our enemy,
our scourge, and the greatest danger for the future existence of
the Communist party itself.

In order to do away with the bureaucracy that is finding its
shelter in the soviet institutions, *we must first of all get rid of all
bureaucracy in the party itself.* That is where we face the immediate struggle against this system. As soon as the party—not
in theory but in practice—recognizes self-activity of the masses
as the basis of our state, the soviet institutions will again automatically become those living institutions which are destined to
carry out the communist project, and will cease to be the institutions of red tape, laboratories for dead-born decrees, into which
they had very rapidly degenerated. . . .

The second condition, fulfillment of which with all determination is insisted upon by the Workers' Opposition, is the *expulsion
from the party* of all non-proletarian elements. The stronger becomes the soviet authority the greater is the number of middle
class, and sometimes even openly hostile elements, joining the
party. The elimination of these elements must be complete and
thorough, and those in charge of it must take into account the
fact that all the most revolutionary elements from the non-
workers had joined the party during the first period of the October revolution. The party must become a *workers' party* for
only then will it be able to repeal with force all the influences
that are being brought to bear upon it by the petty-bourgeois
elements, peasants, or by the faithful servants of capital—the
specialists.

The Workers' Opposition proposes to register all members who
are non-workers and who had joined the party since 1919, and
reserve for them the right to appeal within three months from

the decisions arrived at, in order that they might join the party again.

At the same time it is necessary to establish "a working status" for all non-working elements which will try to get back into the party, by providing that every applicant to membership in the party must have worked a certain period of time at manual labor under general working conditions before he becomes eligible for enrollment into the party.

The third decisive step toward democratization of the party is the elimination of all non-workers' elements from all the administrative positions; in other words, the central, provincial, and county committees of the party must be composed so that workers closely connected with the working masses would have the preponderant majority therein.

In close connection with this point of the Oppositions' demands stands the other of converting all our party centres, beginning from the Central Executive Committee and including the provincial county committees, from institutions taking care of routine, every day work, into *institutions of control over the soviet policy*. . . .

The fourth basic demand of the Workers' Opposition is this: *the party must reverse its policy to the elective principle.*

Appointments must be permissible only as exceptions, but lately they began to prevail as a rule. Appointments are very characteristic of bureaucracy, and yet at present they are a general, legalized and well recognized daily occurrence. The procedure of appointments produces a very unhealthy atmosphere in the party, and disrupts the relationship of equality among the members by rewarding friends and punishing enemies as well as by other no less harmful practices in our party and soviet life. Appointments lessen the sense of duty and responsibility to the masses in the ranks of appointees, for they are not responsible to the masses. This condition makes the line of division between the leaders and the rank and file members still sharper.

Every appointee, as a matter of fact, is beyond any control, for the leaders are not able to watch closely his activity while the masses cannot call him to account, and discharge him if necessary. As a rule every appointee is surrounded by an atmosphere of officialdom, servility and blind subordination, which infects all subordinates, and discredits the party. . . .

BIBLIOGRAPHY

Works by Kollontai

Communism and the Family (New York, 1920). Also other editions.
La femme nouvelle et la classe ouvrière (1918), trans. by Marie Bor (Paris-Brussels, 1932). Also in German as *Die neue Moral und die Arbeiterklasse* (Berlin, 1920).
Free Love, trans. by C. J. Hogarth (London, 1932). Also as *Red Love* (New York, 1927).
A Great Love, trans. by Lily Lore (New York, 1929). Contains also "Sisters" and "The Love of Three Generations."
La juventud comunista y la moral sexual (1922; Madrid, 1933, and Barcelona, 1937).
–*The Peasant and Working Woman in Soviet Russia* (Moscow, 1921). Also in French and German.
–*Wenn nützt der Krieg?* (Bern, 1918).
The Workers' Opposition in Russia (Chicago, 1921?).

Biography

Palencia, Isabel de, *Alexandra Kollontay* (New York, 1947).

Exposition

Bell, Daniel, "One Road from Marx: On the Vision of Socialism and the Fate of Workers' Control, in Socialist Thought," *World Politics*, Vol. 11 (July, 1959), pp. 491-512.
Bryant, Louise, *Mirrors of Moscow* (New York, 1923). Contains chapter, "Madame Alexandra Kollontai and the Women's Movement."
Chaplet, Pierre, *La famille en Russie soviétique* (Paris, 1929).
Daniels, Robert V., *The Conscience of the Revolution. Communist Opposition in Soviet Russia* (Cambridge, Mass., 1960).
–*Labour Conditions in Russia* (London, 1921). Published by the Russian Economist.

Riazanov, D. (Goldendach, D. B.), *Communisme et mariage* (Paris, 1929).

Schapiro, Leonard, *The Origin of the Communist Autocracy. Political Opposition in the Soviet State—First Phase, 1917-1922* (London, 1955).

Schlesinger, Rudolf, *The Family in the U.S.S.R. Documents and Readings* (London, 1949).

Sverdlov, G. M., *Legal Rights of the Soviet Family; Marriage, Motherhood and the Family in Soviet Law* (London, 1945).

Tomski, M., *Abhandlungen über die Gewerkschaftsbewegung in Russland* (Hamburg, 1921). Through 1918.

7

Bukharin:
Marxism as Equilibrium Economics

BUKHARIN is less widely known than the revolutionary triumvirate, Lenin, Trotsky, and Stalin, and as a theorist he was less
voluntaristic and perhaps narrower; but so much of his career
was spent in opposition, and so many of his ideas, good and
bad, failed of adoption, that evaluation is difficult. He had a
university education (rare among the Bolsheviks), and from
1918 to 1929, although younger than his colleagues, he was a
valued member of the Politbureau of the Bolshevik Party. Lenin,
in his testament, described him as "the most valuable and biggest
theoretician" and "the favorite of the whole party" although there
was "something scholastic in him (he never has learned, and
I think never has fully understood, the dialectic)." [1]

Born into the intelligentsia in Moscow, Nikolai I. Bukharin
(1888-1938) led a student demonstration at the university there
in 1905, and continued his activities as a subversive organizer
and propagandist until 1911 when, after a third arrest, he joined
the émigrés. Supporting Lenin against the "social chauvinists"
during the war, he worked in all the Scandinavian countries and
in New York. As an editor and a writer he early demonstrated
his independent grasp of the questions of theory then occupying
the Marxists.

[1] Quoted in Leon Trotsky, *The Real Situation In Russia* (New York,
1928), p. 322.

After the February revolution he returned to Russia via Japan
and Siberia. Established in the executive committee of the Moscow soviet, he was named to the Bolshevik Central Committee
and became editor of *Pravda*. In Petrograd he led his first fight,
brief and bitter, against Lenin himself, for rejection of the German ultimatum. He insisted on Lenin's own previous program
of converting the imperialist war into an international civil war
against the exploiting classes (see p. 98). This apparently un-
realistic and untenable position he took not as a patriotic Russian
but as an optimistic international Marxist. Retreating into the
depths of Siberia before the German aggression, if need be, the
revolution, he believed, would both rally the support of the Russian people and exert irresistible influence upon the proletariat
abroad to rise up and throw off its yoke of militaristic capitalism.
This somewhat reckless plan, ready to risk even loss of the power
already obtained in the interest of international revolution,
seemed to him and to almost half the Central Committee to flow
logically from the then accepted belief that the weak proletariat
of Russia ultimately must depend, not on the petty-bourgeois
peasants, but upon the workers of western Europe. In 1918
Bukharin's position, and not Trotsky's, was the one consistent
with the theory of permanent revolution.

At the same time Bukharin and Osinski attacked a second
aspect of Party policy. Lenin's use of "bourgeois experts" as
managers of factories, his reintroduction of piece rates, incentive
wages, and labor discipline, and his approaches to foreign capitalists (see p. 61) provoked a sense of betrayal among the more
idealistic and doctrinaire socialists. The "Left Communists" led
the attack on this program in the name of the revolution. Bukharin
argued that, just as at Brest-Litovsk the international revolution
was abandoned to save Russia, so, in such programs, socialism
was being abandoned in favor of production. He denounced them
in prophetic words he was later to forget:

The introduction of labour discipline in connection with the restoration of capitalist management of industry . . . threatens to enslave
the working class; it will rouse discontent among the backward elements as well as among the vanguard of the proletariat. In order to
introduce this system . . . the Communist Party would have to rely

on the petty bourgeoisie, as against the workers, and in this way would ruin itself as the party of the proletariat.[2]

When the Third International was started, in March, 1919, he was elected to its executive committee, and in 1926 he succeeded Zinov'ev as its chairman. No longer hoping for immediate uprisings abroad, he was, after 1923, a firm advocate of the "popular front" tactic (including support for the Kuomintang, over the opposition of Trotsky) on the ground, borrowed from Lenin, that attack on imperialism, and not direct striving for socialism, was the first objective and could be led by a bourgeois group.

Well trained in Marxian economics, he was a firm advocate also of "War Communism." As early as November, 1917, he favored the immediate nationalization and planning of industry, whereas Lenin wanted agreements with the old captains of industry, if possible, and planning limited at first to electrification. With Trotsky he supported compulsory labor, calling it the "self-organization of the working class," and, again like Trotsky, wanted to make the labor unions part of the state machinery (see p. 128ff).

Nevertheless, when the N.E.P. was adopted in 1921, the task of fitting it into Marxist economic theory fell to Bukharin. This he did with such success that he became popularly identified as the theorist of free trade and later as the defender of the kulaks. In this conversion from a "Left Communist" to a "rightist" he parted company with Trotsky, supporting the "troika" of Zinov'ev, Kamenev, and Stalin. Later he again cooperated with Stalin in the elimination of Zinov'ev and Kamenev, reaching thus the pinnacle of power. Yet when Stalin decided to abandon the N.E.P. Bukharin opposed him. So deeply was he convinced that, in a socialist state, even the bourgeoisie will evolve toward socialism, that he sacrificed his personal position of leadership in trying to defend the revolution against the dangers of Stalin's new policies.

During this dispute Stalin removed him from the Politbureau, from the editorship of *Pravda,* and from the presidium of the

[2] Bukharin in *Kommunist,* No. 1, p. 8, quoted in Lenin, " 'Left-Wing' Childishness and Petty-Bourgeois Mentality," *Selected Works,* Vol. 7 (London, 1937), p. 373.

Comintern. Thus disciplined, he capitulated, but was not restored to his old offices. In 1934 he became editor of *Izvestia*, and from February, 1935, he worked with Stalin, Radek, and others on the new constitution of the Soviet Union, which was adopted in November, 1936.

Stalin's suspicion regarding his reliability did not diminish, however. He was arrested as a "rightist" in March, 1937, charged with "fiendish crimes," and tried with others a year later. In a spirited defense as his own attorney, instead of confessing, he flatly denied conspiring against Lenin or the Soviet Union. He explained his opposition to Stalin in terms of "a retardation of reflexes" and "a dual psychology," and said that "this was due not to the absence of consistent thought, but to the objective grandeur of socialist construction." He was convicted and shot.

Like those of Trotsky, the career and thought of Bukharin illustrate the ideological turmoil within the Bolshevik leadership and the changing role of an "opposition." As an economist he understood and depended upon economic forces more than most of his colleagues, and tended more toward schematic, deterministic analyses that led him to extreme positions. A few examples may indicate both Bukharin's importance as a theorist and the reversals of position possible within Bolshevik orthodoxy.

In wartime debates on the "national question," which decided the Bolshevik attitude toward the national minority groups of the tsarist empire, Bukharin proposed the "self-determination of the workers" in place of the "self-determination of nations," which he believed unrealizable under capitalism and unnecessary under socialism. Lenin, however, insisted on the latter formula, supporting even bourgeois revolts against colonial or feudal regimes; and through his influence in 1917 independence was granted as a Christmas present to a bourgeois government in Finland. By January, 1918, however, a new bourgeois government was stamping out the soviets in the Ukraine, and Stalin, moving against it as Commissar of Nationalities, changed the Party line to "self-determination, not of the bourgeoisie, but of the laboring masses."

On a more abstract plane, Bukharin in 1916 analyzed the Marxist attitude toward the state, finding that Marx frequently wanted to "blow up" the state while Engels usually wanted to "seize" it. He concluded that the objective of the revolution was not to capture the bourgeois state machinery but to smash it, and that the "withering away" must apply to the proletarian state which would replace it. Lenin promptly attacked him, reiterating that the revolution must use the "existing machinery of government." This interchange, however, led Lenin to a reinvestigation of the problem, to consequent agreement with Bukharin, and to the writing of his *State and Revolution* (1917).[3] In this process he revised his attitude toward the soviets, returning to his (and Trotsky's) earliest opinion that the soviet was "the embryo of the provisional revolutionary government." The result was his determination not to try to capture the existing provisional government, but to build a new one on the basis of the soviets—the theory put into practice after the October revolution.

Attempting to explain the origin of the war and the patriotism that had wrecked the Second International, Bukharin advanced in 1915 the thesis that under capitalism the elimination of competitors eventually results in the formation of giant national combines of cooperating capitalists, "and the State Authority executes the will of these directors of banks and syndicates." The competition within nations is thus transformed into a much fiercer competition among nations. In this process the proletariat of each country appears temporarily to share with its bourgeoisie the advantages of victory in this competition and of the exploitation of colonial peoples. The upper strata of the proletariat are thus bribed away from revolution, and capitalism becomes stabilized as State Capitalism. This thesis was largely incorporated into Lenin's *Imperialism* the following year (see p. 72ff), although Lenin differed from Bukharin in finding the anarchy of capitalism within the separate countries less completely eliminated by state capitalism and the class war less dependent upon international war. With slight modification in Lenin's direction, however, Bukharin repeated this analysis in his and Preobrazhenski's *A B C of Communism* (1920), a very widely disseminated text-

[3] For Stalin's distortion of this episode see "The Right Deviation in the C.P.S.U.(B.)" in his *Works*, Vol. 12 (Moscow, 1955), pp. 72-83.

book, and went on to develop it in 1927 in *Capitalist Stabilization and Proletarian Revolution.*

This doctrine of the stabilization of capitalism transferred the
Marxian expectation of ever more severe economic crises from
the national arena to the arena of international conflict. It formed
the basis for his popular front policy in the Comintern and
provided an economic foundation for Stalin's theory of socialism
in one country. As the competition of capitalism took the form
of political and military competition among nations, Bukharin
held, periods of relative stability could be expected to follow
the periods of war. During and immediately after the wars the
tide of revolution would rise, but in periods of receding crises,
such as existed after 1923, that tide would ebb. At such times
revolution in western Europe should not be looked for and could
not be induced. Abroad, Communists should cooperate with left-
ist parties of reform; at home, Russia would have to build socialism with her own resources, would have to depend upon her
own peasantry and not upon the proletariat of the West.

The revolution, therefore, could not afford the long-anticipated
desertion of the petty-bourgeois peasants. The N.E.P. was correct, and Bukharin embraced it heartily and became its leading
apologist, seeing in returning prosperity an indication that the
kulaks and private businessmen were becoming reconciled to the
workers' government. Pursuing their own economic interests,
these elements, he believed, would expand production and thus
would provide the surplus needed for industrialization. He therefore advanced the slogan "Enrich yourself!" which went too far
for most of his colleagues. This was not, in his mind, an abandonment of socialism but the shortest route to it, because the
new capitalists would also become inextricably enmeshed in the
networks of credit, markets, and supplies directly controlled by
the state. Holding the "commanding heights" of the government,
the cities, foreign trade, etc., the socialists need not fear the
kulaks and nepmen. They would gradually "grow into socialism." Thus Bukharin came to the doctrine of the withering away
of the class struggle.

Prosperity in the countryside, he believed, was a precondition for prosperity in the cities, because "the development of industry is dependent on the development of agriculture." The peasant market for consumer goods was the "direct driving force" behind industrial production. On the other hand, it was also a limitation upon the rate of expansion of industry because all elements of the national economy must be kept in equilibrium and agriculture could not expand rapidly. "The reverse side of the upsetting of the necessary economic proportions is the shaking of the *political* balance of the country."

In order to ensure the most advantageous possible course of social reproduction, of the systematic growth of socialism (the most free of crises), and consequently the relations of class forces in the country most advantageous to the proletariat, there must be the most correct possible combination of the fundamental elements of national economy. These must balance one another, must be so arranged as best to fulfil their purpose; an active influence must be exercised on the process of economic life and the class struggle.[4]

This theory of equilibrium was so similar to classical economic thought that Bukharin was branded by the left opposition as a "physiocrat" of the "Soviet Manchester school." Like Marx, however, he found the difference between capitalism and socialism precisely in the impossibility of attaining such an equilibrium in the anarchy of capitalistic production, while under socialism

the conditions for the correct co-ordination of the various spheres of production, or, in other words, the conditions of *dynamic economic equilibrium,* may be ascertained. This is the essential part of the task of working out a *plan of national economy* which resembles more and more the balance of the entire national economy, a consciously drawn up plan, which is at the same time a prognosis and a directive.[5]

In practice this meant a rate of growth of industrial production geared to the rate of growth in agriculture. Bukharin wanted "the fastest possible tempo of industrialization," but the support of the peasants must not be sacrificed.

As the N.E.P. progressed and the Party seemed to favor the

[4] Bukharin, "Observations of an Economist," *International Press Correspondence,* Vol. 8, No. 75 (Oct. 26, 1928), p. 1377; slightly emended.
[5] *Ibid.,* No. 73 (Oct. 19, 1928), p. 1329.

capitalists more and more, the advocates of rapid industrialization, especially the Trotskyists, became increasingly dissatisfied. Before the end of 1921, Preobrazhenski, who had supported Trotsky and Bukharin at the Tenth Party Congress (see p. 128), had criticized the working of N.E.P. and wanted the Party to develop the state farms and to encourage collective farms "as the basic form of the transformation of a peasant economy into a socialist economy." [6] The most original of the opposition economists, he expounded his views in 1924 as the doctrine of "primitive socialist accumulation." [7] This phrase was parallel to Marx's "primitive capitalist accumulation," in which the early capitalists gathered the resources for industrialization not by "abstinence" but by the plunder of colonies, by piracy and the slave trade, by the enclosure of the common lands, and other political techniques before they were in a position to expand industry by exploiting the workers. Having come to power in a nation not adequately industrialized, the socialists also had to accumulate capital, but they could not yet depend upon the socialized industrial sector of the economy to do its own accumulating through competitive prices, nor could they exploit the workers as capitalism had done. Private accumulation, contrary to Bukharin's view, did not contribute to socialist accumulation; it did the opposite: it strengthened the class enemy. The socialized sector must, therefore, by taxes and by monopoly prices draw resources in great quantity from the private sector. This meant exploiting the peasantry, although Preobrazhenski withdrew the impolitic word "exploiting" and spoke of "an exchange of the smaller quantity of labor of one economic system or country for the greater quantity of labor of another economic system or country." [8]

He expected resistance from the private sector, and more than anyone else he realized the bitterness of the antagonism that real industrialization would engender among the peasants. Whereas Bukharin wanted to retain the support of the peasants,

[6] Theses printed in V. I. Lenin, *Sochineniia*, 3rd ed., Vol. 27 (Moscow, 1932), p. 446.
[7] The phrase itself he credited to V. M. Smirnov. Preobrazhenski, *Bumazhnye Den'gi v Epokhu Proletarskoi Diktatury* (Tiflis, 1921), p. 71.
[8] Preobrazhenski, *Novaia Ekonomika*, 2nd ed. (Moscow, 1926), p. 102.

Preobrazhenski thought this impossible. He was haunted by the expectation that the rich peasants, strengthened by the N.E.P., would join with world capitalism in a new economic, political, and military drive to crush the Bolsheviks. In a single socialist country capital could be accumulated, he thought, but the dangers from the peasantry were so great that he continued to feel the need for revolution abroad, the "necessity to break out of our socialist isolation, not only for political but also for economic reasons."[9]

Russia, Preobrazhenski believed, could compensate for the absence of revolution in Europe only by rapidly building up the numbers and strength of its own proletariat. Industrialization must be pushed with much greater speed. The great contest between capitalism and socialism, both internally and internationally, would ultimately be decided by the productive efficiency and wealth of the two systems.[10] Between the revolution and the achievement of socialism there was a period in which the incentives and controls of capitalism were lost and the rationalized economy of socialism was not yet attained, a period of great danger to the workers' state from both internal and external enemies. "To run quickly through this period, swiftly to reach the moment when the socialist system will unfold all its natural advantages over capitalism—this is a question of life and death for the socialist state."[11] It should be rushed through by central planning, by rapid industrialization with emphasis on heavy industry, and by collectivization of agriculture. Failure of the Party to do these things would retard production, alienate both workers and peasants, and endanger the revolution itself. He believed, however, that primitive socialist accumulation was an objective law of the economy whose logic would force the adoption of his policies in spite of the subjective desire of the

[9] Preobrazhenski, "Khoziaistvennoe Ravnovesie v Sisteme SSSR," *Vestnik Kommunisticheskoi Akademii*, Vol. 22 (Moscow, 1927), p. 70.

[10] This was an anticipation of Khrushchev's view (see p. 257). Preobrazhenski saw the United States as the pace-setting capitalist country, and held that primitive socialist accumulation would be necessary within the socialist camp until the United States was overtaken, even if revolution occurred in western Europe.

[11] Preobrazhenski, *Novaia Ekonomika*, p. 99.

leadership to continue its encouragement of the capitalist sector
of the economy.[12]

Preobrazhenski, irreconcilable toward the N.E.P., stood close
to Trotsky in the political wilderness as long as economic conditions appeared to improve. The Fifteenth Party Congress (1927)
found it to be "incorrect" to demand "a maximum pumping over
of means from the sphere of peasant economy into the sphere of
industry," but also incorrect "to exclude the villages in the recruitment of means toward the construction of industry." [13] The building of socialized industry remained a primary objective, nevertheless, and Bukharin had agreed to a differential between the
prices paid by and those received by the farmers, a differential
deliberately designed to drain funds from agriculture to support
industrialization, but not at the rate advocated by Preobrazhenski.
By the end of 1927, however, an acute shortage of grain again
developed in the cities, the growers having held it off the market
in an effort to force the government to raise its fixed price, to
revise the differential. On a foraging mission through Siberia
Stalin became convinced that Bukharin's policy of conciliating
the peasants had broken down, that "so long as there are kulaks,
so long will there be sabotage of the grain procurements." He
had strongly supported Bukharin, but now he turned to the left,
toward Preobrazhenski and Trotsky. He resolved to push the
collectivization of agriculture and planned industrialization. Collective farms with modern machinery had long been a generally
accepted Bolshevik answer to the inefficiencies of separate small
holdings and an essential step toward socialization; but their
introduction had heretofore been thought to depend upon the
prior development of industry to supply them with machines.
Similarly, an economic plan had always been accepted in theory,
but Lenin's scepticism had blighted the idea and the N.E.P.
had taken a different road. Now Stalin proposed both to plan
and to collectivize in earnest.

Against Stalin stood Bukharin, the Politbureau's leading econ-

[12] Cf. *Ibid.*, p. 222. For a more complete summary of Preobrazhenski's
views see Alexander Erlich, *The Soviet Industrialization Debate, 1924-1928*
(Cambridge, Mass., 1960), pp. 31-59.

[13] *Piatnadtsatyi S"ezd VKP(B), Stenograficheski Otchet* (Moscow, 1935)
p. 1248.

omist, convinced that these tactics, by alienating the peasants, would destroy the revolution. Confident in the automatic adjustments of a free market, he believed the "sabotage" was a reflection of errors in price policy and would rapidly disappear if a freer play of prices were permitted. He proposed the purchase of grain abroad, even if this made it necessary to reduce purchases of machinery, rather than a resort to forced collections of grain from resisting peasants. He was sure that the socialized sector of the economy was so much stronger than the sector held by private capital that the latter would gradually succumb in the unequal competition, and that, therefore, the civil peace need not be broken.

For over a year they argued, but in the meantime forced collections were ordered. The peasants responded by refusing to plant beyond their own needs—confirming in Stalin's mind his idea that the class struggle, far from withering away, was becoming more intense. In a similar situation Lenin had yielded to the peasants in the N.E.P.; Stalin began the "offensive against the kulaks," with its deportations, starvation, and bloodshed. Moreover, the tempo of industrialization became hectic, far beyond anything previously advocated. Preobrazhenski, reconciled with the leadership in 1929 on the basis of Stalin's left turn, was soon a conservative arguing on economic grounds against the more extreme planners. He fell behind because he did not accept, as did Stalin, Lenin's concept of the priority of politics over economics—he was not prepared for "revolution from above."

Had Bukharin's view prevailed, the price in human suffering that Russia paid for collectivization and industrialization, and the reputation for ruthlessness that Stalin earned, might have been reduced. But who knows if, had it followed Bukharin's policy, the Soviet Union would have had sufficient time to industrialize before war came?

In any event, his view still seems to have some viability. The pace of collectivization in east European agriculture has none of the desperate urgency of Stalin's drive. China's policy of toleration toward its "national bourgeoisie" is based on thinking similar to Bukharin's. In international terms, Krushchev's doctrine of "peaceful coexistence" is an application toward world capitalism of Bukharin's policy toward capitalists within the Soviet Union. These policies are based, as was Bukharin's, on confidence in the strength already held by the communists and in the competitive superiority of socialism over capitalism. It was Bukharin's misfortune that in his day socialism held only one underdeveloped country against the "capitalist encirclement," and that Stalin did not believe capitalism could be defeated by economic competition alone.

[THE WITHERING AWAY

OF THE CLASS STRUGGLE]

Bukharin, *Put' k Sotsializmu i Raboche-Krestianskii Soiuz* (Moscow-Leningrad, 1925), trans. by Eugene Hardy. Numbers in brackets refer to pages of this edition.

The more the national economy as a whole will progress, and the more quickly our state industry will grow, the more powerful will be the support for those strata of the peasantry whose standard of living will catch up to the prosperous top village class, but who at the same time will grow not at the price of exploitation, not at the price of someone else's labor, but by virtue of the improvement of the means of carrying on their economy and the unification of the efforts of a series of peasant households through cooperative organization which will, subsequently, be transformed more and more into a collective type of farming. In this manner the basic network of our cooperative peasant organizations will consist of cooperative cells not of a kulak but of a "laboring" type, cells growing in the system of our nation-wide organs and becoming thus links of a single chain of socialist economy. On the other hand, kulak cooperative nests will, of course, through banks, etc., grow in this same system; but they will be to an important degree foreign bodies, similar, for example, to concession businesses. What will become of this kind of kulak cooperation later on? Let us suppose, for example, that we have a credit association headed by kulaks having full authority. This kulak cooperative, if it wishes to prosper, must of necessity be linked, like all the others, with the state economic organs; it, for example, will deposit its free cash in our banks to receive a fixed interest rate. Even if their own banking organizations should arise of a sort similar to the cooperative, nevertheless, inevitably they would have to be tied with the powerful credit establishments of the proletarian state, having at their disposal the basic credit resources of the country. In any event there will be nowhere for the kulak and the kulak organizations to go, for the general pattern of development in our country *has already been determined as the system of the proletarian dictatorship, and that dictatorship's economic organizations are already in a significant stage of development.* If the kulak willy-nilly becomes a depositor in our banks, if he willy-nilly begins to be tied by a whole series of relations to our economic organs, then he inevitably will be squeezed into the defined framework. . . . To suppose that kulak farms will grow faster than the entire state industry would require supposing something directly opposed to reality. In the development of our national economy as a whole the already established *large-scale industry*, which is found wholly in the hands of the proletarian state, *will develop fastest of all.* This growth itself will determine everything and will serve as a sufficient guarantee that the kulak or the prosperous peasant, employing several agricultural workers, will have to submit to our general system. . . .

In our country at present there are three classes of which two classes—the workers and peasants—are the basic classes of our society and of our system, but the third class—the bourgeoisie (kulaks, nepmen, etc.)—exists only so far as it is "tolerated" to a certain degree and on certain conditions "of collaboration" with the working class and the peasantry. . . . From that position, which the working class now occupies as the ruling class, emerges a whole series of fundamental conclusions for the policy of the workers' state. The basic and main conclusion, . . . is the following: *in the period of capitalism the task of the working class was the overthrow of society, [while] in the conditions of*

*the proletarian dictatorship the task of the working class is not
the overthrow of the system of the proletarian dictatorship and
the new society being created, but, on the contrary, all-out support of it, the strengthening of it, the guidance of it.* From this,
in their turn, other conclusions inevitably follow, namely conclusions concerning the very form of the class struggle in our society.
The class struggle, as we know perfectly well, does not end and
does not die out at once, but will continue for a very, very long
time, as long as the division into classes does not wholly disappear forever. But even now we see how the question concerning the main path of the class struggle and the question of the
forms of that struggle inevitably change. In a capitalistic society,
where the concern of the proletariat is in trying to overthrow
that society, the constant task consists of every kind of aggravation and kindling of the class struggle until that class struggle
assumes the fiercest of its forms, namely the form of civil war
and armed struggle on the part of the toiling masses against the
ruling capitalist regime. . . . The party of the working class
within the capitalistic system is the party of civil war. The position is completely reversed when the working class takes power
into its hands, basing itself on the broad strata of the peasantry.
In so far as the dictatorship of the bourgeoisie is smashed, and
in its place has already arisen the dictatorship of the proletariat,
the task of the working class becomes the strengthening of that
dictatorship and the defense of it against any sort of encroach-
ment. The party of the working class under such circumstances
becomes *the party of civil peace,* i.e., it requires *submission to
the working class* by the former ruling classes, strata and groups;
it requires civil peace from them and the working class now
prosecutes and punishes all disturbers of this civil peace, all
conspirators, saboteurs—in a word, all who interfere in the matter of peaceful construction of the new society.

. . . In accordance with this there appears also a change in
the very *forms* of the class struggle. We shall illustrate this with
a series of examples. We shall take, first of all, relations with
the bourgeoisie. Under capitalism we extended the development
of the struggle against it right up to the use of armed force.
Of course, if the bourgeoisie attempted now to come out against

us with arms in hand just as it did in 1917, 1918, 1919, etc.,
we would immediately apply our armed force and make short
work of such an opponent in a way that it would deserve. But
now we are in a completely different position. The strength of
the Soviet power and its stability are so evident that the complete
hopelessness of launching any active and sharp political struggle
against the new system is perfectly obvious to the bourgeois
strata of our society (the nepmen). Willy-nilly, these strata will
have to make their peace with the existing order of things. Economic activity is permitted to this bourgeoisie within definite
limits. In general we do not now prohibit private trade; we
permit a series of private enterprises; we do not seal up private
shops any more; we give these circles, therefore, a substantial
possibility of existence. Does this mean that the class struggle
has ended? No, by no means. But this struggle has very essentially
changed its form. It continues to be conducted by the working
class: our legislation, guaranteeing the workers' interests, ensuring the definite rights of trade unions, forcing the private
owners to pay insurance rates, depriving these owner circles of
electoral rights in the political organs of power, etc.—this is a
new form of class struggle. The system of taxation, by which
the income and profits of capitalistic enterprises are assessed,
taxation of the bourgeoisie such as is not found in a single [other]
country,—this is precisely a new form of class struggle. The competition from state industry, state trade, cooperatives—this again
is a new form of class struggle. When our state gives special
privileges and advantages to cooperative enterprises, when this
state especially finances, i.e., subsidizes by monetary means, the
cooperative organizations, when it through legislation provides
broad rights for them,—all this is a new form of class struggle.
If in the process of competition in the market place state industry, commerce, cooperatives gradually force out the private
owner—that is a victory in the class struggle, but a victory not
in a mechanical clash of strength, not through the help of armed
seizure, but wholly within the new framework which did not
exist earlier, which in the capitalist regime was completely unthinkable for the working class and the peasantry.

Exactly in this manner *the form of the class struggle changes*

in the countryside. True, here and there the class struggle in the
countryside breaks out in its former manifestations, in which the
aggravation is usually caused by kulak elements. . . . However,
such instances usually occur where the local soviet apparatus is
still weak. . . . Several years ago the main form of the class
struggle in the countryside was direct administrative pressure
on the top rural class: at first constant confiscation and requisition among the more prosperous peasantry and the transfer of
this confiscated property to the use of the poverty-stricken (in
the period of the Committees of the Poor). . . . While in the
city from the very beginning of the new economic policy we
permitted economic activity by the private traders and owners,
in the country, as a matter of fact, the rural bourgeoisie were
confronted with obstacles which severely restricted this activity
or made it practically impossible. At present (summer, 1925)
we are on the point of changing this system and we are giving
great freedom of movement to the rural bourgeois elements. But
this does not in the least mean that we are ceasing to carry on
the class struggle against the rural bourgeoisie. This does not
in the least mean that we refuse to support the poor and middle
strata against the exploiting strata. We only are changing the
form of our class struggle against the petty rural capitalists. We
are turning to a new form of this class struggle, more expedient
under the present circumstances.

In the city we do not at all seal up the shops of the private
trader; we allow his "work." As a result we have a great revival
of commodity circulation in the entire country. And this trader
also becomes a buyer in our state industry and in our wholesale
state trade; on the other hand he sells our wares in the various
corners of our country—so long as our own state and cooperative
commodity distribution network is very weak. By this, of course,
he obtains commercial profit or a share of that commercial profit.
But, nevertheless, independently of his will he furthers—thanks
to the general revival of commodity circulation and the growth
of our state industry and growth of our state trade—the quicker
turnover of the general capital of the country including the
capital of our state industry and our state trade. For that reason
the machine of production itself revolves faster, the process of

accumulation [of capital] goes faster, and for that reason the power of our state industry increases faster—that fundamental base, fundamental foundation, or socialist society. On the other hand, by taxing the bourgeois strata we at the same time obtain additional means which go into our state treasury. . . . Such a policy is thus a class policy on our part. This class policy has as its aim the support of the toilers against the remains of the exploitative world. But the form of this policy, the form of that class struggle, as we see, is completely different from that of simply sealing up the shops of the private traders. . . .

Now we can also transfer such a policy to our countryside, persuading our rural workers not to practice the system of direct administrative "suppression" and "pressure" with respect to the more prosperous strata of the countryside. But again, does this mean that here we wish to give up the class struggle with this agricultural bourgeoisie? Not at all. Just as we do not give up the class struggle with the city bourgeoisie (the nepmen) when we permit it to occupy itself with its "interests," so the corresponding policy in the country by no means signifies the giving up of the struggle. We are only changing its form. Against the shops of the rural traders we have to employ not the organs of direct coercion and violence, but our excellent cooperative shops. Against the rural usurer who lends money at outrageous interest rates, or who rents his horse to the horseless peasant under bondage conditions, we should bring forward first and foremost a battery of our credit associations, an excellent organization of cheap cooperative credit and help on the part of the state power. Our merchandise should be better and cheaper than the merchandise of the private trader, our credit loans should be larger and much cheaper than the loans which the usurer gives, the cooperative should trade better and be more accommodating to the local rural demand than private trade. These are the weapons we should bring to the front in our struggle with the exploiting elements of the countryside.

It is possible, however, to ask oneself: is it correct to transfer to the countryside such a policy which is suitable for the city? Of course, for this question there is an important and extremely substantial difference between the conditions of the economic struggle in the city and the conditions of that economic struggle in the countryside. In the city we already have "the commanding heights" more or less well organized and working well; this, of course, is our heavy artillery in the struggle with the city nepmen. But where are such "commanding heights" in the countryside? . . . Will conditions not be such that the kulak elements will show themselves to be immeasurably stronger economically than the remaining peasantry and, by the same token, will they not be able to whip through us and consequently find themselves the directors and masters of all rural life?

To this quite valid question we must give this answer: *the commanding height in relation to the rural bourgeoisie is the proletarian city.* It is impossible to imagine a state of affairs wherein the countryside develops completely independently of the city. We have already said that with the growth of productive forces in the nation the influence of the city will be more and more decisive in the development of our agriculture. And the core of this city, its proletarian industry, its banking system, its legislation, etc., all this is a "turning of the face to the country," i.e., all this serves as the most powerful support to the middle and poor elements of the countryside, support against its kulak strata.

The connecting link between the proletarian city and the toiling countryside is *the cooperative system* which stands exactly at the junction between this city and countryside, itself embodying above all that economic bond between the working class and the peasantry, the strengthening of which is the basic task of the working class and our party. . . . Step by step state industry and state trade, uniting with the rural cooperative system, which, in turn, being extended from trade to production itself, will force out private capital: industrial, trade, and usurious. The peasant farms will be drawn into the general state-cooperative organization and will be absorbed through the various forms of cooperative organizations, primarily the producers' cooperatives, exactly as the petty artisans and handicraftsmen here [in the city] will be drawn in and absorbed. . . .

The partial development of capitalistic relations in the countryside, which will occur in the immediate years ahead, will of necessity, however, also call forth other forms of the class struggle besides the purely economic struggle, i.e., besides the struggle of various economic forms against each other. . . . The struggle between the kulak and the farm laborer involves questions concerning the conditions of hired labor (length of the work day, wages, forms of payment for work, general conditions of work, etc., etc.). But here also the class struggle of the farm laborers, who are a part of the working class now in power, has forms entirely different from those forms of the class struggle which had been peculiar to the capitalistic regime. This is because the farm laboring group, which on the kulak farm finds itself, so to say, under its master, at the same time, as a part of the ruling class, stands over him even though individual farm laborers have not realized this. In what does this fact find its expression? In that the entire legislation of our country is aimed at the exploiters and each of its paragraphs defends the interests of the workers, in that the trade unions of the working class and the trade unions of the farm laborers enjoy by law recognized rights such as they do not have in a single capitalist country, in that the courts of our country punish employers for violation of these laws, etc., etc. For this reason the class struggle of the farm labor group in the final analysis is not at all directed towards ruining the farm of the kulak and dividing it among themselves. . . . The farm labor group carries on its class struggle in other forms, forcing proper conditions of work through its trade organizations and through its state power, the Soviet power, and it has recourse to the courts of its class if it is necessary to curb the farm owners. . . . [48-59]

. . . In the final analysis the development of market transactions destroys itself because, in so far as through these market transactions . . . the state industry and cooperatives absorb all the remaining economic forms and gradually squeeze them out to the end through the market, to that extent the market itself will sooner or later die out, for all will be replaced by state-cooperative distribution of manufactured products.

In that way our conception of the development towards socialism has been changed to a significant extent, but these changes do not express in the slightest a retreat from the proletarian policy; on the contrary, they express the accounting of a colossal revolutionary experiment. For the first time we found in the new economic policy the correct combination between the private interests of the petty producer and the general interests of socialist construction. *The new economic policy is not a betrayal of the proletarian line but the only correct proletarian policy.* That has now become clearer than clear. [65-66]

[THE ALLIANCE OF

WORKERS AND PEASANTS]

Bukharin, *Put' k Sotsializmu i Raboche-Krestianskii Soiuz* (Moscow-Leningrad, 1925), trans. by Eugene Hardy.

Thus, in the proletarian dictatorship in relation to the peasantry there is the sort of tie which can be designated by the word alliance (*soiuz*). In this alliance, as we already know, leadership belongs to the working class organized into the state power.

In order to present the situation as it is, quite clearly and exactly, a strict distinction between two things is necessary: between the collaboration *in society* on the one hand and on the other hand the collaboration *in power*, i.e., *the division* of this power between the classes. The collaboration and even the alliance, an alliance strong and inviolable, is not as yet a division of power. Between the working class and the peasantry there is complete collaboration in society, there is the relationship of a union. This means that the state industry and the peasant economy should help one another; this means that the working class and the peasantry fight together against the landlords and capitalists if they campaign against the soviet republics; this means that the working class and the peasantry fight together on the economic front against private capital. But this still does not mean that we have a *division of power*, that we do not have a dictatorship of the working class but a dictatorship of two classes, i.e., both the working class and the peasantry. Well then, this is an alliance between whom? Between the working class, organized as the state power, and the peasantry; in the state power itself the peasantry is not a participant, but this workers' power is found in the alliance with the peasant class. Why is that so, and why under our conditions, i.e., under the conditions of the transition of society to socialism, is it necessary to have the dictatorship of one class only, i.e., of the proletariat? This is necessary because *only* the proletariat presents that kind of social strength which can quite consciously and firmly lead all of society to socialism. . . . But the dictatorship of the proletariat, i.e., the organization of the proletariat into the state power, is also the organization of *leadership* in relation to the broad masses of the peasantry. However, the working class by no means sets as its aim an eternal "kingdom of the proletariat," it by no means sets as its goal the perpetual existence of the proletarian dictatorship, nor its own existence as being forever that of a dominant class.

The working class sets as its real goal, towards which it slowly but steadfastly goes and leads after it all society, *the transformation of wide strata of people* and, first of all, the transformation of *the peasantry itself*, its re-education in the socialist manner, its continual development and elevation to that level, material, economic, and cultural-political, at which are found the most advanced strata of the proletarian population. . . . The difference between classes will disappear more and more. And in that way the widest strata of the peasantry, "remaking its own nature," will blend with the workers of the city; the dictatorship of the proletariat, as of a separate class, will more and more die away.

It is also possible to a certain extent to say of the bourgeoisie in capitalistic society that it, the bourgeoisie, was the *leader* of all society, its foremost and most educated class; but leadership by the bourgeoisie and leadership by the proletariat differ from each other in the sharpest, deepest, most fundamental manner. For the development of capitalistic society, at the head of which

stood the bourgeoisie, led to the difference between the bourgeoisie on the one hand [and] the working class and the peasantry on the other, increasing and becoming more and more
aggravated. It is impossible even to think that within the framework and limits of the capitalistic system the working class and
the peasantry could achieve equality with the bourgeoisie in
their material position, the level of their life, their education,
their social position. This would contradict the most fundamental basis of bourgeois society. On the contrary, the very
essence of this bourgeois society lies in its sharpest division into
classes . . . : the bourgeoisie in the countries where it rules
has a monopoly (i.e., exclusive ownership) not only of the
means of production, factories, mills, railroads, etcetera; it has
a monopoly not only over the state power, into which it allows
no one; but it also has a complete actual monopoly over higher
education, over the press (newspapers, magazines), over science,
etc. . . . The bourgeoisie never set and could not set as its
aim the uplifting, systematically and steadily, of the new peoples'
strata towards a cultural life, for that would mean the downfall
of its own power.

The working class pursues exactly the opposite, a completely
different policy. Its goal is not the perpetuation of the same
relationship between classes: its goal is the overcoming of class
differences, the abolition of those class differences by re-educating
the broad masses of the people; for that [purpose] it utilizes all
the means at its disposal and all the might of its state power.
The basis of that transformation is the transformation of the
economic relationships of society, the development of that society
on the path to socialism. . . . Attracting a larger and larger number of non-party peasants to soviet work and helping them in
that work to re-educate themselves, to grow, to transform their
nature, to acquire habits necessary for the affairs of public
administration, to acquire an understanding not only of local
but also of nationwide goals, etc., the working class by the same
token gradually begins to wipe out the boundary between itself
and the foremost strata of the peasantry. Through these foremost
strata other strata, new groups of peasants, will pass to a higher
stage and will lift themselves to a new life, active and aware;

and, little by little, on the basis of the proletarian leadership, the peasantry will coalesce with the working class in its customs, habits, thoughts, hopes and aims. Likewise, through the co-operative the peasant economy will coalesce with the state economy of the proletariat and, in the final analysis, having remade itself, will flow into a single planned socialist economy, just as in all walks of life the peasantry will grow together with the working class. . . . This will also be the destruction (dying away) of the proletarian dictatorship itself as "not wanted." But to arrive at that goal a persistent and firm policy is necessary, which, bearing that goal in mind, powerfully directs the course of social development. That is why at the present stage of development it is necessary to preserve in full the only actual guarantee of the correct policy, which guarantee is the system of the proletarian dictatorship, resting on the peasantry and being in an alliance with that peasantry. [70-74]

BIBLIOGRAPHY

Works by Bukharin

La bourgeoisie internationale et son apôtre Karl Kautsky (Paris, 1925). Also in German.
Capitalist Stabilisation and Proletarian Revolution (Moscow, 1926).
Le chemin du socialisme et le bloc ouvrier-paysan (Paris, 1925). Also in German.
The Economic Theory of the Leisure Class (1919; New York, 1927).
Historical Materialism, A System of Sociology (1921; New York, 1925).
Imperialism and World Economy (1915; New York, 1929).
Der Imperialismus und die Akkumulation des Kapitals (Berlin, 1927). Reprinted from *Unter dem Banner des Marxismus*, Vol. 1 (March, July, 1925), pp. 21-63 and 231-290.
"Der imperialistische Raubstaat," *Jugend-Internationale*, No. 6 (December 1, 1916), pp. 7-9. Trans. in part in Olga H. Gankin and Harold H. Fisher, eds., *The Bolsheviks and the World War* (London, 1940), pp. 236-239.
"The New Economic Policy of Soviet Russia," in Lenin, V. I., *et al.*, *The New Policies of Soviet Russia* (Chicago, 1921).

"New Forms of the World Crisis," *Labour Monthly,* Vol. 10 (September-October, 1928), pp. 533-543 and 610-618.

"Notes of an Economist" (1928), in Bertram D. Wolfe, *Khrushchev and Stalin's Ghost* (New York, 1957), pp. 295-315.

Die Oekonomik der Transformationsperiode (1920; Hamburg, 1922).

–*Les problèmes fondementaux de la culture contemporaine* (Paris, 1936).

–*Proletarische Revolution und Kultur* (Hamburg, 1923).

La question paysanne (Paris, 1925). Also in German.

"Ueber die Theorie der permanenten Revolution," in *Um den Oktober* (Hamburg, 1925), pp. 179-211. Also in French in *Cahiers du Bolchevisme,* Vol. 1 (March 1, 1925), pp. 886-900.

Also numerous articles in English in the periodical, *International Press Correspondence.*

Biography

–Flaherty, John E., "The Political Career of Nicholas Bukharin," unpublished Ph.D. dissertation, New York University, 1954.

Exposition

Beelen, Ernst, "Nikolaj Bucharin," *Deutsche Republik,* Vol. 2 (December 23, 1927), pp. 378-380.

Daniels, Robert V., *The Conscience of the Revolution. Communist Opposition in Soviet Russia* (Cambridge, Mass., 1960).

————, "The Left Opposition in the Russian Communist Party to 1924," unpublished Ph.D. dissertation, Harvard University, 1951.

Erlich, Alexander, "Preobrazhenski and the Economics of Soviet Industrialization," *Quarterly Journal of Economics,* Vol. 64 (February, 1950), pp. 57-88.

————, *The Soviet Industrialization Debate, 1924-1928* (Cambridge, Mass., 1960).

Kaufman, Adam, "The Origin of 'The Political Economy of Socialism.' An Essay on Soviet Economic Thought," *Soviet Studies,* Vol. 4 (January, 1953), pp. 243-272.

Knirsch, Peter, *Die ökonomischen Anschauungen Nikolaj I. Bucharins* (Berlin, 1959).

Lenin, V. I., " 'Left-Wing' Childishness and Petty-Bourgeois Mentality" (May, 1918), in his *Selected Works,* Vol. 7 (New York, 1943), pp. 351-378.

————, "The Nascent Tendency of 'Imperialist Economism'," *Bolshevik*, No. 15 (August 15, 1929). Reprinted in Olga H. Gankin and Harold H. Fisher, eds., *The Bolsheviks and the World War* (Stanford and London, 1940), pp. 228-236.

————, "Once Again on the Trade Unions, the Present Situation and the Mistakes of Comrades Trotsky and Bukharin" (January, 1921), in his *Selected Works*, Vol. 9 (New York, 1943), pp. 40-80.

————, "The Trade Unions, the Present Situation and the Mistakes of Comrade Trotsky" (December, 1920), *ibid.*, Vol. 9, pp. 3-27.

Lukács, Georg, Review of Bukharin's *Theorie des historischen Materialismus*, in *Archiv für die Geschichte des Sozialismus und der Arbeiterbewegung*, Vol. 11 (1923), pp. 216-224.

–Nelson, Daniel J., "Views of N. Bukharin on the Future Communist Society." Unpublished Certificate essay, Russian Institute, Columbia University, 1952.

Stalin, Joseph, "The Right Deviation in the C. P. S. U. (B.)" (1929) in his *Problems of Leninism* (Moscow, 1953), pp. 287-373.

Vandervelde, Émile, *La psychologie du socialisme*, in the *Mémoires du Academie Royale de Belgique*, Classe des Lettres, Collection in 8°, 1er série, tome 23, fasc. 3 (Brussels, 1928).

8

Stalin:

Revolution from Above

STALIN's pose as Lenin's mere lieutenant has tended to divert attention from his own contributions to political thought. Moreover, the violence with which he sometimes achieved his ends has obscured the theoretical bases of these ends and the lines by which they were connected with the thinking of Marx and Lenin. Stalin was, in fact, one of the most practical and one of the least abstract of the molders of Marxist theory in Russia, and in his hands Marxism became more realistic and more dynamic than even Lenin had made it.

Born in the Caucasus, the son of a religious but illiterate mother and a drinking and perhaps sadistic shoemaker father, both former serfs, Stalin (Joseph V. Dzhugashvili, 1879-1953) was a good student in the church school of his home town, Gori (Georgia). At fourteen he earned a scholarship to the Orthodox theological seminary in Tiflis, a school known as a hotbed of Georgian nationalism. He later claimed that "the harsh intolerance and Jesuitical discipline" of this institution helped to convert him to Marxism. In the city itself he met a number of socialist leaders and joined, in 1898, the moderate Marxist "Third Group," with which he worked for several years (between escapes and exiles) as an organizer and propagandist among working men. Already an organization man, he was drawn to Lenin after the Party Congress of 1903 by the latter's emphasis on a tightly disciplined movement of professional revolutionaries.

In 1905, when Lenin was almost alone in the Party, Stalin

attracted his attention as the leader of a Leninist minority of the Georgian Social Democrats. In this role he first entered the national arena, attending the Bolshevik conference at Tammerfors late in 1905 and the Stockholm unity congress early the next year. Returning to the Caucasus he continued to work with Lenin in arranging armed "expropriations," an activity which, disapproved by the Party, strengthened the ties between them.

Stalin was coöpted to the Bolshevik Central Committee in 1912 as a second Georgian member at the instance of Lenin, who was then leaning heavily upon the Caucasian party in his struggle with the Mensheviks (see p. 54). Seeing in Stalin an able and yet not too independent follower, Lenin asked him to write on the important question of national minorities within Russia, an assignment for which his origin seemed to qualify him. The result was "The National Question and Social Democracy" (see p. 219), which stated essentially Lenin's position in favor of a right of self-determination but not a practice of secession. Lenin also commissioned him to launch the publication of *Pravda*, but, finding its resulting tone too conciliatory, Lenin soon thought it necessary to relieve him tactfully of these editorial duties.

Arrested and exiled again in 1913, Stalin spent the war years in Siberia, whence he was able to return to Petrograd in March, 1917, three weeks ahead of Lenin. As the only member of the Central Committee present he resumed the editorship of *Pravda* and leadership of the Bolsheviks in the city soviet. He also presided at a nationwide conference of Bolsheviks convened in connection with the conference of provincial soviets called by the Petrograd soviet. Here he sought, through compromise rather than through any resolution of differences, to hold together the radical wing led by Molotov and the conservatives of Kamenev. Young Molotov, as editor of *Pravda* before Stalin's arrival, had enunciated the provocative slogan, "All power to the soviets," but Stalin avoided either accepting or rejecting it. He did not, as Trotsky and Lenin were to do, think of the soviet of Petrograd as the focus of power, although he was already on its executive committee. Still hampered by Marx's expectation of two distinct stages of revolution, which had been underlined by Lenin's re-

jection of the theory of permanent revolution, he continued to
think in terms of an extended period of bourgeois politics. The
Bolsheviks, he thought, should use their new freedom to extend
their influence among the peasants. Additional soviets should
be formed in the provinces and affiliated in an All-Russian soviet.
But even a national soviet would not be sufficient; only a constituent assembly would "enjoy authority in the eyes of all sections of society." He thus moved toward the broadly based party
of Axelrod and Martov; he even opened negotiations with the
Mensheviks. To this conservative leadership, preparing neither a
practical nor a theoretical basis for an early bid for power,
Lenin's "April Theses" provided a radical transfusion of ideas.

In May Stalin was elected to a new Party Central Committee
of nine. In July the suburbs overflowed in a spontaneous uprising for which the Bolshevik leadership was not ready but
which it could not repudiate since its propaganda had identified
the Party with such movements. Soon all the more conspicuous
leaders were either under arrest or in hiding, and Stalin again
attained relative importance as the liaison between the Central
Committee and Lenin, who had taken cover. He was also dele-
gated, along with four others, to represent the Bolsheviks on
the Military Revolutionary Committee of the Petrograd soviet;
but, since Lenin still thought that the seizure of power should
be made in the name of the Party rather than of the soviet (as
the Committee was planning—cf. p. 125), his lieutenant seems
to have done little of the real work of the uprising.

To Lenin, however, he appeared dependable if not brilliant,
and he continued in the inner circle even after the October
revolution. He was appointed Commissar of Nationalities, which
gave him great influence in the affairs of the minority peoples,
and from 1919 he also served as Commissar of the Workers' and
Peasants' Inspectorate, which exercised "control from below"
over the whole bureaucracy. In addition he was the only member
of the Politbureau who was also a member of the Orgbureau,
the organ in charge of the distribution of party personnel. In
April, 1922, he was appointed General Secretary of the Party,
a position which gave him leverage on all Party organs. He
instituted a practice of appointment from above, in place of

election from below, for secretaries in the lower echelons of the Party, with the result that by 1924 his appointees controlled the Party and his position was impregnable.

At Lenin's death Stalin's stature was not yet recognized by his colleagues and he was able, by party manipulation and by skillful exploitation of circumstances, to eliminate the leading Old Bolsheviks before they realized the extent of his ambition or of his ability. With the centralized power thus achieved he industrialized Russia at a hectic pace, collectivized her agriculture, repulsed Hitler's invasion, and extended communism in eastern Europe. He also impressed the dark qualities of his personality upon his government, his Party, and the international Marxist movement, leaving to his successors a heritage of unnecessary antagonisms in addition to the unavoidable conflicts with the capitalists.

Stalin's earliest contribution to Bolshevik theory was his solution to the land problem. The Marxists, well aware both of the inefficiencies of small scale farming and of the individualistic, uncooperative psychology of the small landowner, had long regarded redistribution of the land as a step that would reinforce capitalism and would convert the peasants from dissatisfied revolutionaries into tenacious counterrevolutionaries. They knew, however, that the peasantry constituted a useful auxiliary in the struggle against the tsar's régime, and one whose demands for land could not be ignored. The Socialist Revolutionaries believed that redistribution as private holdings could be largely avoided through strengthening the village communes, so they advocated "socialization" of the land—collective possession by the communes and abolition of all private ownership. Against this Stalin argued that it would "combat the further *development* of capitalism and turn back the wheel of history. . . . Science, however, tells us that the victory of socialism depends upon the *development* of capitalism, and whoever combats this development is combating socialism." [1] Lacking faith in the commune, the Marxists could not escape from the dilemma by that path.

[1] Stalin, "The Agrarian Question," in his *Works*, Vol. 1 (Moscow, 1952), p. 222.

The Mensheviks proposed "municipalization"—transference of ownership to the local (*volost* or *uezd*) governments, which would redistribute the use but not ownership to the tillers. Lenin, the centralist, advocated nationalization instead, and redistribution on a rental basis. Many party members, however, feared that this would strengthen the bourgeoisie, which was expected to dominate the central government.

At the Stockholm Party Congress, in 1906, Stalin spoke against all three solutions, socialization, "municipalization," and nationalization, one of the few times he opposed Lenin openly. He proposed that the peasants' own seizures and redistributions of land as private property be sanctioned, and their support for the revolution thereby assured, at least for a time. This policy he defended with a very literal reading of Marx: the coming revolution was to be capitalistic, not socialistic, and the small peasant holdings would rapidly succumb to capitalistic agriculture, leaving a rural proletariat and hastening the next, the socialistic, revolution. The Menshevik-controlled Congress adopted municipalization, but Lenin retained his doubts about this policy and at the Bolshevik-led London Congress (1907) he secured the adoption of his and Stalin's programs as alternatives. In the revolution of 1917 both were, officially, rejected; the central government decreed socialization, the Socialist Revolutionary program, but in the countryside the peasants largely carried out Stalin's plan. This history of ambivalence of both theory and practice within the Party may have increased the peasants' later opposition to collectivization, but it did accomplish the Party's purpose of insuring temporary support. No Marxist had yet imagined that the peasants in general could be induced to support the revolution permanently.

Stalin's second theoretical venture, "The National Question and Social Democracy" [2] (1913), on a subject then being hotly debated, was written against the Bund, the Jewish Marxist organization. In it he attempted a difficult reconciliation of the right of nations to self-determination with international working-class solidarity. He accepted the former, even "the right to complete

[2] This was later published separately, and is now known as *Marxism and the National Question.*

secession"; but he accepted it only as a means to "combat the policy of national oppression" employed by the tsar against minority peoples, a means which, he implied, would not be necessary after the revolution. Regarding nationalism as "essentially a bourgeois movement," he denied that Marxists should support movements for secession: "The obligations of Social-Democracy, which defends the interests of the proletariat, and the rights of a nation, which consists of various classes, are two different things." [3] Such movements, and even demands for national (ethnic, as distinguished from territorial) cultural autonomy, were pernicious since they retarded and handicapped proletarian organization on internationalist lines. For Russia, therefore, "the only correct solution is *regional* autonomy," not separation, because "it does not divide people according to nations, it does not strengthen national barriers; on the contrary, it breaks down these barriers and unites the population in such a manner as to open the way for division of a different kind, division according to classes." [4] Then he concluded, with characteristic intolerance, "There is no middle course: principles triumph, they do not 'compromise'." After he became Commissar of Nationalities he permitted Finland to secede, but he forcibly prevented the secession of Georgia and Ukraina. The former, and not the latter, marked a deviation from his 1913 position.

Stalin's most momentous contribution to Marxist theory, however, was his doctrine of socialism in one country. This doctrine was not new to socialism. It had been enunciated in 1879 by Georg von Vollmer in an article, "The Isolated Socialist State"; [5] but Stalin could not lean upon Vollmer since he had been a right-wing socialist, an adherent of Bernstein. He leaned instead on Lenin who had foreseen such a situation in 1915 when he opposed the "United States of Europe" slogan: "Uneven economic and political development is an absolute law of capitalism. Hence, the victory of Socialism is possible first in a few or even

[3] Stalin, *Marxism and the National Question,* in his *Works,* Vol. 2 (Moscow, 1953), pp. 321-322.

[4] *Ibid.,* p. 375.

[5] Georg von Vollmer, "Der isolirte socialistische Staat," *Jahrbuch für Sozialwissenschaft und Sozialpolitik,* Vol. 1 (1879), pp. 54-75.

in one single capitalist country." [6] Lenin had nevertheless retained his hope of international working class cooperation.

When the Bolsheviks abandoned Marx's plan of revolution
based on a majority of proletarians and accepted instead Trotsky's
notion that backward Russia could lead the way to socialism
(see p. 122), they based their seizure of power on an expectation
of support from two sources: the proletariat of western Europe
and the peasantry of Russia. Since the latter were regarded as
petty-bourgeois and were expected to desert the cause, revolution in the West was considered essential. In the beginning
Stalin shared that conviction, but he was, perhaps, less of an
internationalist by temperament than his fellows. Unlike the
other leading Bolsheviks, he had spent little time outside of
Russia and had little feeling of familiarity with or confidence
in European revolutionary movements. On the other hand, his
early belief that peasant support could be earned by party approval of their seizures of land caused him to place less emphasis
than did Lenin or Trotsky upon the proletariat of the West.

He saw his scepticism of the West confirmed by the collapse
of the Second International in 1914 and by the failure of the
Western revolutionaries, in spite of their vast numbers, to achieve
a single success comparable with the October revolution. The
failure of Trotsky's propaganda campaign at Brest-Litovsk was
no surprise to him. Voting with Lenin for the German treaty,
he summed up the view which continued to guide him: "There
is no revolutionary movement in the West, there is no evidence
of a revolutionary movement. It exists only in potential, and in
our practical activities we cannot rely merely on potentials." [7]
The subsequent failures of revolt in Germany, in Hungary, and
elsewhere served to strengthen him in his negative opinion. Even
for Bukharin, one of the most inveterate internationalists, these
failures led to the economic doctrine that capitalism had entered
a period of stabilization, and that, therefore, the tide of revolution was ebbing. Stalin concluded by 1924 that six years was

[6] V. I. Lenin, "The United States of Europe Slogan," in his *Selected Works*, Vol. 5 (London, 1936), p. 141.

[7] Minutes of the Central Committee, January 11, 1918, in Stalin, *Works*, Vol. 4 (Moscow, 1953), p. 28.

enough of waiting for leadership by the Western proletariat, and that Russia both could and must proceed alone to the building of socialism. Stalin was careful, however, to give this drastic change of policy an appearance of continuity and to relate it to Lenin's early controversies with Trotsky. Magnifying Lenin's "law" of the uneven development of capitalism, and combining it with Bukharin's stabilization theory,[8] he provided respectable background for an idea which was psychologically appealing to revolutionaries-turned-bureaucrats who were tired of looking westward. Reviving Lenin's polemics against "permanent" revolution, he altered their emphasis: where Lenin had been thinking of a majority revolution and therefore stressed peasant support rather than revolution in the West, Stalin interpreted him as denying the dependence of Russia upon the West. He thus armed himself with a patriotic weapon against his principal rival, Trotsky. He made it appear that Trotsky, by proposing to proceed with only a minority in hope of Western support, had disparaged the proletariat and peasantry of Russia.[9]

In making this basic revision of Marxist internationalism Stalin proceeded gradually. In 1924 he limited himself to a modest statement that the "building" of socialism could proceed in one country, and affirmed that for the "final victory" of socialism, revolution, "at least in several countries, will be requisite." By 1926 he thought that socialism could be "established" in a single country, but that it could not be safe while the "capitalist encirclement" remained. This view he expressed again in 1938, when socialism was held to be already achieved. Before the second World War he extended the doctrine again: the building of communism, too, was possible within a single state.

With the determination to build socialism in one country, four closely linked consequences became inescapable. Their influences, in Russia and outside, are even now far from being exhausted.

In the first place, the West was converted from a focus of

[8] It should be noted that this was a cyclical theory and, therefore, could not provide permanent support for socialism in one country. But Stalin never expected this situation to be permanent.

[9] As a matter of fact, in believing in 1905 that a minority could carry the revolution on into socialism in a backward country, Trotsky had displayed greater confidence in the Russians than any of the Bolsheviks had shown.

hope and expectation into a focus of fear. Its proletarian potentialities were discounted and attention was centered upon its
capitalistic actualities. The armed intervention in Russia by Britain, France, Japan, Poland, and the United States had already
convincingly demonstrated, to Stalin and his colleagues, that
the capitalists would not stop short of war in their desire to
eradicate Bolshevism. Russia was caught in a capitalist encirclement which, sooner or later, would again become an armed
attack. The old, defensive, outpost psychology of Muscovy, which
had long been fading among both liberals and radicals, returned
with renewed vigor.

This imminent attack required, in the second place, the military
strengthening of the nation. "We are fifty or a hundred years
behind the advanced countries," Stalin said in 1931. "We must
make good this distance in ten years. Either we do it, or we
shall go under." [10] Hence the hectic pace of industrialization in
the five-year plans and the great emphasis on heavy industry.
This policy, more than Marxism and quite apart from its theoretical basis, changed the face of Russia.

Thirdly, the abandonment of all expectation of revolutionary
help from the West meant the acceptance of dependence upon
the peasantry. The traditional assumption that the peasants
would ultimately desert the revolution had, therefore, to give
place to a determination to prevent that desertion. The forcible
collectivization of the 1930's, in Stalin's mind the only alternative
to the liquidation of the revolution when a withdrawal of peasant support seemed threatened, was the result. It had been
implicit in socialism in one country since 1924. Thus, the dis-
counting of the international Marxist movement led to this and
other policies which permanently undermined the moral authority of the régime abroad and greatly handicapped those supporters whom it did not repel.

And finally, the aim of the Communist International was
narrowed from the achievement of socialism in other countries
through revolution to the defense of the Soviet Union by any
expedient means. Stalin never developed confidence in the revo-

[10] Stalin, "The Tasks of Business Executives," in his *Works*, Vol. 13
(Moscow, 1955), p. 41.

lutionaries of the West, and preferred to avoid any attempt by them to take power which might stimulate a capitalist attack upon Russia. Even at the end of the Second World War he restrained the French and Italian communists, then enjoying great prestige in very fluid situations, rather than risk the consequences. Communism, therefore, was not to be extended by the other national parties but by the more reliable Red Army.

Toward the end of his life Stalin produced two theoretical works of importance, *Marxism and Problems of Linguistics* (1950) and *Economic Problems of Socialism in the U.S.S.R.* (1952).

In the former he reexamined the antique Marxist question of the relation of the institutional superstructure to the economic base.[11] From his analysis the superstructure emerged as "an exceedingly active force" capable of affecting its base in a manner that no economic determinist would accept. This conclusion, reaffirming the voluntaristic tendency of Russian Marxism, illustrates the continuity in Stalin's thought. As early as 1904, writing against Plekhanov, he had insisted that the theory of socialism "is engendered *outside* of the spontaneous [labor] movement," even "in spite of that movement," and is "then *introduced* into that movement *from outside, correcting* it in conformity with its content."[12] He had quickly absorbed Lenin's idea that, by its own efforts, the working class could not escape "ideological enslavement" to the bourgeoisie, could not develop class consciousness (see p. 47). Like Lenin, he never ceased to use this idea when needed as justification for his own and his Party's disregard for economic determinants in history.[13] In earlier years this voluntaristic concept of leadership had frequently called for conspiracy and radical, even violent, change. By 1950, however, its role within Russia had become pacific: through its influence

[11] Marx had discussed this relation in *The Poverty of Philosophy* (1847) and more exactly in *The Critique of Political Economy* (1859).

[12] Stalin, "A Letter from Kutais" (October, 1904), in his *Works*, Vol. 1, pp. 56-57.

[13] See especially his arguments for the socialization of agriculture without waiting for the agricultural machinery that should provide the appropriate economic base, in his *Works*, Vols. 11 and 12.

"contradictions" in society could be prevented from becoming "antagonistic" as the economic base evolved, and peaceful "revolution from above" would obviate violent change.

In his *Economic Problems* two years later Stalin found it necessary to utter a word of caution to "comrades" who had been led by his *Linguistics* to "believe that in view of the specific role assigned to the Soviet state by history, the Soviet state and its leaders can abolish existing laws of political economy and can 'form,' 'create,' new laws." [14] In the process he attempted to establish some more definite limits for Russian voluntarism. Even under socialism, he held, economic laws are objective, beyond human will; therefore, only by stimulating and encouraging changes in the economic base can the superstructure (i.e., the Communist Party) achieve changes in the relations of production and thus in the superstructure itself.

He then went on to elaborate upon some of the related problems of the transition from socialism to communism. In 1939 he had thought the prime requisite for this transition lay in the "country being fully saturated with consumer goods," but he now rebuked those who thought this sufficient. The relations of production must be altered; specifically, the "group property" of the collective farms must become "public" property. Yet this must not be done by confiscation. It must, instead, be accomplished by replacing the market in farm commodities with direct "products-exchange." [15] His meaning is not entirely clear, but apparently he meant that it must be done by changing the productive forces, the economic base itself. Through the "products-exchange" of an expanded industrial output for farm products, and through the diversification of skills by "compulsory polytechnical education," the productive forces of the cities must be so blended with those of the countryside that no difference in economic base remained to justify a separate "group" ownership of agricultural products. Agriculture, like industry, could then be planned, and an incipient restraint upon the ex-

[14] Stalin, *Economic Problems of Socialism in the U.S.S.R.* (Moscow, 1952), pp. 5-6.

[15] It might be noted that Stalin had once thought that the introduction of socialism itself would mean the abolition of "commodity production." See "The Agrarian Question," (1906) in his *Works*, Vol. 1, p. 221.

pansion of production, inherent in decentralized farm management, could be removed. The "contradictions" and "essential distinctions" between town and country and between mental and physical labor would then be eliminated.

It would seem that, in spite of his reputation for inflexibility and dogmatism on one hand, and the accusations of opportunism (a deadly sin for a Marxist) hurled against him on the other, in Stalin's mind Marxism remained a dynamic theory, adaptable and yet indispensable. The problems of government required the reformulation and extension of theory, he thought, and the scriptures were subject to flexible interpretation permitting administration to cope with problems as they arose.

[SOCIALISM IN ONE COUNTRY]

From Stalin, a) "The October Revolution and the Tactics of the Russian Communists" (1924), and b) "The Foundations of Leninism" (1924), in his *Works*, Vol. 6 (Moscow, 1953), and c) "On the Problems of Leninism" (1926), in his *Works*, Vol. 8 (Moscow, 1954), as indicated in following notes.

In his study of imperialism, especially in the period of the war, Lenin arrived at the law of the uneven, spasmodic economic and political development of the capitalist countries. . . . This law proceeds from the following:

1) "Capitalism has grown into a world system of colonial oppression and of the financial strangulation of the overwhelming majority of the population of the world by a handful of 'advanced' countries" (Lenin, Preface to French edition of *Imperialism,* [*Collected Works,* 4th Russian edition,] Vol. XIX, p. 74) [English edition, Vol. 19 (1942), p. 87];

2) "This 'booty' is shared between two or three powerful world marauders armed to the teeth (America, Great Britain, Japan), who involve the whole world in *their* war over the sharing of *their* booty" (ibid.);

3) In consequence of the growth of contradictions within the world system of financial oppression and of the inevitability of armed clashes, the world front of imperialism becomes easily vulnerable to revolution, and a breach in this front in individual countries becomes probable;

4) This breach is most likely to occur at those points, and in those countries, where the chain of the imperialist front is weakest, that is to say, where imperialism is least consolidated, and where it is easiest for a revolution to expand;

5) In view of this, the victory of Socialism in one country, even if this country is less developed in the capitalist sense, while capitalism is preserved in other countries, even if these countries are more highly developed in the capitalist sense—is quite possible and probable.

Such, briefly, are the foundations of Lenin's theory of the proletarian revolution.[16]

But the overthrow of the power of the bourgeoisie and establishment of the power of the proletariat in one country does not yet mean that the complete victory of Socialism has been ensured. After consolidating its power and taking the peasantry in tow, the proletariat of the victorious country can and must build up a socialist society. But does this mean that it will thereby achieve the complete and final victory of Socialism, i.e., does it mean that with the forces of only one country it can finally consolidate Socialism and fully guarantee that country against intervention and, consequently, also against restoration? No, it does not. For this the victory of the revolution in at least several countries is needed. Therefore, the development and support of revolution in other countries is an essential task of the victorious revolution. Therefore, the revolution in the victorious country must regard itself not as a self-sufficient entity but as an auxiliary, as a means of hastening the victory of the proletariat in other countries.[17]

It goes without saying that for the *complete* victory of Socialism, for *complete* security against the restoration of the old order, the united efforts of the proletarians of several countries

16 a), pp. 386-387.
17 b), pp. 110-111.

are necessary. It goes without saying that, without the support given to our revolution by the proletariat of Europe, the proletariat of Russia could not have held out against the general onslaught, just as without the support the revolution in Russia gave to the revolutionary movement in the West the latter could not have developed at the pace at which it has begun to develop since the establishment of the proletarian dictatorship in Russia. It goes without saying that we need support. But what does support of our revolution by the West-European proletariat imply? Is not the sympathy of European workers for our revolution, their readiness to thwart the imperialists' plans of intervention—is not all this support? Is this not real assistance? Unquestionably it is. If it had not been for this support, if it had not been for this assistance, not only from the European workers but also from the colonial and dependent countries, the proletarian dictatorship in Russia would have been in a tight corner. Has this sympathy and this assistance, coupled with the might of our Red Army and the readiness of the workers and peasants of Russia to defend their socialist fatherland to the last—has all this been sufficient to beat off the attacks of the imperialists and to win us the necessary conditions for the serious work of construction? Yes, it has been sufficient. Is this sympathy growing stronger, or is it waning? Unquestionably, it is growing stronger. Hence, have we favourable conditions, not only to push on with the organizing of socialist economy, but also, in our turn, to give support to the West-European workers and to the oppressed peoples of the East? Yes, we have. This is eloquently proved by the seven years history of the proletarian dictatorship in Russia. Can it be denied that a mighty wave of labour enthusiasm has already risen in our country? No, it cannot be denied.

After all this, what does Trotsky's assertion that a revolutionary Russia could not hold out in the face of a conservative Europe signify?

It can signify only this: first, that Trotsky does not appreciate the inherent strength of our revolution; secondly, that Trotsky does not understand the inestimable importance of the moral support which is given to our revolution by the workers of the West and the peasants of the East; thirdly, that Trotsky does not perceive the inherent infirmity which is consuming imperialism today. . . .

Well, then, since there is still no victory in the West, the only "choice" that remains for the revolution in Russia is: either to rot away or to degenerate into a bourgeois state.

It is no accident that Trotsky has been talking for two years now about the "degeneration" of our Party.

It is no accident that last year Trotsky prophesied the "doom" of our country.

Lack of faith in the strength and capabilities of our revolution, lack of faith in the strength and capabilities of the Russian proletariat—that is what lies at the root of the theory of "permanent revolution." [18]

This does not mean, of course, that Leninism has been or is opposed to the idea of permanent revolution, without quotation marks, as proclaimed by Marx in the forties of the last century. On the contrary, Lenin was the only Marxist who correctly understood and developed the idea of permanent revolution. What distinguishes Lenin from the "permanentists" on this question is that the "permanentists" distorted Marx's idea of permanent revolution and transformed it into lifeless, bookish wisdom, whereas Lenin took it in its pure form and made it one of the foundations of his own theory of revolution.[19]

Very well, we may be told; but if this be the case, why did Lenin combat the idea of "permanent (uninterrupted) revolution"?

Because Lenin proposed that the revolutionary capacities of the peasantry be utilized "to the utmost" and that the fullest use be made of their revolutionary energy for the complete liquidation of tsarism and for the transition to the proletarian revolution, whereas the adherents of "permanent revolution" did not understand the important role of the peasantry in the Russian revolution, underestimated the strength of the revolutionary energy of the peasantry, underestimated the strength and ability of the Russian proletariat to lead the peasantry, and thereby hampered the work of emancipating the peasantry from

[18] a), pp. 391-395.
[19] c), p. 20.

the influence of the bourgeoisie, the work of rallying the peasantry around the proletariat. . . .

Consequently, Lenin fought the adherents of "permanent" revolution, not over the question of uninterruptedness, for Lenin himself maintained the point of view of uninterrupted revolution, but because they underestimated the role of the peasantry, which is an enormous reserve force for the proletariat, because they failed to understand the idea of the hegemony of the proletariat.[20]

[THE CLASS STRUGGLE]

Stalin, "The Right Deviation in the C.P.S.U.(B.)" (1929), in his *Works*, Vol. 12 (Moscow, 1955), pp. 35-41.

Bukharin thinks that under the dictatorship of the proletariat the class struggle must *die down* and *come to an end* so that the abolition of classes may be brought about. Lenin, on the contrary, teaches us that classes can be abolished only by means of a stubborn class struggle, which under the dictatorship of the proletariat becomes *even fiercer* than it was before the dictatorship of the proletariat.

"The abolition of classes," says Lenin, "requires a long, difficult and stubborn *class struggle,* which, *after* the overthrow of the power of capital, *after* the destruction of the bourgeois state, *after* the establishment of the dictatorship of the proletariat, *does not disappear* (as the vulgar representatives of the old socialism and the old Social-Democracy imagine), but merely changes its forms and in many respects becomes even fiercer" ([*Collected Works,* 4th Russian edition,] Vol. XXIV, p. 315).

That is what Lenin says about the abolition of classes.

The abolition of classes *by means of the fierce class struggle of the proletariat*—such is Lenin's formula.

The abolition of classes *by means of the extinction of the class*

[20] b), pp. 106-107.

struggle and by the capitalists growing into socialism—such is Bukharin's formula.

What can there be in common between these two formulas? . . .

It may be said that it is not worth while dwelling at length on Bukharin's theory of the kulaks growing into socialism, since it itself speaks, and not only speaks, but cries out, against Bukharin. That is wrong, comrades! As long as that theory was kept hidden it was possible not to pay attention to it—there are plenty of such stupid things in what various comrades write. Such has been our attitude until quite lately. But recently the situation has changed. The petty-bourgeois elemental forces, which have been breaking out in recent years, have begun to encourage this anti-Marxist theory and made it topical. . . .

What is the point at issue here? Is it that the capitalist elements are growing faster than the socialist sector of our economy, and that, because of this, they are increasing their resistance, undermining socialist construction? No, that is not the point. Moreover, it is not true that the capitalist elements are growing faster than the socialist sector. If that were true, socialist construction would already be on the verge of collapse.

The point is that socialism is successfully attacking the capitalist elements, socialism is growing *faster* than the capitalist elements; as a result the relative importance of the capitalist elements is *declining*, and for the very reason that the relative importance of the capitalist elements is *declining* the capitalist elements realise that they are in mortal danger and are increasing their resistance.

And they are still able to increase their resistance not only because world capitalism is supporting them, but also because, in spite of the decline in their relative importance, in spite of the decline in their relative growth as compared with the growth of socialism, there is still taking place an absolute growth of the capitalist elements, and this, to a certain extent, enables them to accumulate forces to resist the growth of socialism.

It is on this basis that, *at the present stage of development and under the present conditions* of the relation of forces, the intensification of the class struggle and the increase in the resistance of the capitalist elements of town and country are taking place. . . .

There have been no cases in history where dying classes have voluntarily departed from the scene. There have been no cases in history where the dying bourgeoisie has not exerted all its remaining strength to preserve its existence. Whether our lower Soviet apparatus is good or bad, our advance, our offensive will diminish the capitalist elements and oust them, and they, the dying classes, will carry on their resistance at all costs.

That is the basis for the intensification of the class struggle in our country.

The mistake of Bukharin and his friends is that they identify the growing resistance of the capitalists with the growth of the latter's relative importance. But there are absolutely no grounds for this identification. There are no grounds because the fact that the capitalists are resisting by no means implies that they have become stronger than we are. The very opposite is the case. The dying classes are resisting, not because they have become stronger than we are, but because socialism is growing faster than they are, and they are becoming weaker than we are. And precisely because they are becoming weaker, they feel that their last days are approaching and are compelled to resist with all the forces and all the means in their power. . . .

Wherein lies the harm of the Bukharin theory of the capitalists growing into socialism and of the Bukharin conception of the intensification of the class struggle?

It lies in the fact that it lulls the working class to sleep, undermines the mobilised preparedness of the revolutionary forces of our country, demobilises the working class and facilitates the attack of the capitalist elements against the Soviet regime.

[THE WITHERING OF THE STATE]

Stalin, *Report to the Eighteenth Congress of the C.P.S.U.(B.) on the Work of the Central Committee* (1939), (Moscow, 1951), pp. 80-93.

It is sometimes asked: . . . "The exploiting classes have already been abolished in our country; Socialism has in the main been built; we are advancing towards Communism. Now, the Marxist doctrine of the state says that there is to be no state under Communism.—Why then do we not help our socialist state to die away? Is it not time we relegated the state to the museum of antiquities?"

These questions show that those who ask them have conscientiously memorized certain tenets of the doctrine of Marx and Engels about the state. But they also show that these comrades have not grasped the essential meaning of this doctrine; that they do not realize in what historical conditions the various tenets of this doctrine were elaborated. . . .

Is this proposition of Engels' correct?

Yes, it is correct, but only on one of two conditions: (1) *if* we study the socialist state only from the angle of the internal development of a country, abstracting ourselves in advance from the international factor, isolating, for the convenience of investigation, the country and the state from the international situation; or (2) *if* we assume that Socialism is already victorious in all countries, or in the majority of countries, that a socialist encirclement exists instead of a capitalist encirclement, that there is no more danger of foreign attack, and that there is no more need to strengthen the army and the state.

Well, but what if Socialism has been victorious only in one, separate country, and if, in view of this, it is quite impossible to abstract oneself from international conditions—what then? Engels' formula does not furnish an answer to this question. . . .

Since the October Revolution, our socialist state has passed through two main phases in its development.

The first phase was the period from the October Revolution to the elimination of the exploiting classes. The principal task in that period was to suppress the resistance of the overthrown classes, to organize the defence of the country against the attack of the interventionists, to restore industry and agriculture, and to prepare the conditions for the elimination of the capitalist elements. Accordingly, in this period our state performed two main functions. The first function was to suppress the overthrown classes within the country. In this respect our state bore a superficial resemblance to previous states whose functions had also been to suppress recalcitrants, with the fundamental difference, however, that our state suppressed the exploiting minority in the interests of the labouring majority, while previous states had suppressed the exploited majority in the interests of the exploiting minority. The second function was to defend the country from foreign attack. In this respect it likewise bore a superficial resemblance to previous states, which also undertook the armed defence of their countries, with the fundamental difference, however, that our state defended from foreign attack the gains of the labouring majority, while previous states in such cases defended the wealth and privileges of the exploiting minority. Our state had yet a third function: this was the work of economic organization and cultural education performed by our state bodies with the purpose of developing the infant shoots of the new, socialist economic system and re-educating the people in the spirit of Socialism. But this new function did not attain to any considerable development in that period.

The second phase was the period from the elimination of the capitalist elements in town and country to the complete victory of the socialist economic system and the adoption of the new Constitution. The principal task in this period was to establish the socialist economic system all over the country and to eliminate the last remnants of the capitalist elements, to bring about a cultural revolution, and to form a thoroughly modern army for the defence of the country. And the functions of our socialist state changed accordingly. The function of military suppression within the country ceased, died away; for exploitation had been abolished, there were no more exploiters left, and so there was no one to suppress. In place of this function of suppression the state acquired the function of protecting socialist property from thieves and pilferers of the property of the people. The function of armed defence of the country from foreign attack fully remained; consequently, the Red Army and the Navy also fully remained, as did the punitive organs and the intelligence service, which are indispensable for the detection and punishment of the spies, assassins and wreckers sent into our country by foreign espionage services. The function of economic organization and cultural education by the state organs also remained, and was developed to the full. Now the main task of our state within the country is peaceful economic organization and cultural education. As for our army, punitive organs, and intelligence service, their edge is no longer turned to within the country but to without, against external enemies.

As you see, we now have an entirely new, socialist state, one without precedent in history and differing considerably in form and functions from the socialist state of the first phase.

But development cannot stop there. We are moving ahead, towards Communism. Will our state remain in the period of Communism also?

Yet, it will, unless the capitalist encirclement is liquidated, and unless the danger of foreign military attack has been eliminated, although naturally, the forms of our state will again change in conformity with the change in the situation at home and abroad.

No, it will not remain and will wither away if the capitalist encirclement is liquidated and is replaced by a socialist encirclement.

That is how the question stands with regard to the socialist state.

[BASIS AND SUPERSTRUCTURE]

Stalin, *Marxism and Problems of Linguistics* (1950), (Moscow, 1954), pp. 7-15, 38-39.

The basis is the economic structure of society at the given stage of its development. The superstructure is the political, legal, religious, artistic, philosophical views of society and the political, legal and other institutions corresponding to them.

Every basis has its own corresponding superstructure. The basis of the feudal system has its superstructure, its political, legal and other views, and the corresponding institutions; the capitalist basis has its own superstructure, so has the socialist basis. If the basis changes or is eliminated, then, following this, its superstructure changes or is eliminated; if a new basis arises, then, following this, a superstructure arises corresponding to it. . . .

Further, the superstructure is a product of the basis, but this by no means implies that it merely reflects the basis, that it is passive, neutral, indifferent to the fate of its basis, to the fate of the classes, to the character of the system. On the contrary, having come into being, it becomes an exceedingly active force, actively assisting its basis to take shape and consolidate itself, and doing its utmost to help the new system to finish off and eliminate the old basis and the old classes.

It cannot be otherwise. The superstructure is created by the basis precisely in order to serve it, to actively help it to take shape and consolidate itself, to actively fight for the elimination of the old, moribund basis together with its old superstructure. The superstructure has only to renounce this role of auxiliary, it has only to pass from a position of active defence of its basis to one of indifference towards it, to adopt an equal attitude to all classes, and it loses its virtue and ceases to be a superstructure. . . .

Further, the superstructure is the product of one epoch, the epoch in which the given economic basis exists and operates. The superstructure is therefore short-lived; it is eliminated and disappears with the elimination and disappearance of the given basis. . . .

Lastly, one other radical distinction between the superstructure and language. The superstructure is not directly connected with production, with man's productive activity. It is connected with production only indirectly, through the economy, through the basis. The superstructure therefore reflects changes in the level of development of the productive forces not immediately and not directly, but only after changes in the basis, through the prism of the changes wrought in the basis by the changes in production. This means that the sphere of action of the superstructure is narrow and restricted. . . .

It should be said in general for the benefit of comrades who have an infatuation for explosions that the law of transition from an old quality to a new by means of an explosion is inapplicable not only to the history of the development of languages; it is not always applicable to other social phenomena of a basis or superstructural character. It applies of necessity to a society divided into hostile classes. But it does not necessarily apply to a society which has no hostile classes. In a period of eight to ten years we effected a transition in the agriculture of our country from the bourgeois, individual-peasant system to the socialist, collective-farm system. This was a revolution which eliminated the old bourgeois economic system in the countryside and created a new, socialist system. But that revolution did not take place by means of an explosion, that is, by the overthrow of the existing government power and the creation of a new power, but by a gradual transition from the old bourgeois system in the countryside to a new system. And it was possible to do that because it was a revolution from above, because the revolution was accomplished on the initiative of the existing power with the support of the bulk of the peasantry.

CHARACTER OF ECONOMIC LAWS
UNDER SOCIALISM

Stalin, *Economic Problems of Socialism in the U.S.S.R.* (Moscow, 1952), pp. 5-13.

Some comrades deny the objective character of laws of science, and of the laws of political economy particularly, under socialism. They deny that the laws of political economy reflect law-governed processes which operate independently of the will of man. They believe that in view of the specific role assigned to the Soviet state by history, the Soviet state and its leaders can abolish existing laws of political economy and can "form," "create," new laws.

These comrades are profoundly mistaken. . . .

Marxism regards laws of science—whether they be laws of natural science or laws of political economy—as the reflection of objective processes which take place independently of the will of man. Man may discover these laws, get to know them, study them, reckon with them in his activities and utilize them in the interests of society, but he cannot change or abolish them. Still less can he form or create new laws of science. . . .

The same must be said of the laws of economic development, the laws of political economy—whether in the period of capitalism or in the period of socialism. Here, too, the laws of economic development, as in the case of natural science, are objective laws, reflecting processes of economic development which take place independently of the will of man. Man may discover these laws, get to know them and, relying upon them, utilize them in the interests of society, impart a different direction to the destructive action of some of the laws, restrict their sphere of action, and allow fuller scope to other laws that are forcing their way to the forefront; but he cannot destroy them or create new economic laws.

One of the distinguishing features of political economy is that its laws, unlike those of natural science, are impermanent, that they, or at least the majority of them, operate for a definite historical period, after which they give place to new laws. However, these laws are not abolished, but lose their validity owing to the new economic conditions and depart from the scene in order to give place to new laws, laws which are not created by the will of man, but which arise from the new economic conditions. . . .

Reference is made to the specific role of Soviet government in building socialism, which allegedly enables it to abolish existing laws of economic development and to "form" new ones. That also is untrue.

The specific role of Soviet government was due to two circumstances: first, that what Soviet government had to do was not to replace one form of exploitation by another, as was the case in earlier revolutions, but to abolish exploitation altogether; second, that in view of the absence in the country of any ready-made rudiments of a socialist economy, it had to create new, socialist forms of economy, "starting from scratch," so to speak.

That was undoubtedly a difficult, complex and unprecedented task. Nevertheless, the Soviet government accomplished this task with credit. But it accomplished it not because it supposedly destroyed the existing economic laws and "formed" new ones, but only because it relied on the economic law that the relations of production *must necessarily conform* with the character of the productive forces. The productive forces of our country, especially in industry, were social in character, the form of ownership, on the other hand, was private, capitalistic. Relying on the economic law that the relations of production must necessarily conform with the character of the productive forces, the Soviet government socialized the means of production, made them the property of the whole people, and thereby abolished the exploiting system and created socialist forms of economy. Had it not been for this law, and had the Soviet government not relied upon it, it could not have accomplished its mission.

The economic law that the relations of production must necessarily conform with the character of the productive forces has
long been forcing its way to the forefront in the capitalist countries. If it has failed so far to force its way into the open, it is
because it is encountering powerful resistance on the part of
obsolescent forces of society. Here we have another distinguishing feature of economic laws. Unlike the laws of natural science,
where the discovery and application of a new law proceeds
more or less smoothly, the discovery and application of a new
law in the economic field, affecting as it does the interests of
obsolescent forces of society, meets with the most powerful
resistance on their part. A force, a social force, capable of overcoming this resistance, is therefore necessary. In our country, such
a force was the alliance of the working class and the peasantry,
who represented the overwhelming majority of society. . . .

It is said that some of the economic laws operating in our
country under socialism, including the law of value, have been
"transformed," or even "radically transformed," on the basis of
planned economy. That is likewise untrue. Laws cannot be
"transformed," still less "radically" transformed. If they can be
transformed, then they can be abolished and replaced by other
laws. The thesis that laws can be "transformed" is a relic of the
incorrect formula that laws can be "abolished" or "formed."
Although the formula that economic laws can be transformed
has already been current in our country for a long time, it must
be abandoned for the sake of accuracy. The sphere of action of
this or that economic law may be restricted, its destructive
action—that is, of course, if it is liable to be destructive—may
be averted, but it cannot be "transformed" or "abolished."

Consequently, when we speak of "subjugating" natural forces
or economic forces, of "dominating" them, etc., this does not
mean that man can "abolish" or "form" scientific laws. On the
contrary, it only means that man can discover laws, get to know
them and master them, learn to apply them with full understanding, utilize them in the interests of society, and thus subjugate
them, secure mastery over them.

Hence, the laws of political economy under socialism are objective laws, which reflect the fact that the processes of economic

life are law-governed and operate independently of our will. People who deny this postulate are in point of fact denying science, and, by denying science, they are denying all possibility of prognostication—and, consequently, are denying the possibility of directing economic activity. . . .

COMMODITY PRODUCTION
UNDER SOCIALISM

Stalin, *Economic Problems of Socialism in the U.S.S.R.* (Moscow, 1952), pp. 13-21.

Certain comrades affirm that the Party acted wrongly in preserving commodity production after it had assumed power and nationalized the means of production in our country. They consider that the Party should have banished commodity production there and then. In this connection they cite Engels, who says:

"The seizure of the means of production by society puts an end to commodity production, and therewith to the domination of the product over the producer." (See *Anti-Dühring* [English edition (Moscow, 1954), p. 392].)

These comrades are profoundly mistaken. . . .

But here is a question: what are the proletariat and its party to do in countries, ours being a case in point, where the conditions are favourable for the assumption of power by the proletariat and the overthrow of capitalism, where capitalism has so concentrated the means of production in industry that they may be expropriated and made the property of society, but where agriculture, notwithstanding the growth of capitalism, is divided up among numerous small and medium owner-producers to such an extent as to make it impossible to consider the expropriation of these producers?

To this question Engels' formula does not furnish an answer. . . .

And so, what is to be done if *not all*, but only part of the means of production have been socialized, yet the conditions are favourable for the assumption of power by the proletariat—should the proletariat assume power and should commodity production be abolished immediately after this? . . .

The answer to this question was given by Lenin in his writings on the "tax in kind" and in his celebrated "cooperative plan."

Lenin's answer may be briefly summed up as follows:

a) Favourable conditions for the assumption of power should not be missed—the proletariat should assume power without waiting until capitalism succeeded in ruining the millions of small and medium individual producers;

b) The means of production in industry should be expropriated and converted into public property;

c) As to the small and medium individual producers, they should be gradually united in producers' cooperatives, i.e., in large agricultural enterprises, collective farms;

d) Industry should be developed to the utmost and the collective farms should be placed on the modern technical basis of large-scale production, not expropriating them, but on the contrary generously supplying them with first-class tractors and other machines;

e) In order to ensure an economic bond between town and country, between industry and agriculture, commodity production (exchange through purchase and sale) should be preserved for a certain period, it being the form of economic tie with the town which is *alone acceptable* to the peasants, and Soviet trade —state, cooperative, and collective-farm—should be developed to the full and the capitalists of all types and descriptions ousted from trading activity.

The history of socialist construction in our country has shown that this path of development, mapped out by Lenin, has fully justified itself. . . .

It is said that commodity production must lead, is bound to lead, to capitalism all the same, under all conditions. That is not true. Not always and not under all conditions! Commodity pro-

duction must not be identified with capitalist production. They
are two different things. Capitalist production is the highest form
of commodity production. Commodity production leads to capitalism only *if* there is private ownership of the means of production, *if* labour power appears in the market as a commodity
which can be bought by the capitalist and exploited in the
process of production, and *if*, consequently, the system of exploitation of wageworkers by capitalists exists in the country. . . .

It is said that, since the domination of social ownership of
the means of production has been established in our country,
and the system of wage labour and exploitation has been abolished, commodity production has lost all meaning and should
therefore be done away with.

That is also untrue. Today there are two basic forms of socialist production in our country: state, or publicly-owned production, and collective-farm production, which cannot be said to be
publicly owned. In the state enterprises, the means of production
and the product of production are national property. In the
collective farm, although the means of production (land, machines) do belong to the state, the product of production is the
property of the different collective farms, since the labour, as
well as the seed, is their own, while the land, which has been
turned over to the collective farms in perpetual tenure, is used
by them virtually as their own property, in spite of the fact
that they cannot sell, buy, lease or mortgage it.

The effect of this is that the state disposes only of the product
of the state enterprises, while the product of the collective farms,
being their property, is disposed of only by them. But the collective farms are unwilling to alienate their products except in
the form of commodities, in exchange for which they desire to
receive the commodities they need. At present the collective
farms will not recognize any other economic relation with the
town except the commodity relation—exchange through purchase
and sale. Because of this, commodity production and trade are
as much a necessity with us today as they were thirty years ago,
say, when Lenin spoke of the necessity of developing trade to
the utmost.

Of course, when instead of the two basic production sectors, the state sector and the collective-farm sector, there will be only one all-embracing production sector, with the right to dispose of all the consumer goods produced in the country, commodity circulation, with its "money economy," will disappear, as being an unnecessary element in the national economy. But so long as this is not the case, so long as the two basic production sectors remain, commodity production and commodity circulation must remain in force, as a necessary and very useful element in our system of national economy. How the formation of a single and united sector will come about, whether simply by the swallowing up of the collective-farm sector by the state sector—which is hardly likely (because that would be looked upon as the expropriation of the collective farms)—or by the setting up of a single *national* economic body (comprising representatives of state industry and of the collective farms), with the right at first to keep account of all consumer product in the country, and eventually also to distribute it, by way, say, of products-exchange —is a special question which requires separate discussion. . . .

[COLLECTIVE-FARM PROPERTY

AND PUBLIC PROPERTY]

Stalin, *Economic Problems of Socialism in the U.S.S.R.* (Moscow, 1952), pp. 96-103.

What measures are necessary to raise collective-farm property, which, of course, is not public property, to the level of public ("national") property?

Some comrades think that the thing to do is simply to nationalize collective-farm property, to proclaim it public property, in the way that was done in the past in the case of capitalist property. Such a proposal would be absolutely wrong and quite unacceptable. Collective-farm property is socialist property, and we simply cannot treat it in the same way as capitalist property.

From the fact that collective-farm property is not public property, it by no means follows that it is not socialist property. . . .

Assuming for a moment that we accepted Comrades Sanina's and Venzher's proposal and began to sell the basic implements of production, the machine and tractor stations, to the collective farms as their property, what would be the outcome? . . .

The outcome would be, secondly, an extension of the sphere of operation of commodity circulation, because a gigantic quantity of instruments of agricultural production would come within its orbit. What do Comrades Sanina and Venzher think—is the extension of the sphere of commodity circulation calculated to promote our advance towards communism? Would it not be truer to say that our advance towards communism would only be retarded by it?

Comrades Sanina's and Venzher's basic error lies in the fact that they do not understand the role and significance of commodity circulation under socialism; that they do not understand that commodity circulation is incompatible with the prospective transition from socialism to communism. They evidently think that the transition from socialism to communism is possible even with commodity circulation, that commodity circulation can be no obstacle to this. That is a profound error, arising from an inadequate grasp of Marxism. . . .

But we, Marxists, adhere to the Marxist view that the transition from socialism to communism and the communist principle of distribution of products according to needs preclude all commodity exchange, and, hence, preclude the conversion of products into commodities, and, with it, their conversion into value. . . .

But what, then, should be done to elevate collective-farm property to the level of public property?

The collective farm is an unusual kind of enterprise. It operates on land and cultivates land which has long been public, and not collective-farm property. Consequently, the collective farm is not the owner of the land it cultivates.

Further, the collective farm operates with basic implements of production which are public, not collective-farm property. Consequently, the collective farm is not the owner of its basic implements of production.

Further, the collective farm is a cooperative enterprise: it utilizes the labour of its members, and it distributes its income among its members on the basis of workday units; it owns its seed, which is renewed every year and goes into production.

What, then, does the collective farm own? Where is the collective-farm property which it disposes of quite freely, at its own discretion? This property of the collective farm is its product, the product of collective farming: grain, meat, butter, vegetables, cotton, sugar beet, flax, etc., not counting the buildings and the personal husbandry of the collective farmers on their household plots. The fact is that a considerable part of this product, the surplus collective-farm output, goes into the market and is thus included in the system of commodity circulation. It is precisely this circumstance which now prevents the elevation of collective-farm property to the level of public property. It is therefore precisely from this end that the work of elevating collective-farm property to the level of public property must be tackled.

In order to raise collective-farm property to the level of public property, the surplus collective-farm output must be excluded from the system of commodity circulation and included in the system of products-exchange between state industry and the collective farms. That is the point.

[TOWN AND COUNTRY,

MENTAL AND PHYSICAL LABOR]

Stalin, *Economic Problems of Socialism in the U.S.S.R.* (Moscow, 1952), pp. 29-33.

Abolition of the antithesis between town and country, between industry and agriculture, is a well-known problem which was discussed long ago by Marx and Engels. The economic basis of this antithesis is the exploitation of the country by the town,

the expropriation of the peasantry and the ruin of the majority
of the rural population by the whole course of development of
industry, trade and credit under capitalism. Hence, the antithesis
between town and country under capitalism must be regarded
as an antagonism of interests. This it was that gave rise to the
hostile attitude of the country towards the town and towards
"townfolk" in general.

Undoubtedly, with the abolition of capitalism and the exploiting system in our country, and with the consolidation of the
socialist system, the antagonism of interests between town and
country, between industry and agriculture, was also bound to
disappear. And that is what happened. The immense assistance
rendered by the socialist town, by our working class, to our peasantry in eliminating the landlords and kulaks strengthened the
foundation for the alliance between the working class and the
peasantry, while the systematic supply of first-class tractors and
other machines to the peasantry and its collective farms converted the alliance between the working class and the peasantry
into friendship between them. Of course, the workers and the
collective-farm peasantry do represent two classes differing from
one another in status. But this difference does not weaken their
friendship in any way. On the contrary, their interests lie along
one common line, that of strengthening the socialist system and
attaining the victory of communism. It is not surprising, therefore, that not a trace remains of the former distrust, not to speak
of the former hatred, of the country for the town.

All this means that the ground for antithesis between town
and country, between industry and agriculture, has already been
eliminated by our present socialist system. . . .

We have a similar situation as regards the problem of the
abolition of the antithesis between mental and physical labour.
This too is a well-known problem which was discussed by Marx
and Engels long ago. . . .

Of quite a different character is the problem of the disappearance of distinctions between town (industry) and country (agriculture), and between physical and mental labour. This problem
was not discussed by the Marxian classics. It is a new problem,
one that has been raised practically by our socialist construction.

Is this problem an imaginary one? Has it any practical or theoretical importance for us? No, this problem cannot be considered an imaginary one. On the contrary, it is for us a problem of the greatest seriousness.

Take, for instance, the distinction between agriculture and industry. In our country it consists not only in the fact that the conditions of labour in agriculture differ from those in industry, but, mainly and chiefly, in the fact that whereas in industry we have public ownership of the means of production and of the product of industry, in agriculture we have not public, but group, collective-farm ownership. It has already been said that this fact leads to the preservation of commodity circulation, and that only when this distinction between industry and agriculture disappears, can commodity production with all its attendant consequences also disappear. It therefore cannot be denied that the disappearance of this essential distinction between agriculture and industry must be a matter of paramount importance for us.

The same must be said of the problem of the abolition of the essential distinction between mental labour and physical labour. It, too, is a problem of paramount importance for us. . . . What should we have had if not only isolated groups, but the majority of the workers had raised their cultural and technical level to that of the engineering and technical personnel? Our industry would have risen to a height unattainable by industry in other countries. It therefore cannot be denied that the abolition of the essential distinction between mental and physical labour by raising the cultural and technical level of the workers to that of the technical personnel cannot but be of paramount importance for us.

[THE TRANSITION TO COMMUNISM]

Stalin, *Economic Problems of Socialism in the U.S.S.R.* (Moscow, 1952), pp. 74-77.

In order to pave the way for a real, and not declaratory transition to communism, at least three main preliminary conditions have to be satisfied.

1. It is necessary, in the first place, to ensure, not a mythical "rational organization" of the productive forces, but a continuous expansion of all social production, with a relatively higher rate of expansion of the production of means of production. The relatively higher rate of expansion of production of means of production is necessary not only because it has to provide the equipment both for its own plants and for all the other branches of the national economy, but also because reproduction on an extended scale becomes altogether impossible without it.

2. It is necessary, in the second place, by means of gradual transitions carried out to the advantage of the collective farms, and, hence, of all society, to raise collective-farm property to the level of public property, and, also by means of gradual transitions, to replace commodity circulation by a system of products-exchange, under which the central government, or some other social-economic centre, might control the whole product of social production in the interests of society.

Comrade Yaroshenko is mistaken when he asserts that there is no contradiction between the relations of production and the productive forces of society under socialism. Of course, our present relations of production are in a period when they fully conform to the growth of the productive forces and help to advance them at seven-league strides. But it would be wrong to rest easy at that and to think that there are no contradictions between our productive forces and the relations of production. There certainly are, and will be, contradictions, seeing that the development of the relations of production lags, and will lag, behind the development of the productive forces. Given a correct policy on the part of the directing bodies, these contradictions cannot grow into antagonisms, and there is no chance of matters coming to a conflict between the relations of production and the productive forces of society. . . .

The task of the directing bodies is therefore promptly to discern incipient contradictions, and to take timely measures to resolve them by adapting the relations of production to the growth of the productive forces. This, above all, concerns such economic factors as group, or collective-farm, property and commodity circulation. At present, of course, these factors are being successfully utilized by us for the promotion of the socialist economy, and they are of undeniable benefit to our society. It is undeniable, too, that they will be of benefit also in the near future. But it would be unpardonable blindness not to see at the same time that these factors are already beginning to hamper the powerful development of our productive forces, since they create obstacles to the full extension of government planning to the whole of the national economy, especially agriculture. There is no doubt that these factors will hamper the continued growth of the productive forces of our country more and more as time goes on. The task therefore is to eliminate these contradictions by gradually converting collective-farm property into public property, and by introducing—also gradually—products-exchange in place of commodity circulation.

3. It is necessary, in the third place, to ensure such a cultural advancement of society as will secure for all members of society the all-round development of their physical and mental abilities, so that the members of society may be in a position to receive an education sufficient to enable them to be active agents of social development, and in a position freely to choose their occupations and not be tied all their lives, owing to the existing division of labour, to some one occupation.

What is required for this?

It would be wrong to think that such a substantial advance in the cultural standard of the members of society can be brought about without substantial changes in the present status of labour. For this, it is necessary, first of all, to shorten the working day at least to six, and subsequently to five hours. This is needed in order that the members of society might have the necessary free time to receive an all-round education. It is necessary, further, to introduce universal compulsory polytechnical education, which is required in order that the members of society might be able freely to choose their occupations and not be tied to some one occupation all their lives. It is likewise necessary that housing conditions should be radically improved, and that real wages of workers and employees should be at least doubled, if not more, both by means of direct increases of wages and salaries, and, more especially, by further systematic reductions of prices for consumer goods.

These are the basic conditions required to pave the way for the transition to communism. . . .

Only after *all* these preliminary conditions have been satisfied in their entirety will it be possible to pass from the socialist formula, "from each according to his ability, to each according to his work," to the communist formula, "from each according to his ability, to each according to his needs."

BIBLIOGRAPHY

Works by Stalin

Works, 13 vols. (Moscow, 1952-1955). Contains works written through January, 1934.
Anarchism or Socialism? (1906-1907; Moscow, 1950).
Economic Problems of Socialism in the USSR (Moscow, 1952).
Marxism and the National Question (1913-1936; New York, 1942). A collection.
Marxism and Problems of Linguistics (1950; Moscow, 1954).
Problems of Leninism (Moscow, 1953). Contains works from 1924 to 1939, including the following which are also available separately.
Dialectical and Historical Materialism (1938). Also in *History of the C. P. S. U. (B.).*
Foundations of Leninism (1924).
The October Revolution and the Tactics of the Russian Communists (1924).
On the Problems of Leninism (1926).
The Right Deviation in the C. P. S. U. (B.) (1929).

Biography

Deutscher, Isaac, *Stalin* (London, 1949).

Souvarine, Boris, *Staline. Aperçu historique du bolchévisme* (Paris, 1940). Contains a lengthy bibliography not found in the English edition.

Exposition

Bataille, Georges, "Le Communisme et le Stalinisme," *Critique,* Vol. 9 (May and June, 1953), pp. 415-428, 514-535.

Beyer, Wilhelm R., "Stalins sprachwissenschaftliche Arbeit," *Archiv für Rechts- und Sozialphilosophie,* Vol. 40 (1952), pp. 436-447.

Deutscher, Isaac, "Dogma and Reality in Stalin's 'Economic Problems'," *Soviet Studies,* Vol. 4 (April, 1953), pp. 349-363.

Djilas, Milovan, "Staline dans l'impasse," *Questions actuelles du Socialisme,* No. 14 (October-November, 1952), pp. 1-49. In English as —*Is Stalin Turning in a Circle?* (New York, n.d. [1952?]).

Giusti, Wolf, *Due secoli di pensiero politico russo* (Florence, 1943), pp. 297-312.

Historicus (*pseud.*), "Stalin on Revolution," *Foreign Affairs,* Vol. 27 (January, 1949), pp. 175-214.

Korey, William, "Zinoviev's Critique of Stalin's Theory of Socialism in One Country, December, 1925—December, 1926," *American Slavic and East European Review,* Vol. 9 (December, 1950), pp. 255-267.

Mehnert, Klaus, *Stalin vs. Marx* (London, 1952).

—Sager, Peter, *Die theoretischen Grundlagen des Stalinismus und ihre Auswirkungen auf die Wirtschaftspolitik der Sowjetunion* (Bern, 1953).

Sarel, Benno, "Lénine, Trotski, Staline et le problème du parti révolutionnaire," *Temps Modernes,* Vol. 7 (November, 1951), pp. 848-879.

Stern, Viktor, *Stalin als Philosoph* (Berlin, 1949).

Trotsky, Leon, *Stalin, An Appraisal of the Man and His Influence* (London, 1947).

———, "Stalin as a Theoretician" (1930), *New International,* Vol. 7 (October and November, 1941), pp. 247-254, 280-283. On agricultural policy.

Wetter, Gustav A., *Dialectical Materialism, A Historical and Systematic Survey of Philosophy in the Soviet Union,* trans. by Peter Heath (London, 1958).

9

Khrushchev:

Marxism Means Material Abundance

STALIN's dictatorship, coupled with his didactic and distrustful personality, progressively stifled the relative freedom of discussion prevalent among the party leaders in the old days of Lenin, and thus engendered dissatisfaction at the top of the hierarchy as well as among the lower ranks. Experiencing the tensions of the war years, his closest associates saw ever more clearly the dangers inherent in too great dependence upon one man. Stalin's immediate successors, therefore (wishing also to delay a showdown among themselves), drew a sharp distinction between "the cult of the individual" (their euphemism for those features of his rule which they chose to reprobate) and "collective leadership," the magic formula which would "reestablish the Party standards worked out by Lenin." Khrushchev described the new leadership as "a working collective of leaders whose relations are based on ideas and principles permitting neither of mutual forgiveness nor personal antagonism." [1]

To the Yugoslav theorist Milovan Djilas this meant that, with the death of Stalin "the epoch of great Communist monarchs and of great ideas came to an end, and the reign of mediocre Communist bureaucrats began." [2] Yet there is an unavoidable conflict between the belief that, for Russia, Marxism has only one correct interpretation and the belief that several coordinate

[1] Khrushchev, *Report of the Central Committee of the C.P.S.U. to the 20th Party Congress* (Moscow, 1956), p. 119.

[2] Milovan Djilas, *The New Class* (New York, 1957), p. 183.

253

minds can interpret it. In the past this conflict has led to the
emergence of one pre-eminent interpreter and the voluntary or
involuntary subordination of all others. The process seems to
have repeated itself, and the man who emerged was Nikita
Khrushchev (1894-   ).

Of Cossack ancestry, Khrushchev was born a peasant in the
village of Kalinovka near the Ukraine north of Kharkov. His father, however, left the land when Nikita was fifteen, became a
miner in the Donbas, and set his son to learn the skilled trade
of a fitter. Working at this trade in several factories and mines,
owned by German, French, and Belgian capital, Khrushchev also
learned at first hand the life of the proletariat—the first of the
top Soviet leaders to do so. Like other Russian proletarians he
retained his farm roots, and in 1917 he returned to Kalinovka
and assumed the leadership in the redistribution of land. Even
so, he was careful of his political commitments and did not
formally join the Bolsheviks until 1918, when they had already
held power for six months or more.

After three years in the civil war he entered a workers' technical school in Kharkov in 1921, and was chosen secretary of the
school's Party cell. He graduated four years later, aged thirty-
one, and his abilities as a Party organizer soon attracted the attention of Kaganovich, Stalin's new appointee as secretary of the
Ukrainian party, a connection which was to prove very useful to
Khrushchev in his climb up the Party ladder. Kaganovich employed him as a propagandist in the Ukraine and in 1929 secured
his transfer to Moscow. Once in the center of party activity, he
rose rapidly. By 1934 he was second secretary of the Moscow
regional Party, directly under Kaganovich (who had become
Stalin's brother-in-law), and the next year first secretary. These
posts brought membership in the national Central Committee.
He was chosen in 1938 a deputy member of the Politbureau, and
a year later he became a full member.

Sent in 1938 to direct Stalin's purge in Ukraina, he consolidated
his own party position in the process. He was among the advocates of the agreement with Hitler in 1940, using the argument
that the annexations would reunite and secure the Ukrainian
people. During the war and the reconstruction he continued to

work there in various military, Party, and governmental capacities until relieved and brought back to Moscow in 1949.

In the process of reconstruction Khrushchev became perhaps too enamoured with the idea of replacing the scattered villages by building large "agro-towns" with extensive community facilities. This urbanization was a step toward the removal of the Marxist "contradiction" between town and country, and was in line with the movement, also pushed by Khrushchev and adopted by the Party early in 1950, for the amalgamation of the smaller collective farms into more efficient units. The consolidation movement has continued, but Stalin frowned upon the "agro-town," and at the Party Congress of 1952 Malenkov condemned it as a "wrong, consumer, approach": "The mistake . . . was to forget the major production tasks of the collective farms, and give prominence to tasks that derive from them, to consumer tasks connected with welfare amenities in the collective farms." [3]

Khrushchev was hardly discarded, however; in that same year the Central Committee chose him as one of its secretaries, and Stalin directed him to draw new Party statutes eliminating the Politbureau and the Orgbureau and replacing them with a Presidium. He was a member of this Presidium which, on Stalin's death, proclaimed the collective leadership.

Malenkov having become chairman of the Council of Ministers, Khrushchev was elected in September, 1953, as first secretary of the Party Central Committee, not, significantly, "general secretary" as Stalin's title had read. In January, 1955, he induced the Central Committee to reject Malenkov's budget on the ground that its emphasis on consumer goods would prevent the fulfillment of capital goods commitments to China. Malenkov thereupon resigned, and his replacement by Khrushchev's old friend Bulganin indicated where the preponderance of forces lay.

At the Twentieth Party Congress a year later Khrushchev delivered his famous secret speech on the crimes of Stalin. While condemning Stalin's conduct of the war and some of his purge activities, Khrushchev by no means denounced the whole of Stalin's career nor rehabilitated all of his victims. Stalin's per-

[3] Georgi Malenkov, *Report to the Nineteenth Party Congress on the Work of the Central Committee of the C.P.S.U.(B.)* (Moscow, 1952), p. 75.

sonal qualities of suspicion, vindictiveness, and unwillingness to take advice, rather than his theories or methods, were the chief objects of attack.

Khrushchev's position was not yet secure, however. Although he controlled a majority of the Central Committee, its Presidium became disturbed by his intention to decentralize control of industrial production. In June, 1957, four of its members, Kaganovich, Malenkov, Molotov, and Shepilov, attempted to remove him as first secretary. The army, under Zhukov, however, refused to support the removal, and the full Central Committee instead removed these four men from the Presidium. Zhukov himself was soon demoted, and in March, 1958, Khrushchev displaced Bulganin as head of the government. Like Stalin he also retained the headship of the Party.

Because of his volubility, his vigorous sense of humor (unusual in a dictator), and his lack of early formal schooling, there is a widespread tendency to underestimate Khrushchev's mental ability and to credit his rise to ruthlessness. The documents which are accumulating over his signature (see, for example, Bibliography, p. 283), however, indicate stature beyond that of a "mediocre Communist bureaucrat." His volatility, and that of the situation over which he presides, make the ideas he has expressed subject to correction, contradiction, or supplementation at any time, yet strong convictions, if not fixed opinions, are evident.

The fundamental point of difference between Khrushchev's and Stalin's interpretations of Marxism lies in their attitudes toward the class war. Khrushchev apparently believes that the most acute phase of the struggle between capitalism and socialism has passed, both within the Soviet Union and in the international arena. He has, therefore, expressly repudiated Stalin's contrary opinion and has shown an inclination to relax some of the tensions generated under the latter's regime.

Great harm to the cause of socialist construction and the development of democracy inside the party and the state was inflicted by Stalin's erroneous formula that as the Soviet Union moved toward socialism *the class struggle would allegedly become more and more acute.* This formula, which is only correct *for certain stages of the transition* period, . . . was put forward in 1937 at a moment *when socialism had already triumphed* in our country. . . .[4]

This was the formula Stalin had used against Bukharin in 1929 (see p. 231f), and presumably it was then correct; but by 1937 it was obsolete, and, by implication, Bukharin's "withering of the class struggle" has since been more nearly right. Khrushchev has not rehabilitated Bukharin but he seems to be convinced that

We have entered a stage in the contest between labour and capital, between socialism and capitalism, when the relation of forces is de-cided by peaceful co-existence and peaceful competition. And this competition shows which of the two systems can best develop the productive forces and raise labour productivity; which of the two sys-tems can best satisfy the material and spiritual requirements of the people.[5]

This pragmatic approach, inviting comparison in precisely the area where capitalism has thought itself strongest, is the keynote of the present régime.

In domestic policy efforts have been made to stimulate local initiative and to provide individual incentives through correlating salaries with productivity. Industry has been decentralized and the educational system reorganized. The collective farms, now fewer and larger, are to operate on price incentives rather than on quota assignments. They are entrusted with their own build-ing and electrification programs and the ownership of their ma-chinery, formerly owned by the state through the Machine and Tractor Stations. Although some of these steps may strengthen the collective farms, Khrushchev has not lost sight of Stalin's desire to eliminate "commodity production" by converting the collective farms into state farms. He has his eye on the large undistributed funds that some of the farms have accumulated

[4] Quoted (with italics) in Myron Rush, *The Rise of Khrushchev* (Wash-ington, 1958), p. 29, from a statement issued by the Central Committee on June 30, 1956. Courtesy of Public Affairs Press.

[5] Khrushchev, "Accelerated Development of the Chemical Industry," *New Times* (Moscow), No. 19 (May, 1958), supp. p. 7; a report to the Central Committee, May 6, 1958.

through the sale of grain, and he has stressed that "the wealth of every collective farm has been created with the decisive help of the state and that this wealth essentially belongs to the entire people. . . . In present-day conditions the collective farms' indivisible funds essentially approach [the status of] public property." [6]

Moreover, in his program for the development of virgin lands in Kazakhstan preference has been given to the state farm system. Yet "property forms cannot be changed at will," so for the present the kolkhozes will remain, even though less efficient than the state farms.

Khrushchev has announced the end of two old fixtures of the régime, the capitalist encirclement and the dictatorship of the proletariat, both dating from 1917. Early in 1958, with his characteristic humor, he suggested that the concept of encirclement required "serious clarification," since, with the formation of the world socialist system, "you cannot tell who is encircling whom —whether the capitalist countries encircle the socialist countries, or vice versa." [7] This view, which was reaffirmed more seriously at the Twenty-first and Twenty-second Party Congresses, does not imply any reassessment of the motives of the capitalist countries. They remain predatory:

It is true that the nature of imperialism, its aggressive character, has not changed. But the possibilities it now has are different from those it had at the time of its undivided rule. As matters stand, imperialism can no longer dictate its will to all, or pursue its policy of aggression without hindrance. [8]

Unlike Stalin, Khrushchev argues that "war is not fatalistically inevitable." The growing economic and military strength of the socialist states has changed the situation. "Developments indicate that it may actually be feasible to banish world war from the

[6] "M.T.S. Reorganization: Khrushchev's Theses," *Current Digest of the Soviet Press*, Vol. 10, No. 9 (April 9, 1958), p. 10, from *Pravda* and *Izvestia*, March 1, 1958.

[7] Interview with correspondent of *Le Figaro*, in Khrushchev, *For Victory in Peaceful Competition with Capitalism* (New York, 1960), pp. 206-207.

[8] Khrushchev, "Concluding Speech at the 22nd Congress of the C.P.S.U.," in *The Road to Communism, Documents of the 22nd Congress of the C.P.S.U.* (Moscow, 1962), p. 332. This was in answer to Chinese criticism.

life of society even before the complete triumph of socialism on earth, with capitalism surviving in part of the world." [9]

The liquidation of the dictatorship of the proletariat at last frees the nation from that obnoxious phrase, if not from its substance. Quite logically, with the disappearance of class distinctions among the people, the concept of rule by a class loses its meaning. The state becomes a "state of the whole people," a new stage in the transition to self-government by the people without the state, the final form of government under communism. It is interesting, however, and another indication of his acute public relations sense, that Khrushchev has made this distinction of state forms while distinctions of class are still present—the workers and peasants being regarded as "friendly" classes. Again, the new state does not imply any reassessment of the needs of internal control or of external defense.

It is in the international field, rather than in the domestic, that the most difficult problems of Marxist theory have arisen in the post-Stalin period. Marx's vision of proletarian unity has been subjected to the strains arising from its interpretation by separate sovereignties, and the forces of nationalism and the potential power of China have helped to complicate matters. Khrushchev has tried both repression and flexibility in his efforts to maintain unity. At times, as in the Hungarian uprising of 1956, his means resemble those of Stalin at his worst.[10] At others, as in the temporary reconciliation with Yugoslavia, he has reversed established policy in the interest of unity. This search for unity is evident not only in Europe but also in his relations with China. So frequently has he veered to meet the ideas of the Chinese communists that a doubt may arise as to whether Russian policy is made in Moscow or in Peking, but there seem to be limits to this process. While hardly granting to Mao Tse-tung a succession to

[9] Khrushchev, "Report of the Central Committee," in *ibid.*, p. 57.

[10] "We did not criticize Stalin for being a bad Communist. We criticized him for certain deviations, negative qualities, for committing grave mistakes. . . . Stalin's name is inseparable from Marxism-Leninism. Therefore, each one of us . . . strives to be as faithful to the cause of Marxism-Leninism, the struggle for the interests of the working class, as Stalin was faithful to this cause." Khrushchev at the Chinese Embassy, January 17, 1957, in his *Speeches and Interviews on World Problems, 1957* (Moscow, 1958), pp. 16-17.

Stalin as the oracle of Marxism, Khrushchev has avoided a rivalry with him in the interpretation of the faith. If this results in an avoidance of antagonism between the two countries it may well emerge as the most important feature of his policy.

The appearance of additional socialist states has led to the doctrine, advocated especially by Yugoslavia, that several different paths, and not solely that followed by Russia, may lead from capitalism to socialism. For a time under Stalin this doctrine appeared to find favor even in Moscow; but the suspicion that leaders travelling on other paths might, through malice or error, not really approach socialism, or might cause difficulties for Moscow, subsequently led to a narrowing of the limits of acceptable variation. Khrushchev has again widened them, although the career of Imre Nagy indicates that the toleration does not extend to neutrality between the socialist and the capitalist blocs. He agrees that "a stage through which we passed does not necessarily have to be repeated in other Socialist countries," and in some of his criticisms of Stalin he has, at least by implication, even suggested that the path followed by Russia was not always the best of all possible paths. More important, at the Twentieth Party Congress he made the statement, reminiscent of Bernstein, that the transition to socialism need not be violent, that a "stable majority in parliament" might be sufficient.

Because of the large bloc of socialist states, this transition is independent of the particular country's stage of economic development. "Today practically any country, irrespective of its level of development, can enter on the road leading to socialism." Moreover, as in the old theory of permanent revolution, "In the present epoch the tasks of the popular-democratic, the national-liberation and the socialist revolutions are drawing closer and becoming more interwoven," since all three are aimed against one foe—"imperialism, the monopolist bourgeoisie." [11]

The most significant new theory stimulated by the emergence of new socialist countries is Khrushchev's "law of the even development of socialism." Lenin's "law of the uneven development

[11] Khrushchev, "On the Programme of the C.P.S.U.," in *The Road to Communism*, p. 274. Thus, although not rehabilitated, a strange triumvirate is waiting in the wings—Bernstein, Bukharin, and Trotsky.

of capitalism" (see p. 71), which had served as the foundation for Stalin's doctrine of socialism in one country, was based on the anarchic, unplanned methods of production under capitalism, which permitted some countries to outstrip others in economic development. Socialism, on the other hand, by deliberate planning and mutual aid within the bloc can speed up the advance of backward countries so that the existing differences in stages of development are progressively narrowed, and all the socialist countries enter full communism, not simultaneously, but "within one historical epoch." The U.S.S.R., having the greatest industrial capacity, should not rush ahead into luxury; it should forego some consumer goods in the interest of international solidarity and make use of a more efficient international division of labor to increase the total output of goods for all.

But what about China? Her vast population and poverty seem to defy such a "law." To raise her to Russia's level would demand too great sacrifices from the Russian people and delay the achievement of communism. This line of objection lay behind the suggestion made by Stepanian that the law of even development might be applied separately in two groups of socialist countries, a European and an Asiatic group. The differences between countries within each group were much less than those between the groups, and the law would not demand such great sacrifices.[12]

Khrushchev, however, branded this suggestion as revisionism. He may not succeed in implementing his theory as public policy, but it has clear long-range advantages. It aims to avoid stimulating in the socialist camp the "have" and "have not" jealousies of capitalistic international relations and the moral bankruptcy in the eyes of the poor to which selfishness leads. Having confidence in the constructive powers of socialism, Khrushchev is acutely aware that China will not always be weak. One day she will be either an overwhelming antagonist or a resourceful and contributing partner. And besides, the sacrifices may not be so great. The long emphasis on heavy industry is giving Russia a capacity to produce producers' goods that will soon need an

[12] T. A. Stepanian, "Oktiabr'skaia revoliutsiia i stanovlenie kommunisticheskoi formatsii," *Voprosy Filosofii*, No. 10 (1958), p. 34.

outlet elsewhere, since they cannot easily be left idle in the manner of capitalism. "Even development," therefore, is not only good proletarian solidarity; it is also good, hard-headed politics and economics.

Another significant theory, not new, to which Khrushchev gives much emphasis is his doctrine of the peaceful coexistence of states with "different social systems." While for their own safety capitalist governments may legitimately doubt the sincerity of the resulting peaceful professions, this doctrine is founded on three important considerations. In the first place, a sufficient segment of the world's resources has come under socialist control so that the socialist countries now have great confidence in their own military strength. They no longer think themselves (as they once did) dependent on revolution in western Europe, and therefore feel less need to promote, for their own protection, the subversion of foreign governments. In the second place, the breakdown of colonialism has greatly weakened the capitalist powers. While the newly emerging nations may not be socialist, they constitute important subtractions from the resources of the former colonial powers and collectively they form a strong body of world public opinion that is generally neutral if not adverse toward the West. And in the third place, the doctrine of peaceful coexistence rests on similar confidence in the long-range superiority of socialism over capitalism in economic competition. If Marx's economics is correct, the capitalist countries will fall like ripe fruit (as the deterministic Marxists long ago pointed out), victims of their own internal contradictions and external conflicts. There is evidence, however, that in Khrushchev this confidence does not signify a reversion to the deterministic line. Marx had hinged the future fate of capitalism upon the deepening of the crises within it, with the attendant worsening of the lot of the workers and eventual revolution. The deepening crises remain a part of the dogma, but Khrushchev pragmatically finds that the inherent inefficiences of capitalism are in practice resulting in its inability to match the socialist rate of progress. It no doubt appeals to his sense of humor to contemplate the overthrow of capitalism through economic competition (which capitalism professes to admire) with socialism (which it so scornfully depre-

cates). His repeated emphasis on catching up with and surpassing the United States in per capita production indicates that,
as a materialist, he believes in the propaganda appeal of material
things. Thus, if the standard of living in the Soviet Union comes
to surpass that of the United States, the rest of the world will
take notice of that achievement, he seems to feel, and capitalism
will be overthrown by the cupidity, rather than by the desperation, of the masses.

Three important qualifications to the doctrine of peaceful co-
existence need to be remembered. First, it does not apply in the
realm of ideology. No cessation of the ideological struggle between capitalism and communism is involved, but this should not
be "confused" with "the question of relations between states."
Second, it does not imply the maintenance of the status quo.
There must be no "export of revolution," but also no "export
of counterrevolution." Khrushchev expects, as Marxism predicts,
a series of local revolutions, like that in Cuba, gradually to erode
the area of capitalism. And third, like the doctrine of socialism
in one country, that of peaceful coexistence applies to what the
Russians regard as a temporary stage in the world's transition
to communism. According to the Marxist prophecy of increasingly severe crises periodically erupting into international war,
this stage may meet with a violent end at any time. Barring
major war, however, peaceful coexistence may last until the last
capitalist nation succumbs in the economic competition between
the two systems.

Most of the current thought of the régime is concentrated in
the new Party program adopted at the Twenty-second Congress
in 1961. The first program (1903) was a plan for revolution, to
overthrow the tsar; the second (1919) was a plan for the building of socialism; these ends being achieved, a new program was
needed, a plan for the building of communism. Much attention,
therefore, has recently been given to the problems of the transition from socialism to communism and to the nature of commu-
nistic society itself. For the first time something approaching
a concrete timetable for this transition has been established,
subject to the preservation of peace and even to the drain of the
armaments race: a communist society will "in the main" be built

by 1981. "The Party solemnly proclaims: the present generation of Soviet people shall live in communism!"

The old idea of abundance of consumer goods and services still lies at the heart of the project. It is anticipated that specific items will reach adequate supply before others and will be made free—such as medical service, maintenance of children, education, transportation, housing, utilities, and restaurant meals. Other items will be reduced in price and wages will be increased until eventually, "With the transition to the single communist form of people's property and the communist system of distribution, commodity-money relations will become economically outdated and will wither away." [13] The transition must be gradual; socialism grows into communism by an "objective law" even though capitalism cannot grow into socialism.

Material goods alone, however, will not bring communism. Khrushchev is very much aware of the psychological changes that are needed.

A man steeped in capitalist prejudices cannot be taken into communism. He must first be freed from the burden of the past. It will take time and effort to eliminate the survivals of capitalism in the minds of men, to change in millions of people customs and habits that have evolved in the course of centuries—to complete the change that was begun by our revolution. Survivals of the past are a terrible power that weighs on the minds of people. They persist in the lives and in the minds of millions of people long after the economic conditions that engendered them have disappeared.[14]

In the meantime material and moral incentives to work will be required. Wages will not be levelled, but the acquisition of skill by all will eliminate the lower end of the pay scale and at the same time remove much of the distinction between mental and manual labor. This distinction, in Khrushchev's opinion, will be more difficult to remove than that between town and country.

The latter is expected to yield to technology. Better equipment

[13] Programme of the C.P.S.U. in *The Road to Communism*, p. 536 (Part 2, end of Sec. I).

[14] Khrushchev, "Report of the Central Committee," in *The Road to Communism*, p. 154.

and management will raise productivity and "farm labor will turn into a variety of industrial labor." Both state farms and collective farms are to be improved. This "creates conditions for the gradual *rapprochement* and, in the long run, also for the merging of kolkhoz property and the property of the whole people into one communist property." The collective farms are "schools of communism" for the peasants. "As production on the collective and state farms develops and social relations there advance, agriculture will ascend to a higher level that will make it possible to go over to communist forms of production and distribution." [15]

In this approach to the elimination of distinctions between town and country, as in the broader problem of the contest between communism and capitalism, it is clear that Khrushchev is relying on the psychological impact of material abundance. Stalin saw the solution to this distinction in terms of the elimination of commodity production (see p. 248), and on that ground opposed the sale of machinery to the collective farms. Khrushchev has seen a different vision. He has sold the machinery and hopes to raise the productivity of the kolkhoz peasantry enough to permit them to enter the promised land of communism along with the rest of the population. In the transition to communism, he seems to believe, the ownership of property, hitherto so basic to Marxism, becomes less important than the efficient use and productivity of the property. If industry and the farms can and do in fact produce abundance for all, what does it matter who owns them? In this great drive for more goods and services the old antagonisms of scarcity may be losing their grip—even among Marxists. Yet in Khrushchev's hands Marxism remains, both externally and internally, a messianic movement. He seems to aspire to the role of the messiah of material abundance.

[15] Khrushchev, "On the Programme of the C.P.S.U.," in *ibid.,* p. 231.

SOME FUNDAMENTAL QUESTIONS

OF PRESENT-DAY

INTERNATIONAL DEVELOPMENT

Khrushchev, *Report of the Central Committee of the C.P.S.U. to the 20th Party Congress* (Moscow, 1956), pp. 38-46.

Comrades, I should like to dwell on some fundamental questions concerning present-day international development, which determine not only the present course of events, but also the prospects for the future.

These questions are the peaceful co-existence of the two systems, the possibility of preventing wars in the present era, and the forms of transition to socialism in different countries.

Let us examine these questions in brief.

The Peaceful Co-existence of the Two Systems

The Leninist principle of peaceful co-existence of states with different social systems has always been and remains the general line of our country's foreign policy.

It has been alleged that the Soviet Union advances the principle of peaceful co-existence merely out of tactical considerations, considerations of expediency. Yet it is common knowledge that we have always, from the very first years of Soviet power, stood with equal firmness for peaceful co-existence. Hence, it is not a tactical move, but a fundamental principle of Soviet foreign policy.

This means that if there is indeed a threat to the peaceful co-existence of countries with differing social and political systems, it by no means comes from the Soviet Union or the rest of the socialist camp. Is there a single reason why a socialist state should want to unleash aggressive war? Do we have classes and groups that are interested in war as a means of enrichment? We do not. We abolished them long ago. Or, perhaps, we do not have enough territory or natural wealth, perhaps we lack sources of raw materials or markets for our goods? No, we have sufficient of all those and to spare. Why then should we want war? We do not want it, as a matter of principle we renounce any policy that might lead to millions of people being plunged into war for the sake of the selfish interests of a handful of multi-millionaires. Do those who shout about the "aggressive intentions" of the U.S.S.R. know all this? Of course they do. Why then do they keep up the old monotonous refrain about some imaginary "communist aggression"? Only to stir up mud, to conceal their plans for world domination, a "crusade" against peace, democracy, and socialism.

To this day the enemies of peace allege that the Soviet Union is out to overthrow capitalism in other countries by "exporting" revolution. It goes without saying that among us Communists there are no supporters of capitalism. But this does not mean that we have interfered or plan to interfere in the internal affairs of countries where capitalism still exists. Romain Rolland was right when he said that "freedom is not brought in from abroad in baggage trains like Bourbons." (*Animation.*) It is ridiculous to think that revolutions are made to order. We often hear representatives of bourgeois countries reasoning thus: "The Soviet leaders claim that they are for peaceful co-existence between the two systems. At the same time they declare that they are fighting for communism, and say that communism is bound to win in all countries. Now if the Soviet Union is fighting for communism, how can there be any peaceful co-existence with it?" This view is the result of bourgeois propaganda. The ideologists of the bourgeoisie distort the facts and deliberately confuse questions of ideological struggle with questions of relations between states in order to make the Communists of the Soviet Union look like advocates of aggression.

When we say that the socialist system will win in the competition between the two systems—the capitalist and the socialist—this by no means signifies that its victory will be achieved through

armed interference by the socialist countries in the internal affairs
of the capitalist countries. Our certainty of the victory of communism is based on the fact that the socialist mode of production
possesses decisive advantages over the capitalist mode of production. Precisely because of this, the ideas of Marxism-Leninism
are more and more capturing the minds of the broad masses of
the working people in the capitalist countries, just as they have
captured the minds of millions of men and women in our country
and the People's Democracies. (*Prolonged applause.*) We believe
that all working men in the world, once they have become convinced of the advantages communism brings, will sooner or later
take the road of struggle for the construction of socialist society.
(*Prolonged applause.*) Building communism in our country, we
are resolutely against war. We have always held and continue
to hold that the establishment of a new social system in one or
another country is the internal affair of the peoples of the countries concerned. This is our attitude, based on the great Marxist-
Leninist teaching. . . .

We believe that countries with differing social systems can
do more than exist side by side. It is necessary to proceed further,
to improve relations, strengthen confidence between countries,
and co-operate. The historic significance of the famous Five Principles, advanced by the People's Republic of China and the
Republic of India and supported by the Bandung Conference
and the world public in general, lies in that they provide the
best form for relations between countries with differing social
systems in present-day conditions. Why not make these principles the foundation of peaceful relations among all countries in
all parts of the world? It would meet the vital interests and
demands of the peoples if all countries subscribed to these Five
Principles.

The Possibility of Preventing War in the Present Era

Millions of people all over the world are asking whether
another war is really inevitable, whether mankind which has
already experienced two devastating world wars must still go
through a third one? Marxists must answer this question taking

into consideration the epoch-making changes of the last decades.

There is, of course, a Marxist-Leninist precept that wars are inevitable as long as imperialism exists. This precept was evolved at a time when 1) imperialism was an all-embracing world system, and 2) the social and political forces which did not want war were weak, poorly organized, and hence unable to compel the imperialists to renounce war.

People usually take only one aspect of the question and examine only the economic basis of wars under imperialism. This is not enough. War is not only an economic phenomenon. Whether there is to be a war or not depends in large measure on the correlation of class, political forces, the degree of organization and the awareness and resolve of the people. Moreover, in certain conditions the struggle waged by progressive social and political forces may play a decisive role. Hitherto the state of affairs was such that the forces that did not want war and opposed it were poorly organized and lacked the means to check the schemes of the war-makers. Thus it was before the First World War, when the main force opposed to the threat of war —the world proletariat—was disorganized by the treachery of the leaders of the Second International. Thus it was on the eve of the Second World War, when the Soviet Union was the only country that pursued an active peace policy, when the other Great Powers to all intents and purposes encouraged the agressors, and the Right-wing Social-Democratic leaders had split the labour movement in the capitalist countries.

In that period this precept was absolutely correct. At the present time, however, the situation has changed radically. Now there is a world camp of socialism, which has become a mighty force. In this camp the peace forces find not only the moral, but also the material means to prevent aggression. Moreover, there is a large group of other countries with a population running into many hundreds of millions which are actively working to avert war. The labour movement in the capitalist countries has today become a tremendous force. The movement of peace supporters has sprung up and developed into a powerful factor.

In these circumstances certainly the Leninist precept that so long as imperialism exists, the economic basis giving rise to wars will also be preserved remains in force. That is why we must display the greatest vigilance. As long as capitalism survives in the world, the reactionary forces representing the interests of the capitalist monopolies will continue their drive towards military gambles and aggression, and may try to unleash war. But war is not fatalistically inevitable. Today there are mighty social and political forces possessing formidable means to prevent the imperialists from unleashing war, and if they actually try to start it, to give a smashing rebuff to the aggressors and frustrate their adventurist plans. To be able to do this all anti-war forces must be vigilant and prepared, they must act as a united front and never relax their efforts in the battle for peace. The more actively the peoples defend peace, the greater the guarantees that there will be no new war. (*Stormy, prolonged applause.*)

Forms of Transition to Socialism in Different Countries

In connection with the radical changes in the world arena new prospects are also opening up in respect to the transition of countries and nations to socialism.

As far back as the eve of the Great October Socialist Revolution Lenin wrote: "All nations will arrive at socialism—this is inevitable, but not all will do so in exactly the same way, each will contribute something of its own in one or another form of democracy, one or another variety of the dictatorship of the proletariat, one or another rate at which socialist transformations will be effected in the various aspects of social life. There is nothing more primitive from the viewpoint of theory or more ridiculous from that of practice than to paint, 'in the name of historical materialism,' *this* aspect of the future in a monotonous grey. The result will be nothing more than Suzdal daubing." (*Works* [4th Russian ed.] Vol. 23, p. 58; [cf. 1st English ed., Vol. 19 (1942), p. 256].)

Historical experience has fully confirmed Lenin's brilliant precept. Alongside the Soviet form of reconstructing society on socialist lines, we now have the form of People's Democracy.

In Poland, Bulgaria, Czechoslovakia, Albania, and the other European People's Democracies, this form sprang up and is being utilized in conformity with the concrete historical, social and economic conditions, and peculiarities of each of these countries. It has been thoroughly tried and tested in the course of ten years and has fully proved its worth.

Much that is unique in socialist construction is being contributed by the Chinese People's Republic, whose economy prior to the victory of the revolution was exceedingly backward, semi-feudal and semi-colonial in character. Having taken over the decisive commanding positions, the people's democratic state is using them in the social revolution to implement a policy of peaceful reorganization of private industry and trade and their gradual transformation into a component of socialist economy.

The leadership of the great cause of socialist reconstruction by the Communist Party of China and the Communist and Workers' Parties of the other People's Democracies, exercised in keeping with the peculiarities and specific features of each country, is creative Marxism in action.

In the Federative People's Republic of Yugoslavia, where state power belongs to the working people, and society is based on public ownership of the means of production, specific concrete forms of economic management and organization of the state apparatus are arising in the process of socialist construction.

It is probable that more forms of transition to socialism will appear. Moreover, the implementation of these forms need not be associated with civil war under all circumstances. Our enemies like to depict us Leninists as advocates of violence always and everywhere. True, we recognize the need for the revolutionary transformation of capitalist society into socialist society. It is this that distinguishes the revolutionary Marxists from the reformists, the opportunists. There is no doubt that in a number of capitalist countries the violent overthrow of the dictatorship of the bourgeoisie and the sharp aggravation of class struggle connected with this are inevitable. But the forms of social revolution vary. It is not true that we regard violence and civil war as the only way to remake society.

It will be recalled that in the conditions that arose in April 1917 Lenin granted the possibility that the Russian Revolution might develop peacefully, and that in the spring of 1918, after the victory of the October Revolution, Lenin drew up his famous plan for peaceful socialist construction. It is not our fault that the Russian and international bourgeoisie organized counter-revolution, intervention, and civil war against the young Soviet state and forced the workers and peasants to take up arms. It did not come to civil war in the European People's Democracies, where the historical situation was different.

Leninism teaches us that the ruling classes will not surrender their power voluntarily. And the greater or lesser degree of intensity which the struggle may assume, the use or the non-use of violence in the transition to socialism depends on the resistance of the exploiters, on whether the exploiting class itself resorts to violence, rather than on the proletariat.

In this connection the question arises of whether it is possible to go over to socialism by using parliamentary means. No such course was open to the Russian Bolsheviks, who were the first to effect this transition. Lenin showed us another road, that of the establishment of a republic of Soviets, the only correct road in those historical conditions. Following that course we achieved a victory of history-making significance.

Since then, however, the historical situation has undergone radical changes which make possible a new approach to the question. The forces of socialism and democracy have grown immeasurably throughout the world, and capitalism has become much weaker. The mighty camp of socialism with its population of over 900 million is growing and gaining in strength. Its gigantic internal forces, its decisive advantages over capitalism, are being increasingly revealed from day to day. Socialism has a great power of attraction for the workers, peasants, and intellectuals of all countries. The ideas of socialism are indeed coming to dominate the minds of all toiling humanity.

At the same time the present situation offers the working class in a number of capitalist countries a real opportunity to unite the overwhelming majority of the people under its leadership and to secure the transfer of the basic means of production into the hands of the people. The Right-wing bourgeois parties and their governments are suffering bankruptcy with increasing frequency. In these circumstances the working class, by rallying around itself the toiling peasantry, the intelligentsia, all patriotic forces, and resolutely repulsing the opportunist elements who are incapable of giving up the policy of compromise with the capitalists and landlords, is in a position to defeat the reactionary forces opposed to the popular interest, to capture a stable majority in parliament, and transform the latter from an organ of bourgeois democracy into a genuine instrument of the people's will. (*Applause.*) In such an event this institution, traditional in many highly developed capitalist countries, may become an organ of genuine democracy, democracy for the working people.

The winning of a stable parliamentary majority backed by a mass revolutionary movement of the proletariat and of all the working people could create for the working class of a number of capitalist and former colonial countries the conditions needed to secure fundamental social changes.

In the countries where capitalism is still strong and has a huge military and police apparatus at its disposal, the reactionary forces will of course inevitably offer serious resistance. There the transition to socialism will be attended by a sharp class, revolutionary struggle.

Whatever the form of transition to socialism, the decisive and indispensable factor is the political leadership of the working class headed by its vanguard. Without this there can be no transition to socialism.

[FROM SOCIALISM TO COMMUNISM]

Khrushchev, a) "On the Programme of the C.P.S.U.," in *The Road to Communism,* and b) *Control Figures for the Economic Development of the U.S.S.R. for 1959-1965* (Moscow, 1959), as indicated in following notes.

Socialism does not develop on its own foundation. For all its immense achievements of world historic significance, in many respects—the economic, legal and moral, and in the consciousness of men—it still bears an imprint of the old system,

from which it has emerged. Communism is a higher and more
perfect stage of social life, and can develop only after socialism
is fully consolidated. Under communism all the after-effects of
the capitalist system will be completely eliminated.

The fact that communism develops on its own foundation
predetermines the distinctive features of its construction. The
transition from capitalism to socialism is effected under conditions of class struggle. It involves a radical break-up of social
relations, a sweeping social revolution and the establishment of
the dictatorship of the proletariat. On the other hand, the transition to communism proceeds in the absence of any exploiting
classes, when all members of society—workers, peasants and intellectuals—have a vested interest in the victory of communism,
and work for it consciously. It is natural therefore that the building of communism is effected by the most democratic methods,
by way of improving and developing social relations, with due
account of the departure of the old forms of life and the appearance of new forms, of their interlacement and mutual influence.
Society will no longer experience the difficulties induced by class
struggle within the country. All this will serve to accelerate the
rates of social development in the period of transition to communism.

The historical limits of the draft Programme are 20 years. Why
did we set this term? When the draft Programme was being
discussed, some comrades wondered whether the time allocated
to the task was not too long. No, comrades. To prepare society
for the establishment of the principles of communism we have to
develop the productive forces enormously and create an abundance of material and spiritual values. And that takes a certain
amount of time. The bowl of communism is a bowl of abundance, and it must always be full. Everyone must contribute his
bit to it, and everyone must take from it. It would be a fatal
error to decree the introduction of communism before all the
necessary conditions for it have matured. If we were to proclaim
that we introduce communism when the bowl is still far from
full, we would be unable to take from it according to needs.
In that case we would only discredit the ideas of communism,
disrupt the initiative of the working people and retard the ad-

vance to communism. We base ourselves on strictly scientific esti-
mates, which indicate that we shall, in the main, have built a
communist society within 20 years. (*Prolonged applause.*)

What does it mean to build communism in the main? It means
that:

in the *economic* sphere the material and technical basis of
communism will be created; the economy of the Soviet Union
will surpass that of the most developed capitalist countries and
move into first place for production per head of the population,
the world's highest living standard will be ensured and all the
conditions created to attain an abundance of material and cultural values;

in the sphere of *social* relations the still existing remnants of
distinctions between classes will be eliminated; classes will fuse
into a classless society of communist working people; the essential
distinctions between town and country, and then between physical and mental labour, will, in the main, be eradicated; there
will be greater economic and ideological community among
nations; the features will develop of the man of communist society, a man harmoniously combining ideological integrity, broad
education, moral purity and physical perfection;

in the *political* sphere all citizens will participate in the administration of public affairs, and society will prepare itself for
the full implementation of the principles of communist self-
government through a most extensive development of socialist
democracy.[16]

Marxist-Leninist theory, and our practical experience in building socialist society, enable us to draw some important conclusions concerning the nature of our forward movement to communism.

First, the transition from the socialist to the higher stage is a
law-governed historical process that cannot be violated or by-
passed at will. . . .

Second, notwithstanding all the differences between the communist and socialist phases, there is no wall separating these
two stages of social development. Communism stems from social-

[16] a), pp. 194-196.

ism as its direct continuation. It would be wrong, erroneous, to believe that communism will somehow appear on the scene suddenly. . . .

Third, gradual transition to communism should not be understood as a decelerated movement. On the contrary, it is a period of rapid development of modern industry. . . .

As socialist production is extended on a new material and technical base, and as education is more closely linked with productive labour, the essential distinctions between mental and physical labour will gradually disappear. The all-round development of our people will transform labour into man's prime want. This will be facilitated by the forthcoming reduction of working hours and further improvement of working conditions. When every branch of industry is automated, when man becomes the master of the machine, he will have to devote less time and energy to producing the things he needs. Labour, which at times is still arduous and tiring, will become a source of joy and pleasure for a harmoniously developed healthy person. . . .

The socialist principle of distribution according to work is based on the understanding that, in the socialist stage, equalitarian distribution is impossible. Distribution according to work is the only reasonable and just principle under prevailing conditions. We cannot disregard the fact that levelling would lead to an unjust method of distribution: the bad worker and the good would receive an equal share, which would be to the advantage of slackers. The material incentive for people to work better, raise productivity and produce more, would be dampened. Levelling would mean not transition to communism, but the discrediting of communism. . . .

In communist society there will, of course, be planned and organized allocation of labour among the various branches of production, and social regulation of working time in accordance with the specific features of the different production processes. The machine industry has a set rhythm that calls for a corresponding arrangement of the work.

There is a vulgarized conception of communist society as a loose and unorganized anarchistic mass of human beings. No, it will be a highly organized and closely coordinated common-

wealth of men of labour. For the machine to be properly op-
erated, every worker will have to perform his production job
and social functions in a definite time and according to a definite
system. The highly mechanized and automated industry of the
future will not require long hours of work. There will be ample
time for study, art, literature, sports, and so forth.

The question of how to *develop and bring closer together the
collective-farm and public forms of socialist property* acquires
great theoretical and practical importance in communist construction.

It should be perfectly clear that in the future the collective-
farm-co-operative and state forms of property will merge into an
integral communist property. Why then, it might be asked, are
we not pressing for their merger, and consider that in the present
stage we must develop collective-farm-co-operative property
alongside with state property?

Property forms cannot be changed at will. They develop in
accordance with economic laws and depend on the nature and
level of the productive forces. The collective-farm system fully
accords with the present level and development requirements
of the productive forces in agriculture. It makes for the most
effective use of modern farm machinery, which is impossible
under parcelled-out small peasant farming. . . .

The continued development of the productive forces will tend
to raise the degree of socialization of collective-farm production
and bring collective-farm-co-operative property into closer approximation with public property, gradually obliterating the line
dividing the two. This is shown by the following characteristic
processes:

First, uninterrupted increase of collective-farm non-distribu-
table assets, which are the economic basis for continued expansion of collective-farm production and gradual approximation of
collective-farm and public property.

Second, enlargement of collective-farm production to involve
more and more fully all the branches of agriculture. . . .

Third, inter-farm production ties and diverse forms of cooperation. These are being more widely applied. . . .

Fourth, agricultural electrification, mechanization and automation will lead to the pooling, to a kind of merger, of collective-farm production facilities with state, or public, facilities. Agricultural labour will gradually become a variety of industrial labour.

The merger of the collective-farm and public forms of property is historically inevitable. It will be brought about not by dispensing with collective-farm property, but by raising its level of socialization with the aid and support of the socialist state.

The merger of collective-farm-co-operative property with state property into an integral public property is not a simple organizational and economic measure, but is the solution of the cardinal problem of bridging the essential distinction between town and country. . . .

Parallel with these problems of economic development, we are squarely faced with *the problems of the political organization of society, the state system and administration in the period of extensive building of communism.*

Marxism-Leninism teaches us that under communism the state will wither away and that the functions of public administration will no longer have a political character, and will pass under the people's direct administration. But we should not take an oversimplified view of the process. We should not imagine that the withering away of the state will resemble the falling of leaves in autumn, when the trees are left bare.

The withering away of the state, if we approach the question dialectically, implies the development of the socialist state into communist public self-administration. For under communism, too, there will remain certain public functions similar to those now performed by the state, but their nature, and the methods by which they will be exercised, will differ from those obtaining in the present stage. . . .

It is already clear that many functions of our government agencies will gradually pass to public organizations. Take, for instance, certain aspects of our cultural services. It is not at all obligatory that they remain in the charge of government organizations. Public organizations can handle them just as successfully. . . .

Questions relating to public order and the rules of socialist human relations should likewise come increasingly under the jurisdiction of non-government organizations. . . .

Socialist society forms such voluntary organizations for safe-guarding public order as the people's militia, courts of honour and so forth. They will employ new methods and will follow new patterns in the performance of public functions. The duty of the voluntary people's militia detachments should be to keep public order in their respective communities and to see that the rights and interests of all citizens are properly respected and protected. . . .

The transfer of certain state functions to public organizations should not be carried out with undue haste. In some cases it will be done more resolutely, while in others we shall take only the first, exploratory steps in order to train people to safeguard public order themselves. . . .

The tasks of the socialist state in the defence of peace, in safeguarding the country against the threat of armed attack by the imperialist powers, are of special importance and magni-tude. . . .[17]

FROM THE DICTATORSHIP
OF THE PROLETARIAT TO A STATE
OF THE WHOLE PEOPLE

Khrushchev, "On the Programme of the C.P.S.U.," in *The Road to Communism*, pp. 148-153.

The draft Programme of the Party raises, and resolves, a new important question of communist theory and practice—the development of the dictatorship of the working class into a state of the whole people, the character and the tasks of this

[17] b), pp. 114-116, 119, 123-130.

state, and its future under communism. *The state of the whole people is a new stage in the development of the socialist state, an all-important milestone on the road from socialist statehood to communist public self-government.*

Half a century ago our Party was the only party to put the Marxist-Leninist idea of the dictatorship of the proletariat into its programme. If we managed to survive in the bitter struggle against domestic and world reactionaries, if we managed to translate into reality mankind's age-old dream of socialism, we owe this, to a tremendous degree, to the fact that we possessed a powerful instrument for the transformation of society—a state of the dictatorship of the proletariat. The experience of the Soviet Union and the People's Democracies has fully confirmed the Marxist-Leninist thesis that the victory of socialism is possible only if the dictatorship of the proletariat is established.

The dictatorship of the proletariat is born of the conditions created by the class struggle between the proletariat and the bourgeoisie. In the process of its establishment, socialism has to overcome the resistance, often of a most bitter kind, of the reactionary forces of the old world. . . .

It stands to reason that when socialism had triumphed *completely and finally* in our country and we entered upon the *period of full-scale communist construction,* the conditions which necessitated the dictatorship of the proletariat disappeared, its domestic purposes were fulfilled.

The working class is the only class in history which does not entertain the purpose of perpetuating its domination. When the conditions which gave rise to its dictatorship disappear, when the tasks which society could accomplish solely with its help are consummated, the state gradually develops, under the leadership of the working class, into a nation-wide organisation of all the working people of socialist society. With the victory of socialism and the country's entry into the period of full-scale communist construction, the working class of the Soviet Union has on its own initiative, consistent with the tasks of communist construction, transformed the state of proletarian dictatorship into a state of the whole people. That, comrades, is a fact unparalleled in history. Until now the state has always been an instrument of dictatorship by this or that class. In our country, for the first time in history, a state has taken shape which is not a dictatorship of any one class, but an instrument of society as a whole, of the entire people. . . .

But why, for all that, is the state as such being retained, though the antagonism of classes, the main thing that gave rise to it, has disappeared? It is being retained because the tasks which society can solve only with the aid of the state are not as yet consummated. These tasks and functions of the socialist state are clearly specified in the draft of our Party Programme.

The state will remain long after the victory of the first phase of communism. The process of its withering away will be a very long one; it will cover an entire historical epoch and will not end until society is completely ripe for self-administration. For some time, the features of state administration and public self-government will intermingle. In this process the domestic functions of the state will develop and change, and gradually lose their political character. It is only after a developed communist society is built in the U.S.S.R., and provided socialism wins and consolidates in the international arena, that there will no longer be any need for the state, and it will wither away.

The fact that the dictatorship of the proletariat is no longer necessary does not in any way imply any relaxation of public order and legality. The Party attaches great importance to a further strengthening of legality and of law and order, and to the protection of the rights of citizens. The rights, freedom, honour and dignity of the Soviet citizen will be closely protected by society and by the state. Those who expect that public order in our country will be less rigid, are in for a woeful disappointment. Alongside the state organs, public organisations of working people will play an increasing role in combating anti-social and criminal elements.

[RELATIONS AMONG SOCIALIST STATES]

Khrushchev, a) *Control Figures for the Economic Development of the U.S.S.R. for 1959-1965;* and b) his speech at the Sixth Congress of the Socialist Unity Party of Germany on January 16, 1963, *Moscow News,* January 17, 1963, as indicated in following notes.

How will the socialist countries continue their advance towards communism? Can we envisage a situation where one of the socialist countries passes to communism and introduces the communist principles of production and distribution, while other countries are left trailing behind, somewhere in the early stages of socialist construction?

That prospect is highly improbable, if we take into account the laws governing the development of the socialist system of economy. From the theoretical standpoint it would be more correct to assume that by successfully employing the potentialities inherent in socialism, the socialist countries will more or less simultaneously pass to the higher phase of communist society. We proceed from the fact that the socialist system of economy is subject to new laws of development, laws unknown to human society in the past. For instance, the law operating under imperialism is uneven economic and political development of different countries. . . .

The economic law operating under socialism is balanced, proportional development, with the result that countries economically backward in the past are able rapidly to make up for lost time and raise their economic and cultural levels by drawing on the experience, co-operation and mutual assistance of other socialist countries. In this way the economic and cultural progress of all the socialist countries is evened out. . . .

In surveying the prospect of mankind's advance to communism, we must bear in mind the tremendous variety of historical conditions obtaining in the different countries. And this is bound to produce specific methods, patterns and forms of applying the general laws of mankind's forward movement to communism. But what must be emphasized here is that the principal, determining factor in the advance of all countries to communism is the laws common to all of them, not their specific manifestations. Marxism-Leninism requires ability to apply the theory of scientific communism to the concrete conditions of each individual country at different stages of its development.

The Yugoslav leaders have been voluminous in their allegations that the Communist Parties are coming out against them because they, the Yugoslav leaders, take as their starting-point in building socialism the features peculiar to their own country, and do not emulate the example and experience of other socialist countries. That, of course, is a perversion of the truth. The Marxist-Leninist Parties recognize that every country has its own specific features of socialist development. But that does not mean we can go forward to socialism by some other road, one that lies to the side of the general path indicated by Marxism-Leninism. What has to be taken into consideration are the specific features of the situation and period in which one country or another advances to socialism. For instance, certain steps in socialist construction taken in the past in the Soviet Union cannot be mechanically transplanted to other countries. All the socialist countries are building socialism, but not in a stereotyped way.

The Communist Party of China is employing many original forms of socialist construction. But we have no disagreements with it, nor can there be any disagreement.[18]

Comrades, allow me to deal with some important and pressing issues of the world Communist movement. To begin with, I would like to stress the interconnection of the struggle for peace, for peaceful coexistence, and the revolutionary struggle of the working class and all working people for the triumph of socialism on earth.

As things are in our day, the struggle for peace has become a

[18] a), pp. 133-135.

most important factor in the struggle for socialism. No problem of the revolutionary movement of the working class or the national-liberation movement can now be considered in isolation from the struggle to preserve peace and avert a world nuclear war. This is the important lesson in tactics for the world Communist movement to learn from the recent events in the Caribbean area. . . .

It is typical of our time that the struggle for peace has become, more than ever before, a paramount historic task not only for the working class but for all the other sections of the population. It is a knot in which the interests of all mankind intertwine. In face of the threat of a nuclear war, a single torrent of the most diverse mass movements is arising, movements which can be united by the common desire to deliver mankind from the disaster of war. The international working class and the socialist countries are the leading and organising force of this torrent. Nor is this because the socialist countries have simply taken up the slogan of the struggle for peace which enjoys popularity among the peoples. No, the fact is that the objective interests of the socialist countries, of the international working-class movement and the national-liberation movement are inseparable from the struggle to ward off a nuclear war. . . .

Today some people who call themselves Marxist-Leninists allege that the defence of peace and the struggle against the war danger are contrary to the spirit of Marxism-Leninism and hamper the progress of the revolutionary movement. . . .

The theory of scientific socialism created by Marx and Engels maintains that capitalism inevitably meets its doom in the course of its development, as a result of the antagonistic contradictions arising and growing in society. . . .

Life has proved the Marxist-Leninist doctrine perfectly correct. According to this doctrine, the working class defeats capitalism by its class struggle against the exploiters and not by starting wars between countries.

History willed that the Russian proletariat should achieve victory for the revolution during the First World War. After the Second World War there arose a number of socialist countries.

When a war breaks out between imperialist countries, all the internal and external contradictions of imperialism become aggravated, the machinery of the bourgeois state is shaken and a favourable situation is created for the victory of the working class, particularly in those countries defeated in the war.

It was with due regard to these circumstances that Lenin, at the beginning of the First World War, put forward his historic thesis of turning the imperialist war into a civil war. And the Russian Bolsheviks, the working class of Russia, did it.

But this is not at all to say that the Bolsheviks led by Lenin started a war between countries to bring about the victory of the revolution. On the contrary, Lenin and the Bolsheviks did everything to stave off the war; but since they could not prevent it, they set the task of turning the imperialist war into a civil war.

That has nothing to do with what the newly-fledged theoreticians want who are trying to create a "theory" to the effect that the road to victory for socialism runs through war between states, through destruction, bloodshed and the death of millions of people. Were the Communists to be guided by a "theory" such as that, it would repel the masses instead of attracting them. . . .

We have always considered and still consider the principle of the peaceful coexistence of countries with different social systems—a principle proclaimed by Lenin—to be the only correct one. Its significance has always been confirmed by the entire practice of international relations.

The policy of peaceful coexistence has acquired special significance in present conditions. When there was only one socialist country in the world, one surrounded by imperialist countries, the policy of peaceful coexistence was aimed at gaining time, at winning a respite to strengthen the proletarian state and build socialism in our country. Now that the nature of war has changed and the balance of world forces is favourable to peace and socialism, the policy of peaceful coexistence has far more important tasks to accomplish and goals to attain; it is acquiring what is in effect a new content. Its ultimate objective is to provide the most favourable conditions for the victory of socialism over capitalism through peaceful economic competition.

Some people misrepresent our Marxist-Leninist attitude, alleging that by proclaiming the policy of peaceful coexistence, we are calling on the revolutionary forces, on the Communist Parties of the capitalist countries, to renounce the class struggle, the struggle to establish the rule of the working class, of the working people, to abandon the national-liberation struggle of the peoples. That is not a clever invention and is slander.

The Soviet Union supports the just wars of peoples not only through its declarations and statements; its support has more than once taken the form of concrete assistance. Many peoples have used our arms in their liberation struggle and have won, have freed themselves from colonial oppression. The colonial peoples' wars for their liberation are holy wars, and it is for this reason that we have been, are and will always be on the side of the peoples fighting for their independence.

The advocates of the so-called theory of the victory of socialism through war also deny that socialism can win by peaceful means, saying that this is a departure from Marxism. We must say for the edification of these admirers of the cult of Stalin that it was none other than Stalin who in an interview with British Communists after the Second World War talked about using the peaceful, parliamentary way to bring about the victory of socialism and that is inscribed in the Programme of the Communist Party of Great Britain. British Party leaders know that this formulation was suggested by Stalin. . . .

We must see and appraise all this properly even if we differ on particular issues; we must not be subjective.

Even if we diverge over certain ideological questions, possibly including rather important ones, we must try to ensure that these questions are properly understood. In so doing we must not go to extremes, must not take a subjective stand in appraising the general situation in a particular country. . . .

If we disagreed on certain questions and quarrelled, and then said at once that the socialist country whose leaders differed with us on something was not socialist, we would be showing subjectivism pure and simple. It would be as in the case of the church: when a person ceases to keep religious vows and perform religious rites, he is excommunicated and anathematised. It does not befit us to proceed like churchmen and engage in "excommunicating" from socialism. . . .

In the relations between Communist Parties, it is essential to show tolerance, not to be subjective in appraising this or that development, not to rejoice our class enemies by arguing with each other. To our mind, it is necessary in appraising any development to proceed from the important thing: the attitude of the Communist Party concerned towards the problems of the struggle for the victory of the working class, of socialism. In discussions, particular discretion should be shown by the Parties of those countries whose peoples are already building socialism, are building Communism. It is our common duty not to scatter our forces in the face of the imperialist camp but, on the contrary, vigorously to strengthen them all along the line—economically, militarily, ideologically and politically.

Practice has shown that occasionally we have different opinions of questions bearing on the internal development of a country. In this respect, our relations have been shaping more or less correctly in recent years, and there has been tolerance and moderation, so to speak, as regards lecturing, to say nothing of interfering in the internal affairs of other countries. In foreign policy matters, and in matters concerning the international working-class and Communist movement, we also occasionally approach events and understand them differently. Here there may be a certain difference of opinion, of course, as well as discussions intended to elaborate a correct, agreed policy. But it is particularly essential to show restraint and patience.

The Central Committee of our Party would consider it useful now to call a halt to polemics between Communist Parties, to stop criticising other Parties inside one's own Party and allow some time for the passions to subside.

Some comrades suggest calling a meeting of all the fraternal Parties to discuss the questions that are ripe for it. Our Party has always favoured such meetings. We believe, however, that if we convene that meeting immediately there will probably be little hope of successfully eliminating the existing differences. Such a meeting would lead not to a calm and judicious removal of differences, but to their aggravation and to the danger of a split. We must not forget that there is a logic to every struggle and that political passions run high. . . .

Let us give time a chance to work for us. It will help us understand who is right and who is wrong. Moreover, during this time we should get rid of all that is extraneous and accidental. Then we will be able to come to agreement all the more effectively, to sum up the results achieved and elaborate general provisions expressing a common point of view on the fundamental issues of the development of the world Communist and working-class movement.[19]

BIBLIOGRAPHY

Works by Khrushchev

"Accelerated Development of the Chemical Industry," *New Times* (Moscow), No. 19 (May, 1958), supplement.

Control Figures for the Economic Development of the U.S.S.R. for 1959-1965 (Moscow, 1959). His report to the Twenty-first Party Congress.

Disarmament and Colonial Freedom; Speeches and Interviews at the United Nations General Assembly, September-October, 1960 (London, 1961).

For Victory in Peaceful Competition with Capitalism (New York, 1960). Speeches and interviews in 1958.

Khrushchev in America (New York, 1960). Speeches, September 15-27, 1959. Also as *To Live in Peace and Friendship!*

Measures for the Further Development of Agriculture in the U.S.S.R. (Moscow, 1954).

On Peaceful Co-existence. A Collection (Moscow, 1961). Speeches, articles and interviews, 1956-1960.

On the Further Improvement of Management in Industry and Construction in the U.S.S.R. (Moscow and London, 1957).

Proposals to Reform Soviet Education (London, 1958).

Report of the Central Committee of the C.P.S.U. to the 20th Party Congress (Moscow, 1956).

The Road to Communism (Moscow, 1962). Contains his reports to the Twenty-second Party Congress and the new Party program.

Soviet Policy on Germany; "We propose peace. . . ." Speeches of N. S. Khrushchev, and Documents of the Soviet Government, June to September, 1961 (London, 1961).

Speeches and Interviews on World Problems, 1957 (Moscow, 1958).

[19] b), pp. 10-11, 13-14.

Speeches during Sojourn in India, Burma and Afghanistan, November-December, 1955 (New Delhi, 1956).
World without Arms, World without Wars (Moscow, 1961?). Two volumes of speeches and interviews in 1959.

Biography

Pistrak, Lazar, *The Grand Tactician. Khrushchev's Rise to Power* (New York, 1961).
Rush, Myron, *The Rise of Khrushchev* (Washington, 1958).

Exposition

Achiminow, Herman, "Khrushchev's 'Creative Development' of Marxism-Leninism," *Studies on the Soviet Union*, N.S. Vol. 2, no. 3 (1962), pp. 3-17.
Boffa, Giuseppe, *Inside the Khrushchev Era*, trans. by Carl Marzani (New York, 1959).
Fainsod, Merle, "The 22nd Party Congress," *Problems of Communism*, Vol. 10 (November-December, 1961), special supplement.
Karol, K. S., *Khrouchtchev et l'occident* (Paris, 1960).
Kux, E., "Von Stalin zu Chruschtschew," *Politische Studien* (Munich), Vol. 9 (January-June, 1958), pp. 13-19, 88-89, 161-167, 312-317, 398-402.
Laqueur, Walter, and Labedz, Leopold, eds., *The Future of Communist Society* (New York, 1962). A reprint of *Survey* for October, 1961.
Lippmann, Walter, *The Communist World and Ours* (Boston, 1959). Reprinted from *New York Herald Tribune*, November 10-13, 1958.
Meissner, Boris, *Russland unter Chruschtschow* (Munich, 1960). Especially Chapter 32 on ideology at the 21st Congress.
————, "Die Sowjetunion vor dem XXII. Parteikongress der KPdSU," *Osteuropa*, Vol. 11 (February, September, and October, 1961), pp. 81-97, 601-619, 685-712.
————, "Die Ergebnisse des 22. Parteikongresses der KPdSU," *Europa Archiv*, Vol. 17 (February 10, 1962), pp. 73-92.
"Le rapport Khrouchtchev sur Staline commenté par le IVᵉ Internationale," *Quatrième Internationale*, July, 1956, special number.
Santiago de Pablo, Luis, "El tránsito del socialismo al comunismo en la ideología soviética actual," *Revista de estudios políticos*, No. 121 (January-February, 1962), pp. 23-81.

Swearer, Howard R., "Changing Roles of the CPSU under First Secretary Khrushchev," *World Politics,* Vol. 15 (October, 1962), pp. 20-43.

Vallin, Henri, "De Bernstein à Khrouchtchev," *Quatrième Internationale,* Vol. 14, Nos. 4-6 (June, 1956), pp. 19-26.

Werth, Alexander, *The Khrushchev Phase* (London, 1961). Also entitled *Russia under Khrushchev* (New York, 1962).

Wolfe, Bertram D., *Khrushchev and Stalin's Ghost* (New York, 1956). Contains text of Khrushchev's address, "The Crimes of Stalin."

Index

The names of the "Masters," as subentries, are abbreviated.
"L:" means "Lenin on," etc.

Agrarian programs, 54, 58, 218-9, 244-8
Agro-towns, 255
Alexander II, 2, 7, 10, 11, 21
Alexander III, 11, 44
Alternative paths to socialism, *see* Socialism
Anarchism, 2, 3-5, 32, 66, 114-5
"April Theses," 29, 57, 76-8, 124, 217
Artel, 8
Autocracy, 1, 22, 96
Axelrod, Paul, 8-9, 11, 22, 26, 98, 121
    Iskra, 27, 50, 91
    party organization, 95

Babeuf, F. E. (Gracchus), 122n
Bakunin, Mikhail A., 1, 3-6, 10, 13, 15, 21, 32, 99, 114
Bebel, August, 165
Belinski, Vissarion G., 1
Bentham, Jeremy, 120
Bernstein, Eduard, 25, 118, 121, 220, 260
Black Redistribution, 8, 21
Blanqui, Auguste, 2, 5, 6, 12, 22, 34, 105, 122n; and Lenin, 48-9, 58
Bourgeois experts, 61, 85-7; K: 170, 180-1, 183; B: 191

Bourgeois revolution, *see* Revolution
Brest-Litovsk negotiations, 125, 191, 221
Bronshtein, Lev D., *see* Trotsky
Büchner, Georg, 40
Bukharin, Nikolai I., 48, 58, 152, 190-3, 260n
    class struggle, 195, 201-9, 230-2, 257
    compulsory labor, 128-30
    economics, 195-201
    German ultimatum, 125, 191
    N.E.P., 132, 192, 209
    peasants, 195, 209-14
    stabilization of capitalism, 56, 194-5, 221
    and Stalin, 133, 192-3, 230-2
    state, 193-4
Bund, 28, 90, 219
Bureaucracy, L: 66, 79-80, 84; M: 109; T: 151-2, 160, K: 169-70, 184-7

Cabet, Etienne, 105
Capital, 4, 15, 45
Capitalism, 6, 11-4, 16, 24, 33, 194; L: 56-7, 72-3; T: 152-3
    stabilization of, 194-5, 221-2
    uneven development of, 55-6, 71-2, 153-6, 220, 222, 226, 260

Capitalist encirclement, 201, 222, 235, 258
Catherine II, 3
Chernyshevski, Nikolai G., 1, 13, 33, 34, 120
China, 200, 255, 261, 268, 271, 283
Chinese Communists, 95n, 200, 259
Civil War in France, 109, 111, 113-4
Colonialism, 262
Commodity production, 67; B: 208; S: 225, 241-4, 245, 249-50, 265; Kh: 257, 264
Communism, higher phase of, 83-5
Communism, transition to, *see* Transition
Communist Manifesto, 4, 12, 15, 49, 108, 117, 164
Congress of the Party, First, 25
    Second, 28, 49, 50, 65-7, 90, 93, 101-4, 121
    Fourth, 216, 219
    Fifth, 91, 97, 219
    Sixth, 164
    Eighth, 61, 182
    Ninth, 48, 127, 129, 180
    Tenth, 128, 130, 173, 197
    Eleventh, 164
    Thirteenth, 133-4
    Nineteenth, 255
    Twentieth, 255, 258, 260, 266-73
    Twenty-first, 258, 275-9, 282-3
    Twenty-second, 263, 273-5, 279-81
Consciousness, class, 23, 26; L: 46-8, 51, 68, 123; M: 51, 91-3, 104; S: 224
Credo, 26

Dan, Fedor, 93n
Decembrists, 1, 7, 49
Democracy, L: 64-6, 68-71, 79, 82-3, 112-3, 130; M: 95, 112-3, 117; T: 130, 136; K: 169, 172-3, 186-8; B: 130; Kh: 256
Democratic Centralists, 127
Determinism, 14, 15, 25, 37-41, 46, 135, 238-41
Deutsch, Leo, 22
Deutscher, Isaac, 122n, 134
Dictatorship of the proletariat, 4; L: 68-71, 78, 81, 122, 230; M: 95,

97, 100, 107, 110, 112-8; T: 130-1, 136-8, 157, 158; B: 210, 212; S: 230; Kh: 258-9, 279-81
Djilas, Milovan, 253
Dostoevski, Fedor, 1, 5
Dual power, 78-80
Dzhugashvili, Joseph V., *see* Stalin

Eastman, Max, 133
Economism, 24-7, 47, 51, 93
Eighteenth Brumaire, 109, 111
Emancipation of Labor, 9, 22, 25
Encirclement, capitalist, 201, 222, 235, 258
Engels, Friedrich, 12-4, 48, 241, 246
    family, 164-5
    state, 79, 81, 108, 111-2, 115, 117, 158, 194, 233
Erfurt Program, 46, 112
Even development of socialism, law of, 260-1, 282-3
Experts, *see* Bourgeois experts
Expropriations, 54, 216

Family, 140, 164-9, 175-8
Feminist movement, 165n
Feuerbach, Ludwig A., 1, 106
Fichte, Johann G., 1
Fourier, Charles, 1

Haimson, Leopold H., 51
Hainfeld Program, 46
Hegel, Georg W. F., 1, 3, 13, 37-8
Helfand, Alexander, *see* Parvus
Hervé, Gustave, 105
Herzen, Alexander I., 1, 2, 7, 13
Hitler, Adolf, 218, 254

Imperialism, 56-7, 72-5, 154, 156, 192, 194, 258
Industrialization, 128-31, 195-201, 223
Intelligentsia, 13, 22, 35, 46, 63, 91-2, 101-2
International, First, 4, 13
    Second, 56, 100, 221, 269
    Third, 78, 99-100, 132, 152-8, 164, 192, 195, 223
    Two-and-a-Half, 100
Iskra, 27-8, 50-1, 67, 90, 101, 121

Jaurès, Jean L., 118

Kaganovich, Lazar M., 254, 256
Kamenev, Lev B., 58, 76, 125, 132-3, 192, 216
Kant, Immanuel, 1
Karakozov, D. V., 2
Kautsky, Karl, 46, 56, 75
Kerensky, Alexander F., 29
Khrushchev, Nikita S., 169n, 253-8
  alternative paths to socialism, 260, 270-3, 285-86
  domestic policies, 256-9, 273-81
  even development of socialism, law of, 260-2, 282-3
  peaceful coexistence, 200, 262-3, 266-8, 283-86
  socialism vs. capitalism, 198n, 256-7, 262-3, 267-8
  and Stalin, 253-8, 259n, 265, 286
  transition to communism, 263-5, 273-81
  war, 258, 268-70, 284-86
Kienthal conference, 91, 98
Kollontai, Alexandra M., 163; see also Workers' Opposition
  bureaucracy, 169, 185-8
  democracy, 164, 172-3, 186-8
  family, 164-9, 175-8
  labor organization, 169, 179-85
  new woman, 166-7, 173-5
Kornilov, Lavr G., 125
Kremer, Arkadie, 92
Kulaks, 6, 120, 133, 149; B: 195, 201-2, 205, 207-8; S: 199-200, 231
Kuomintang, 192
Kuskova, Katarina D., 26

Labor, compulsory, 31; T: 126-8, 140-7; B: 128-30; K: 170
Labor, militarization of, T: 126-7, 129, 143-7
Labriola, Antonio, 121, 141
Land and Liberty, 2, 8
Land reform, see Agrarian programs
Lassalle, Ferdinand, 32, 107
Lenin, V. I., 29, 44-62, 156, 168, 170, 230, 270-2, 284-85

agrarian program, 54, 58, 219
consciousness vs. spontaneity, 23, 26, 46, 49, 51, 93
determinism, 46-49
dictatorship of the proletariat, 68-71, 78, 81, 122, 129, 230
economic tactics, 59-62, 85-7, 131; S: 242-3
Economism, 26-8, 51, 93
imperialism, 56-7, 72-5, 99, 226
Iskra, 27-8, 51
party organization, 46-50, 62-7, 94-6, 104
peasantry, 54, 68-70, 97, 122
permanent revolution, 52-3, 121-3; S: 229-30
planning, economic, 59, 131, 199
politics vs. economics, 44, 48, 200
Second Congress of Party, 49-51, 65-7, 93-4
soviets, 52-3, 55, 57, 194
and Stalin, 54, 215-7, 219, 224, 226-7
state, 78-86, 194; M: 108-13, 159
trade unions, 60-1, 128-9, 130n
and Trotsky, 52-3, 121-9, 131-2, 152
Leroux, Pierre, 1
Liberals, 9, 23, 96, 144
Luxemburg, Rosa, 56

Maiski, Ivan, 60
Majority, revolution by, Marx on: 221; L: 49, 222; M: 93, 116-8; Kh: 260, 272, 286
Majority rule, 69, 93-4, 122, 125-6
Maksimovski, V. N., 127n
Malenkov, Georgi M., 255-6
Mao Tse-tung, 54, 259
Martov, Julius (L.), 46, 60, 121, 123, 129
  and bourgeoisie, 96-7
  consciousness vs. spontaneity, 51, 91-3
  determinism, 104-7
  dictatorship of the proletariat, 95, 110, 112-8
  Economism, 26, 51
  International, 98-100
  Iskra, 27, 51, 90, 93

materialism, 104-7
party organization, 49, 66, 93-5,
    101-4
Second Congress of the Party, 49,
    51, 90-1, 93, 101-4
state, 108-18
Marx, Karl, 12-5, 25, 39, 49, 84, 122,
    197
determinism, 38, 40, 106, 159, 262
dictatorship of the proletariat, M:
    113-8
Paris Commune, 57, 114-7
permanent revolution, 122n, 229
state, M: 108-17; B: 193-4
Materialism, P: 37-40; M: 104-7
Mehring, Franz, 115
Mensheviks, 26, 96, 97, 99, 124, 127,
    144-7, 219, *and passim*
Mental and physical labor, 226, 246-
    9; Kh: 264, 275
Meyer, Alfred G., 57n
Militarization of labor, 126-7, 129,
    143-7
Military Revolutionary Committee,
    125, 217
Miliukov, Paul, 56
Mir, see Village community
Molotov, V. M., 216, 256

Nagy, Imre, 260
Naine, Charles, 104
Narodniks, 5-7, 9n, 10-1, 21-2, 24,
    29, 33, 35-6, 46, 68, 92
National question, 193, 216, 219-20
Nechaev, Sergei G., 5, 10, 49
New Economic Policy (N.E.P.), L:
    59, 62, 200; T: 127-9, 131-2,
    150; B: 192, 195, 209; Preo-
    brazhenski on: 197
Nicholas I, 1

Obolenski, V. V., *see* Osinski, N.
Obshchina, see Village community
On Agitation, 25, 51, 92-3
Organization, party, 23, 46-50, 62-7,
    93-6, 101-4, 121
Osinski, N. (V. V.), 127n, 191
Owen, Robert, 105, 106

Paris Commune of 1871, L: 57, 79-
    81, 85; M: 109, 111, 114-8; T:
    135
Party congresses, *see* Congress
Party organization, *see* Organization
Party program, *see* Program
Parvus, 52, 92n, 121-3
Peaceful coexistence, 200; Kh: 257,
    262-3, 266-8, 283-86
Peaceful revolution, *see* Revolution
Peasants, P: 22, 30-2; L: 54, 69, 97;
    M: 97; T: 122, 136-8, 149-51;
    B: 195, 197-8, 201-2, 209-12;
    S: 223, 229-30
People's Will, 5, 9-11, 16, 21-3, 29,
    32, 45, 48-9, 92
Peter I, 31
Petrashevski, M. V., 1
Pilsudski, Józef, 131
Planning, economic, L: 59, 131, 199;
    T: 126, 128-31, 147-9; S: 199,
    225; Kh: 261, 276; Preobra-
    zhenski on: 193
Plekhanov, George V., 12, 56, 91,
    121, 224
    Black Redistribution, 8, 21
    capitalism, 9, 24, 33-5
    class consciousness, 23, 46
    determinism, 37-40
    Economism, 25-8
    Iskra, 27-8
    party organization, 23, 35
    peasantry, 30-2
    terrorism, 8, 11, 21-2
    village commune, 8, 32-6
    voluntarism, 24, 29, 39-41, 45
Pobedonostsev, Konstantine, 11
Politics and economics, 22-4, 29, 44,
    48, 200
Potresov, A. N., 27, 50, 90-1
Pouget, Émile, 104-5
Pravda, 152, 191-2, 216
Preobrazhenski, E. A., 194, 197-200
Primitive socialist accumulation,
    197-8
Program, party, 61, 171, 263, 274,
    279
Pugachev, Emelian, 3, 45

Radek, Karl, 193
Reed, John, 164

Revolution, bourgeois, 9, 12, 14, 26; L: 52, 57, 68; M: 96; T: 121, 137, 139
Revolution from above, 7, 200, 225, 237
Revolution of 1905, 52-3, 70, 94, 124
Revolution of February, 1917, 57, 98, 191
Revolution of October, 1917, 58, 154, 219, 234
Revolution by parliamentary means, 257, 260, 271-3, 286
Revolution, proletarian, 13; P: 32; L: 48, 52, 57, 68, 70, 84, 123; M: 96, 110; T: 123, 139-40, 155-6; Kh: 260, 263, 271-3, 284-85
Rolland, Romain, 267
Rules, point 1 of, 49, 51, 90, 93-4
Rykov, Alexei I., 132, 133

Sapronov, T. V., 127n
Schelling, Friedrich W. J., 1, 37
Schlesinger, Rudolf, 169n
Shepilov, D. T., 256
Shliapnikov, A. G., 164, 172, 184
Slavophils, 13, 15
Socialism, alternative paths to, P: 24-5; L: 54-5, 270; Kh: 260, 270-3, 285-6
Socialism in one country, T: 152-8; B: 195; S: 220-4, 226-30
Socialism, law of even development of, 260-1, 282-3
Socialism, transition to, see Transition
Socialist Revolutionaries, 49, 54, 58, 99, 125, 218
Socialist states, relations among, 282-88
Soviets, 52-3, 57, 77-80, 86-7, 108, 194
Spontaneity, 5, 26, 51, 92, 171, 224
Stabilization of capitalism, 194-5, 221-2
Stalin, J. V., 54, 131, 152, 215-7, 259, 286
    agrarian program, 218-9, 244-8
    and Bukharin, 192-3, 195, 199-201, 230-2

commodity production, 241-4
communism, transition to, 225-6, 233-5, 244-51
determinism, 238-41
and Khrushchev, 255-7, 265
left turn, 62, 133, 192, 199-200
Linguistics, 224-5, 236-7
national question, 216, 219-20
permanent revolution, 52, 222, 228-30
revolution from above, 7, 225, 237
socialism in one country, 132, 220-4, 226-30
state, 233-5
town and country, 246-8
and Trotsky, 52, 122, 127, 132-4, 152-60, 222, 228-30
Stankevich, N. V., 1
State, 5-6; L: 78-86; M: 108-18; T: 158-60; B: 193-4; Kh: 259, 278-81
State and Revolution, 59, 80-5, 109-10, 112, 194
Stepanian, T. A., 261
Stolypin, Peter A., 96
Struve, Peter, 15
Superstructure, 24, 70, 224, 236-7
Syndicalism, 59

Terrorism, 5, 8, 10-1, 22
Tikhomirov, Lev, 16, 32
Tkachev, P. N., 5-8, 32, 34, 49
Tolstoi, Leo, 21
Tomski, M. P., 126, 128
Town and country, T: 148-50; B: 205-12; S: 226, 246-9; Kh: 255, 264-5, 275-8
Trade unions, see Unions
Transition to communism, S: 225-6; 233-5, 244-51; Kh: 263-5, 273-83
Transition to socialism, P: 32-5; L: 270; T: 144-5, 155; B: 207-9; Kh: 257, 260, 270-3, 285-86
Trotsky, Leon, 120-34, 170, 173, 193, 260n
    Brest-Litovsk negotiations, 125, 221
    labor organization, 126-31, 140-7

and Lenin, 48-9, 121-9, 131-2, 152
minority revolution, 7, 29, 48, 92n, 121-3, 135-8
N.E.P., 131-3, 149-51
party democracy, 121, 130-1, 133-4, 151, 158-60
permanent revolution, 16, 52-3, 121-4, 135-40
Petrograd soviet, 124, 125
planning, 126, 128-31, 147-9
and Stalin, 52, 122, 127, 132-4, 152-60, 222, 228-30
trade unions, 121, 127-31, 146, 192
Tsederbaum, Iuri O., *see* Martov

Ul'ianov, Alexander I., 44
Ul'ianov, Vladimir I., *see* Lenin
Ultimatum, German, 98, 125, 134, 191, 221
Uneven development of capitalism, law of, *see* Capitalism
Union of Russian Social Democrats Abroad, 27
Union of Struggle for the Liberation of Labor, 46, 90, 93
Unions, trade, L: 59-61, 126-30; T: 121, 127-31, 146, 192; K: 169-72, 179-85; B: 208
Uspenski, Gleb, 36

Village community, 3, 5, 8, 12, 218; P: 24, 29, 31-6
Vollmer, Georg von, 220

Voluntarism, 14-6, 24, 29, 45, 224, 225

War Communism, 59, 61, 126, 128, 131, 192
War, First World, 28, 55, 76, 91, 98
War, Second World, 224
War and transition to socialism, Kh: 258, 268-70, 283-86
Weitling, Wilhelm, 105
Westerners, 13, 15
What Is To Be Done?, 47, 94
Withering of the class struggle, B: 195-6, 200-9, 257; S: 230-2; Kh: 257
Withering of the family, 167-8, 175-8
Withering of the state, 80-3, 111, 171, 194, 233-5, 278-81
Wolfe, Bertram D., 50n, 124n
Workers' control in industry, 59-60, 169
Workers' Opposition, 48, 128-31; K: 164, 169-73, 179-88
World War, *see* War

Yugoslavia, 259, 260, 271
Yugoslavs, 55, 283

Zasulich, Vera, 10, 12, 22, 27, 50, 91, 121
Zheliabov, Andrei I., 9, 27
Zhukov, Grigori K., 256
Zimmerwald conference, 91, 98
Zinov'ev, Grigori E., 58, 61, 125, 128, 132, 133, 185, 192